STRANGERS WITH MEMORIES

STRANGERS

WITH

MEMORIES

The United States and Canada from
Free Trade to Baghdad

JOHN STEWART

McGill-Queen's University Press
Montreal & Kingston • London • Chicago

© McGill-Queen's University Press 2017

ISBN 978-0-7735-5140-4 (cloth)
ISBN 978-0-7735-5199-2 (ePDF)
ISBN 978-0-7735-5200-5 (ePUB)

Legal deposit third quarter 2017
Bibliothèque nationale du Québec

Printed in Canada on acid-free paper that is 100% ancient forest free
(100% post-consumer recycled), processed chlorine free.

McGill-Queen's University Press acknowledges the support of the Canada
Council for the Arts for our publishing program. We also acknowledge the
financial support of the Government of Canada through the Canada Book
Fund for our publishing activities.

Library and Archives Canada Cataloguing in Publication

Stewart, John, 1960–, author
    Strangers with memories : the United States and Canada
from free trade to Baghdad / John Stewart.

Includes bibliographical references and index.
Issued in print and electronic formats.
ISBN 978-0-7735-5140-4 (cloth). – ISBN 978-0-7735-5199-2 (ePDF). –
ISBN 978-0-7735-5200-5 (ePUB)

    1. Canada – Relations – United States – History – 21st century.
2. United States – Relations – Canada – History – 21st century. I. Title.

FC249.S825 2017   327.7107309'051   C2017-903371-9
                                               C2017-903372-7

This book was typeset by True to Type in 10.5/13 Sabon

*To my parents, Russ and Lucy Stewart, who enjoy history
and have lived some of it*

Contents

Foreword by John Manley   ix

Acknowledgments   xiii

Preface   xv

1 Canada in the American World   3

2 Our Continental Economy: Half Built before the Storm   43

3 From Erasing the Border to the Global War on Terror   87

4 Casualties   125

5 Non-Americanism: Be Careful What You Wish For   167

6 Smaller in the World   223

Epilogue   230

Notes   235

Index   269

Foreword

JOHN MANLEY

As the sun rose over North America on 11 September 2001, I was aboard an Air Canada 747 en route from Frankfurt to Toronto. I was Canada's minister of foreign affairs, returning home after ten days of meetings with counterparts in London, Paris, Riga, and Berlin. At one point, a flight attendant asked me to go to the flight deck; I assumed it was another friendly captain inviting me to experience flying from the cockpit while he shared his views on what our government should or should not be doing. While I enjoyed these visits when they were offered, I was tired from a long trip and would have been happy to relax with a book or a movie.

Little did I know that I was being invited forward so I could hear BBC Radio's live description of events unfolding in New York and Washington on a day that would change history and profoundly affect the United States, Canada, and the world. As my mind struggled to comprehend what had just happened – an effort made even more challenging by radio reports of the chaos and calamity on the ground – I found myself thinking, "This changes everything," and praying, "Please, God, whoever is responsible, may there be no connection to Canada!"

The terrorist strikes of 9/11 did change everything. Although there was never any evidence of a Canadian connection, the repercussions for Canada-US relations were profound and mostly unfavourable. This was a turning point in a relationship that, since the 1965 Auto Pact, had been characterized by ever-closer economic cooperation and convergence. The border between Canada and the United States never formally closed on or after 9/11, but it might as well have done so. Nobody in an operational role seemed to know what to do. Long lines of trucks and other vehicles formed, and commerce stopped.

I soon found myself in a key role as Canada's counterpart to Governor Tom Ridge, the newly designated White House adviser on homeland security. I was also appointed to chair a new cabinet committee on public security and anti-terrorism, and as such became the government's main spokesperson on matters arising from 9/11. I still refer to this period of my political career as my moment of fame. Time Canada named me its 2001 newsmaker of the year, a dubious distinction given that the previous honoree had been the ill-fated John Roth, the CEO of Nortel Networks during its brief tenure as Canada's most valuable corporation.

Managing border issues with a willing and able partner was one thing, but being the point person in a relationship of vital importance to the national interest before and after the invasion of Iraq in March 2003 was something else entirely. US officials did not hide their disappointment when Prime Minister Jean Chrétien declined to send troops to Iraq, or even to offer words of political support, but this was manageable. President George W. Bush had respect for Chrétien and appreciated the prime minister's direct and honest approach. He once told me, "I like your boss! I can work with him." But when a minister, an MP, and even a member of the prime minister's staff make derogatory comments about the president of the United States, some backlash is inevitable.

Fortunately, Tom Ridge and I had built sufficient rapport and mutual trust that we could work through this. It helped that his explicit instructions from President Bush were that security measures at the border should not impede commerce. We signed the Smart Border Declaration on 11 December, exactly three months after 9/11, and met regularly and frequently over the next two years to give the agreement life. I left the government when Paul Martin became prime minister. As John Stewart notes in his account of that period, President Bush was disappointed by Martin's equivocation and dithering, but the Smart Border work continued under my successor, Anne McLellan.

It has been said that the prime minister of Canada has two overriding responsibilities: preserving the unity of the country and managing its relationship with our powerful neighbour. Both of these themes emerge with clarity in this book. John gained a unique perspective as a Canadian employed by the US Embassy from pre-NAFTA days, when Brian Mulroney and George H.W. Bush headed their respective governments, through to the years of Stephen Harper and Barack Obama. *Strangers with Memories* provides a detailed description of the complex relationship between two countries that, for all their similarities, often fail to understand each other.

Special personal relationships between Prime Minister Mulroney and Presidents Ronald Reagan and Bush 41, between Prime Minister Chrétien and President Bill Clinton, and perhaps between Prime Minister Stephen Harper and President Bush 43 all affected the relationship for the better. The tensions between Chrétien and Bush 43 and subsequently Harper and Obama were problematic. So too was Paul Martin's willingness to pander to anti-American sentiment during his brief period as prime minister.

During Canada's constitutional troubles in the 1980s and 1990s, the United States skilfully avoided provocation while discreetly supporting the federalist cause. Meanwhile, Canadians confronted deep-seated insecurities during the great free-trade election of 1988. That our citizens have since shown little desire to reopen the debate no doubt reflects the degree to which cross-border supply chains have reshaped and benefited our economy, contrary to the dire predictions of free-trade opponents. (Full disclosure: yours truly ran for the Liberals in that election.)

Canadians bristle at the perceived American ignorance of all things Canadian. Rick Mercer's long-running "Talking to Americans" – segments in which he ridiculed unsuspecting targets in random interviews on US streets – encapsulated Canadians' complex feelings about our neighbour. We care deeply what Americans think about us but cling to a moral superiority that in my view is both undeserved and embarrassing. Our dependence on a big and powerful neighbour has bred a kind of insecurity in Canadians. We need to remember that it's not all about us!

The new era of Trump/Trudeau will doubtless bring its own challenges and perhaps opportunities. Canadians almost certainly would not have elected Donald Trump, but we cannot allow ourselves to be blinded by smugness. Instead, we might want to develop a better understanding of the factors that led his victory – some of which have relevance in this country. We should remember, too, that when the rest of the world thinks of Canada – admittedly not often – our stature tends to reflect our ability to be both independent from and a close partner of our very consequential neighbour.

There are important lessons to be learned by Canadians in the pages of this book by revisiting the more than two decades John Stewart describes from his special vantage point. Let us hope that today's policy makers are paying close attention.

Acknowledgments

This book grew from my enjoyment of historical documentation, a trait I acquired from my parents and from my studies in history, particularly a research fellowship to which Dr David Pierce Beatty guided me while I was an undergraduate at Mount Allison University. Along with so many other students and colleagues, I fondly remember David as a great lecturer, mentor, and friend. In a conversation around the year 2000, he and I both worried that changing technology and working methods could make diplomatic history hard to trace. That conversation accelerated the effort that led to this book.

The book has been encouraged and helped by my wise, insightful wife, Nadia Daif, and by friends and acquaintances including Michel Vachon, Amy Heron, William Johnson, Laura Dawson, Heather Murray, Emily Andrew, Bud Locklear, Terry Breese, Anne Marie Creskey, Andrew Cohen, and others, along with the team at McGill-Queen's University Press.

The reader will see that I owe much of my professional development to the diverse and talented people of the United States Department of State. I hope I have acquired and returned some small portion of the wisdom so many showed to me, and I wish I were in close touch with more of them, rather than letting them become lost good friends: strangers with memories.

Preface

There is risk in being too confident of one's talent. Some Canadians long ago got the idea that as a nation they are naturally gifted at negotiating the international system and winning friends around the world. But even if this were true, such negotiating would always call for self-critical adaptation rather than complacency.

The international system favours Canada only insofar as the system stays safe and orderly. That safe, orderly international system has been provided for a long time by the United States and the system of alliances of which Canada is part. Canadians, accustomed throughout their history to imperial protection and international rules, have little capacity to protect their interests on their own.

Many Canadians' insight into the power that provides security to them and others is based too much on bits of distilled opinion, perhaps supported by a few visits to one US city or region. More effort is needed to understand a complex global superpower system. To this end, history helps, especially when based on primary material. Memories and opinions get distorted with time, but documents and records preserve with greater accuracy what we knew and thought, and what actually happened. This book is mainly based on such material, accumulated while I worked at the US Embassy in Ottawa from 1990 to 2010, during years of peak US influence and of maximum transparency in US-Canada relations. Beginning in those years, and in the period since, North America has entered a new reality. There is more need than ever to understand the facts and details about the players in this relationship, how they operate, where we have come from, and the kind of path we are on today. Whatever the virtues of my own analysis, the documentary record certainly needs to be opened up and read.

In these pages, the viewpoint of an inside practitioner (rather than a journalist or academic) is presented alongside the documents and the explanatory context, creating a story of how each country dealt with its chief partner during the apogee and turning point of American power. Its value, I believe, lies precisely in this strong interweave of personal experience, contemporary documents, and context. I hope it offers a chronicle of what each country did poorly or well, and how our actions leave each of us positioned a decade or two later, in a less predictable world.

Chapter 1, "Canada in the American World," describes life and work in the US Embassy in Ottawa, where I arrived in 1990 during the post-Cold-War flash of US hegemony and during the premonitory rumblings of international disorder. Canada's constitutional and separatist struggles are seen here, as they were by Bill Clinton, as part of a broader global tension between ethnic and local tribalism, on the one hand, and federalism and international integration, on the other, the latter creating political systems that hold societies together and prevent destructive conflict.

Chapter 2, "Our Continental Economy: Half Built before the Storm," recounts the birth of the Canada-US and North American free-trade agreements (the FTA and NAFTA respectively), and assesses their legacy. Efforts to deepen NAFTA failed after 2001 for three reasons: the FTA and NAFTA had done the easiest work, so what remained were politically tougher problems; after 2001, the United States prioritized security over economics; and progress was later resisted by the anti-trade, anti-globalization backlash.

Chapter 3, "From Erasing the Border to the Global War on Terror," tells the security side of the story. It opens by contrasting the two countries' national cults: for America, other countries are marginal, while for Canada's national cult, the United States has always been central. Attitudes to the United States sway or infect nearly all Canadian popular ideas about defence and security, often not very helpfully. As the border "thinned" – becoming more convenient and affordable to transit – in the late 1990s, it was practical and necessary to think about a customs union and some kind of shared continental-security perimeter, but this thinking was shouted down in the Canadian media. After the terrorist attacks of 9/11, the United States leaped into a wartime mindset, which eventually led to divergence between the State Department and the Bush White House, as well as to the political alienation of many US allies. Canadians increasingly saw international insecurity as a US-generated problem, while in Washington, though Canada was still an ally, it was increasingly seen by some as a critic of – and impediment to – US security measures. This chapter notes the important risk for Canada that some future real or perceived security crisis could result in effective US occupation of part of Canadian territory if US authorities do not consider Canada willing or able to manage a perceived threat. This risk grows as Americans continue to sense that Canadians do not share their security concerns or, even if they do share those concerns, will not have the capacity to address them effectively.

Chapter 4, "Casualties," mainly covers the effects of the war in Iraq on diplomatic operations and relationships. It also mentions Canada's handling of the ballistic missile defence (BMD) and Western Hemisphere Travel Initiative (WHTI) issues. Starting in 2001, the border seemed to "thicken" as a result of US actions, but this was not coordinated on the US side nor even intentional, and there was discussion within the US government on why it was occurring and how to react. The Stephen Harper government made real progress in repairing the bilateral security relationship, but less in restoring the process of economic liberalization. The war in Iraq dragged on, and the occupation (euphemistically, "reconstruction") effort there drained foreign-affairs personnel and other resources. Issues around detainees and torture permanently damaged the global credibility, not just of America, but of the West. Confidence in the Bush administration evaporated, allies were alienated, and ultimately Canadians increasingly came to see Iraq, and even to some extent Afghanistan and global terrorism, as American problems.

Chapter 5, "Non-Americanism: Be Careful What You Wish For," discusses nationalism, loyalty, and Canadian anti-Americanism, and then outlines the history of Canada's cultural-protection policies. The fact that Canadianness was defined in terms of ownership and control, rather than content, made these policies irritating at a business level. Though the United States allowed a cultural exemption in the FTA and NAFTA, commercial disputes came up in the media sector, and the worst of these was the 1997–99 magazine-publishing dispute. The responsible ministry's failure in this misguided crusade led it to pursue an international treaty on cultural diversity, an erratic anti-US diplomatic campaign that, like the magazine dispute, squandered Canadian credibility and resources for years with negligible benefits. In fact, US officials never had a systematic plan or intention to break down Canada's cultural protections, though they did have mixed legal and philosophical views on the issue. Along with other trends, plus the election-trail flailings of the Paul Martin government, this period saw an unnecessary acceleration of the decline in mutual respect and in Canada's influence and prestige in Washington.

The concluding chapter, "Smaller in the World," observes that the United States-Canada relationship seems to have entered a new historical phase since 2001. The two countries are not in direct competition or conflict as they were until the late nineteenth century, but they are no longer building shared institutions as they did in the twentieth. They may even be struggling to maintain what they have built. Meanwhile, Canada matters less than it used to, both globally and to the United States, for both unavoidable and avoidable reasons.

The world is getting bigger and probably less orderly, and there are fewer strong reasons now than there were from the 1940s to the 1990s for another power – whether the United States, Britain, China, or anyone else – to want or need Canada as a friend and ally. On the other hand, while we may be in an era of superpower disengagement or even decline, there remain many strong reasons to want the United States as a friend, and there is, and will continue to be, competitive lobbying among many countries to keep America's engagement, because America will still matter to nearly everyone – even in the Age of Donald Trump, as I explain in the Epilogue. Canadians cannot be complacent about the world's, or America's, good favour. Self-critical adaptation may be required. The examination of recent successes, failures, and mistakes that this book provides will, I hope, be effort well invested to help Canadians manage friendships more wisely than we sometimes have.

STRANGERS WITH MEMORIES

I

Canada in the American World

It was May 1990 and I had just wrapped up a job teaching college economics in Ottawa. The following advertisement appeared in the city's daily newspaper: "Diplomatic mission requires self-starting individual to assist in analyzing trade and energy policy. Reply Box 866."

I did not know what diplomatic mission had placed the advertisement, but the job fit my skills, so I applied. It did not occur to me that the United States Embassy might hire people through this route.

Ten years earlier, I was an undergraduate history student on a summer research fellowship, digging into Canada's relationship with the United States during the 1930s and 1940s. I spent the summer of 1980 deep in federal government archives in both Ottawa and Washington, reading all sorts of Second World War–era documents, including handwritten pencil notes on the margins of memos typed in embassies forty years earlier, notes initialled by diplomats whose roles I knew of and whose photos I had seen. Wartime files had recently been declassified and opened up to non-government researchers for the first time. I had the wonderful experience of leafing through history. So I was already interested in the workings of US foreign policy, though of a different era than my own.

The job interview, in the old US Embassy building at 100 Wellington Street, took the form of an informal chat conducted on big old-fashioned green-leather chairs. I was interviewed by the Embassy's energy officer, a plump, laid-back, friendly US Army veteran who in no way matched my stereotype of a diplomat. The chat was followed by a writing assignment: "Drawing on the press clippings provided, write a short analysis of possible reactions in Canada to the launch of three-way free trade negotiations between the United States, Canada and Mexico. You should assume that your reader knows nothing about Canada."

This was anticipating the North American Free Trade Agreement –
NAFTA – which was likely to be modelled on the US-Canada free-trade
agreement (FTA) that was then being implemented. I had been in Ottawa
during the great free-trade debate two years earlier. In the Canadian federal election in the autumn of 1988, Brian Mulroney's ruling Progressive
Conservative Party tied its fortunes to the issue of a comprehensive free-
trade agreement with the United States, which Mulroney's government
had negotiated during its first term. I had defended the agreement privately in social conversation and so I knew where major segments of
Canadian society stood in the debate.

In response to the assignment, I wrote a short and straightforward
paper outlining who those groups were and how they would have to
adjust their positions now that Mexico was in the picture. My main point
was that the two-hundred-year-old argument *in favour* of trade liberalization stayed roughly the same whether you were liberalizing trade with the
United States or with Mexico: freer trade increased specialization, and it
thus had the potential to make most people better off. On the other hand,
Canadians who *opposed* free trade had to change tack entirely now that
Mexico was at the table. After telling voters for years that big rich American corporations would take their jobs, they had to tell them that under-
paid, exploited Mexican workers would take their jobs. Anti-American
and anti-corporate bias was standard fare in Canadian media, and so the
press had broadcast the argument against the FTA relatively uncritically.
Free trade's opponents had a tougher job with a three-way trade deal.
Switching arguments from what they had been saying through the late
1980s, and suddenly demonizing Mexicans instead of Americans, would
put the agreement's critics at a disadvantage in the debate.

During the two hours I sat writing the paper, a friendly man (who I
later learned was the Treasury Department attaché) stopped by the open
door and made lively, informal conversation with me for a couple of minutes about current events. I suppose this might have been part of the
interview process, but even if so, it gave the impression that this kind of
chatting, apparently without much concern about authority or the clock,
was a normal activity in this office – to the point where one could be
expected to interrupt writing a test to engage in it.

They must have approved of my writing, because I was offered the job,
pending security clearance. I came to the Embassy again for another quick
chat. When my turn came to ask questions, I asked: "What's the worst
thing about this job?"

The answer, after a thoughtful pause, was: "There isn't really anything bad about it. It's a cushy government job."

I took it.

STEPPING INSIDE

I then underwent brutal fingerprinting by a personnel clerk who crushed my fingers into waxy ink. Finally, there was a thorough security interview, in which I divulged my entire life story to a grandfatherly, semi-retired Federal Bureau of Investigation (FBI) agent. At the end of this talk the agent asked me if I could think of any reason why I would not make a loyal employee of the United States government. I said I was convinced that we both lived under reasonably humane and democratic systems of government. My interrogator smiled and recalled the familiar Winston Churchill quote about how democracy is the worst form of government, except for all the others.[1]

While I was a bit nervous about the security-clearance process, I was not at all intimidated by the Americans I had met in the Embassy thus far. The least friendly person was the personnel clerk – a Canadian, in fact – who fingerprinted me. Even ex-FBI interrogators could put me at ease if they were in the habit of quoting Churchill.

Here I glimpsed one of the strange paradoxes of Americans' foreign policy: the seeming mismatch between all the things the world has disliked and feared about the foreign-policy apparatus of the United States, on the one hand, and, on the other, the character of average Americans, who are for the most part honest, direct, outgoing, and thoughtful.

My father, a retired Canadian Forces officer, worried about the security-clearance process. "They can turn you down at the last second and they never even have to tell you why," he said, with a tone of exasperation founded in decades of frustration with government. One of the few things I had not shared with the security officer was that I had worked a few volunteer shifts the preceding summer at a bookstore in Ottawa that (at the time) was a haunt of the far left. I chose the bookstore volunteer stint mainly out of a love of books (political economy in particular) and time on my hands, but I found it a humourless place. I wondered if the Canadian security services monitored who volunteered there. In any case, my background check went through, my new boss invited me to start work, I bought some new clothes, and on 22 June 1990 I entered the building at 100 Wellington Street to begin my career with the United States Department of State.

I still remember how it felt approaching the tall black north-facing door in the sixty-year-old building in the chilly shade of those beautiful early summer mornings. It was like stepping back into the diplomatic world whose yellowing papers I had handled in my undergraduate years.

PROBLEMS OF EMPIRE

Once I left the libraries and archives of my undergraduate life and began living and working in Ottawa as a politically aware young Canadian adult in the 1980s, I had come to hold a suspicious view of contemporary US foreign policy – a view shared with many Canadians and Europeans, and indeed Americans, of my generation. But having studied world history, in particular the Allied experience in the Second World War, I could see Western democracy in the more forgiving context of its full history. I thought that this full history cast the United States in a much better light than did the events of the 1980s, and that there was therefore reasonable promise of improvement in its foreign policies.

The Berlin Wall had fallen just months before my job interview, and the Cold War appeared over. With the Western economic and political system now triumphant, there seemed to be prospects for greater integrity as well as greater opportunities in US foreign relations. Many of the more regrettable instances in which the United States appeared to have compromised its own values since 1945 had been at least partly driven by the anti-communist imperative of the Cold War – an imperative that was vanishing before our eyes in mid-1990. Those of us observing US foreign policy in the first half of 1990 hoped that the compromises of principle that seemed to have been made in the name of winning the Cold War would no longer be needed.

In just a few years during the Second World War, America was vaulted from depression and isolation to world economic, political, and military leadership. Then the Cold War against world communism gripped the United States and its allies, including Canada, in an irreconcilable struggle for military and technological supremacy against the Union of Soviet Socialist Republics (USSR), which operated through and was supported by satellite regimes around the world from Cuba to North Korea to Angola.

In the 1950s, 1960s and 1970s, the United States underwent a great diplomatic expansion, developing and leading multilateral institutions, constructing embassies around the world, going most places fearlessly as a dominant power, and viewing all countries' business as to some extent its own business. Yet there was a deep contradiction between

Americans' confident post-war world building and the imperatives of the Cold War.

My generation – born in the 1960s – knew that fighting the Cold War had led (if not forced) Western governments to invest great economic and scientific resources in developing nuclear weapons, aircraft, guidance systems, bombs, missiles, aircraft carriers, submarines, satellites, and spacecraft. After a few years of apparent progress in the 1970s toward détente (reduced tension) and some arms-limitation agreements, in the 1980s President Ronald Reagan had resumed the race for arms superiority. Horror among my generation of Canadians at the seeming belligerence of the Reagan administration had kept us acutely conscious of, and mostly opposed to, the weapons race. My own position was more reserved since I had taken a strategy course in graduate school and thus understood the logic of deterrence.

The Cold War caused very large resources to be channelled into intelligence gathering, by both human and electronic means. While I did not know much about post-Second World War intelligence activity, it was reasonable to suspect that a great deal of it was going on and that embassies were bases for it. This would, I thought, certainly have included US embassies in the capitals of close allies, such as the one in Ottawa.

Added to this vague awareness of the world of Cold War espionage, my generation knew the actively (though perhaps not accurately) reported details of US efforts to select and sustain the unsavoury regimes of other countries, particularly in Latin America. These episodes had hurt the US claim to be leading a drive for freedom and democracy. During the Cold War, there was an overriding desire in Washington to avoid the emergence of (or to overturn) regimes which might ally themselves with the USSR.

THE BAGGAGE OF REGIME-CHANGE INITIATIVES

This regime-changing activity was not unique to the Cold War. The United States, like Britain before it, had always tried to influence other countries to let its officials, travellers, missionary organizations, and corporations operate freely.[2] This was done through a range of approaches from gentle diplomacy to destabilization or plain military overthrow. A number of Washington's efforts at such interference appeared to have failed in the long run, by degrading the United States' credibility as a promoter of democratic values, and by fomenting anti-American and anti-corporate sentiment in the targeted countries and their neighbours.

The US-assisted regime-changing efforts of which Canadians of my generation were most aware occurred in Guatemala, where the first of a string of US-friendly, military-supported governments was installed in 1954; Cuba, which was the site of a bungled invasion attempt in 1961 and had been subject to US sanctions since then; Chile, where in 1973 an apparently innocuous and democratic leftist leader had been replaced by a military dictator via a US-engineered coup; and Nicaragua, where the United States had intervened in a civil conflict in the mid-1980s.[3]

By one account written by journalist William Langewiesche, the post-war expansion phase of American diplomacy reached a psychological turning point in 1965 when a Vietcong car bomb destroyed the US Embassy in Saigon, Vietnam, killing 22 people and injuring 186. According to Langewiesche, that was the point when outward-oriented, world-building diplomacy began to turn inward and fortify itself and its Embassy buildings.[4]

So the image of post–Second World War US foreign policy that developed in the minds of my generation during our post-graduate years was, in part, one of national ideals gone wrong. Competition with the Soviet Union in the Cold War had produced an interventionist foreign-policy complex that would support ruthless dictators, undercut democratic movements, and run arms to the United States' own enemies – perhaps even illegal drugs to its own people – in order to fund activities of which presidents and elected representatives in Congress might well have disapproved, had they been asked, or that they didn't want to be informed of so they could plausibly deny knowledge.[5]

RESIST OR ENGAGE

Certainly I experienced conflicting attitudes as I approached my new job. Naturally, I struggled with a certain sense of complicity in a system that had seemingly gone so wrong in so many places during the Cold War. But I thought then, and still do now, that whether or not Canadians like the US government and its role in the world does not much alter the need for Canadians to deal with that relationship, nor does it change the value of understanding the relationship clearly and dispassionately.

Even if I hadn't seen value in US leadership in the world, surely one must seek to understand enemies as well as friends. If you object to something, and you really want to resist it, then surely this is a reason to study and understand it as fully as possible, not a reason to avoid it and refuse to learn about it. Shunning an enemy entrenches conflict. Engagement can strengthen the capacity to resist in various ways. Gandhi wrote of his reaction to the outbreak of the First World War: "I could declare open resistance to the war ... or I could seek imprisonment by civil disobedience ... or I could participate in the war on the side of the Empire and thereby acquire the capacity and fitness for resisting the violence of war. I lacked this capacity and fitness, so I thought there was nothing for it but to serve in the war."[6]

Unlike Gandhi's view of the British Empire, generally, and whatever its faults, the United States is a good thing for humanity. One reaches this conclusion by comparing it, not with perfection, nor even with Canada or Denmark or Sweden (which do not bear the same kinds of historical or global burdens), but with actual alternative systems of world power. In her wonderful book on modern-day Islam, Irshad Manji speaks vigorously for the human value of the United States and the West: "America isn't loathed by Muslims so much as it's loved – loved to the point of being needed ... There will always be a contingent of anti-Americans and isolationists, who want Washington to butt out. However, many young Muslims I talked to [after 2001] want Washington to 'butt in' – and follow through – on behalf of human rights. If they could say so without being ostracized, they'd urge America to brandish its influence."[7]

AT THE CENTRE OF A SHIFTING WORLD

The US Embassy that I joined in June 1990 was one small outmoded component of the lone remaining superpower's global information-gathering and national-security apparatus. By the late 1980s, many US diplomatic facilities had become, or were becoming, fortresses, but the one on Wellington Street in Ottawa, opened around 1930 and designed for about seventeen employees, belonged to an earlier diplomatic era and was built on a human scale.

I spent my first morning at 100 Wellington Street on administrative details, being shown around and introduced to various people, and getting to know the files in the big cabinet in my rather dusty corner of the Economic Section (ECON). Along with two other Canadians who had been working there for more than a decade, I occupied a large shared room in the middle of the section on the building's third floor. This room and its occupants served as a library and resource centre for the section's six or seven Foreign Service officers (FSOs) – the American diplomats who came to Ottawa on two- to four-year tours.

In those days before the Internet or e-mail, we kept all the Canadian statutes and a wide range of other government documents on our shelves, and much of our work involved moving pieces of paper around the building and eventually filing some of them in steel cabinets. Locally hired analysts were support staff for the officers, and the institutional memory of the organization. The Political Section on the floor below had no locally engaged staff (LES), so now and then we provided some help to its three to five officers as well.

In 1990 local computers were networked poorly if at all, and few people had mobile phones. Our office circulated stacks of unclassified telegrams each day in thick, pale-green cardboard folders. These "read files" brought information and insights from US diplomatic posts around the world – from news out of the major international organizations' headquarters in New York, Washington, and Geneva, and descriptions of the chaos then reigning in the former Yugoslavia, to the economic and political reports of our six consulates in Halifax, Quebec, Montreal, Toronto, Calgary, and Vancouver. These viewpoints, combined with my conversations with experienced FSO colleagues, rapidly deepened my knowledge of the current state of global affairs and of how the US diplomatic apparatus operated.

For the West, the 1990s were a too-brief period of triumph between the fall of the Iron Curtain (which at the time seemed to end effectively the twentieth century's great ideological conflicts) and the overreach of US power after 2001. The satisfaction produced by the double victories of the Cold War and the First Gulf War left many of us complacent about our forms of democracy, about capitalism, and about our security.

This self-satisfied outlook was not always equipped to evaluate the new international order in a searching, open-minded way. After President Bill Clinton took office early in 1993, there was some criticism of his penchant for endless debate and deliberation, of asking too many questions and taking too long to make decisions. Given the times, I do not think this was such a bad thing. It was a period that called less for bold action than for careful thought, deep understanding, and long vision.

The world was changing all around us and particularly in Europe. The USSR was disintegrating, to be replaced by the Commonwealth of Independent States (CIS), a much looser union, by the end of 1991, leaving Boris Yeltsin's Russia surrounded by a mixed constellation of new neighbours in varying states of disorder. Yugoslavia, too, was slowly beginning its political disintegration, a process that would lead within two years to the Bosnian War. The Berlin Wall had fallen in November 1989, and Germany was reunifying after nearly fifty years of division, as its recently communist east was reabsorbed by its capitalist and democratic west.

FOREBODINGS OF DISORDER

These were immense political dramas that would last for years, with large economic and social implications. They were very difficult for Westerners to assess, individually or holistically, or for Western leaders and diplomats to influence. Analyses coming from US posts in those countries struggled with questions such as whether or not the former Soviet Union could or should remain a single economic area (with German chancellor Helmut Kohl saying yes while others, such as Harvard economics professor Jeffrey Sachs, argued it was impossible).[8] A telegram from October 1992 gives a taste of the atmosphere as viewed by US economic officers in Europe:

> The first and major problem is the continuing decline of output and economic activity in all newly independent states. In Russia, industrial output is projected to decline by 18–20 percent this year and GNP by an even larger percentage, possibly 22–24 percent. It is a matter of concern that the pace of decline has been accelerating in the last few months ... The collapse of production reflects in part continuing disruptions of production and a vacuum of decision-making at the enterprise level ... Such a collapse is making the entire stabilization strategy unsustainable for the government because political and social support is fading away.
>
> The second major issue is the solution of the economic power conflict in Russia and between Russia and other newly independent states ... The third major issue is the break-up of the ruble zone and the fall of trade between the newly independent states ... In the other newly independent states the economic situation is even more difficult and the prospects gloomier. None of them has so far matched either Russia's reforms or its stabilization measures ... [In some of them] internal and external armed conflicts are hampering the progress of economic reforms, and their economies are suffering from all sorts of disruptions and imbalances. These cases indicate how important it is to achieve political stabilization in order to pursue radical economic transformations.[9]

A telegram from London in January 1993 shared highlights of a speech by UK foreign secretary Douglas Hurd on "The New Disorder": "Since the end of the Cold War we are faced with a different world where disorder is spreading ... In almost every continent, including Europe, we find dramas and tragedies which ... contain the danger of wider conflict ... Obviously we cannot be everywhere ... Our armed forces are already stretched ... The United States is unique ... Every major international enterprise will continue to need American support, and probably American participation ... An effort comparable to those of 1815, 1919 and the years after 1945 is needed if the international community is to avert a continuing slide into disorder."[10]

Summarizing an argument made by US senator Richard Lugar, the State Department said in August 1993:

> There is a need for a new strategic bargain between Europe and the United States to deal with the new challenges emerging throughout Europe, challenges that could directly impact vital American national interests. The policy dispute over Bosnia is no longer just about Bosnia, but rather about Allied unity and the willingness of Europeans and Americans to adjust their Cold War political and security institutions and missions to the changing geo-strategic circumstances in and around Europe. In some ways, the details of such adjustments are less important than the pressing need to demonstrate and convince politicians and publics on both sides of the Atlantic that American leadership on European security issues in both possible and advantageous for Europeans as well as for Americans.[11]

It was a dramatic time outside of Europe, too. African National Congress (ANC) leader Nelson Mandela had been freed from prison in February 1990 and, through a miracle of leadership and conciliation, an end to South Africa's apartheid system was being negotiated – without the hideous civil war many had feared. The Japanese asset-price bubble burst in late 1989 and early 1990, and the Nikkei stock index fell to half its peak, beginning Japan's "lost decade" of economic stagnation. As a rising economic giant, Japan would be replaced by China, which, though it saw bloody political repression in Tienanmen Square in 1989, was opening up economically: the Shanghai stock exchange would reopen in late 1990 for the first time in forty years. East Asia's "four tigers" or "four little dragons" – Singapore, Hong Kong, Taiwan, and South Korea – had ridden Japanese-style waves of development to industrial-country status, setting a new model for economic growth. And at home in North America, the information-technology revolution was just beginning to transform how we worked, what we made, how we talked, and how we made money.

In September 1994 former president George H.W. Bush spoke in Berlin on "America's Role in the Post-Cold-War World." According to a report out of Berlin that summarized his speech:

the problems facing the world today ... are nationalism "running amok," proliferation of weapons of mass destruction and conventional arms, drug trafficking and terrorism. A nuclearized North Korea was the greatest danger to stability in Asia, and his "biggest concern"[:] ... Bush regretted that he had not done more during his time in office to stem the international flow of conventional arms. The collapse of the Soviet Union had led to a political and psychological vacuum that created turbulence in many of the former Soviet republics, and in Europe. To meet these challenges, Bush stated, the US should continue to lead internationally ... We won the Cold War but have failed to secure the peace.[12]

A NEW AGE OF AMERICAN LEADERSHIP

The United States was engaging with the world in new ways, particularly in the Cold War's former epicentre – Central and Eastern Europe and the newly independent states – where, as the 1990s went on, the State Department was rapidly setting up new embassies and developing wholly new international relationships. Two telegrams from Brussels that showed up in our office in early 1996 tell part of this story. They compared the West's efforts to aid the post-Soviet economies of the 1990s with the massive and successful Marshall Plan to rebuild post–Second World War Europe in the late 1940s:

> From 1990 through 1994, the world community ... provided 74.7 billion ECU [European Currency Units], or US$97.1 billion, in assistance to Central Europe; and ... 98.3 billion ECU (US$127.4 billion) in aid to the Former Soviet Union (including the Baltics). This ... is two and a half times the US$90 billion (calculated in 1990 dollars) which the U.S. provided Europe after World War II in the Marshall Plan. Since 1989, U.S. and EU leadership has produced the largest assistance project in history to help the former East Bloc nations ... We have mostly provided our asset of greatest value, and the one they need most: our skills, our experience, our knowhow at building and running stable democracies and efficient market economies. As we intended, this is enabling them to fashion the political and economic institutions best suited to their individual priorities and needs, and to attract the domestic and foreign private investment that constitutes the real engine of growth.[13]

Still, the analysts in Brussels complained, the West continued to struggle not only with its image in the East but with a lack of political support for foreign-assistance programs back home.

It is unfortunate that we have not yet been able to explain adequately to either CE-NIS [Central Europe-Newly Independent States] publics or our own taxpayers the magnitude and goals of our CE-NIS aid ... Because this help has come from a number of governments ... as well as the international financial institutions, the large total involved is unknown to, or underappreciated by, both recipients and taxpayers ... Much of the problem also lies in the nature of the aid. Many in the CE-NIS countries expected tangible local infrastructure projects like roads and phone lines ... Since such aid is often not visible on the streets, there is a widespread perception that "all you've done is send us some consultants."[14]

INSIDE THE EMBASSY

In his history of the origins of the Cold War, Daniel Yergin describes the US Foreign Service that formed George F. Kennan and other brilliant officers in the 1930s: a corps of intelligent and experienced people who studied, analyzed, and reported facts dispassionately to Washington.[15] Through my historical studies I already respected this culture; I soon discovered that, while it had evolved somewhat by 1990, it still existed and I was now inside it.

In October 1944, when Winston Churchill visited Joseph Stalin in Moscow and began dividing Europe into spheres of influence, President Roosevelt had asked Churchill not to make decisions without him: "There is in this global war literally no question, either military or political, in which the United States is not interested."[16] Fifty years later, the presumption remained that the US government cared about, and therefore ought to know, everything. In my first weeks in the Economic Section I had asked my supervisor about the justification for maintaining certain subscriptions to little-used statistical publications, and his answer was: "If it's out there, we need access to it."

During my first months at the Embassy, it struck me that there seemed to be no boundaries on the topics on which State Department analysts might research and report. In our function as reporters, we had vast academic freedom. If the choice of subject were questioned, which was rare, it would be because the subject was not important *at all* rather than because it was not relevant to US foreign policy. While other Embassy staffs in Ottawa spent their time working on a small handful of issues that actually affected both their home country and Canada, we looked at nearly anything. Canada was a major, diversified industrial economy and a member of a huge number of international organizations and initiatives (Canadians were considered the ultimate diplomatic "club joiners"), so if we ever had to make a case for the relevance of our work to the United States, one could be found.[17]

This relevance of everything to the United States, and the potential relevance of Canada to most things, did not outlast my twenty years' working life in the Department of State. By the end of the Bush administration, America's foreign-policy establishment would begin to face hard choices about what it could do and what it couldn't.

WORKING DAYS

In the Economic Section, we were surrounded by books, newspapers, magazines, broadcasts, and conversations. There was never any sense of apology for spending time in thought or observation. Nor was there much ideological judgment; rather, on the whole, my colleagues were thoughtful and highly receptive to debate. This made the Embassy, and the Department of State, an intellectually and socially comfortable place.

In the early years, my days, like those of my diplomat colleagues, began with a quick read of several daily newspapers and sometimes a news magazine or two. I selected all the print articles relevant to the economic-policy relationship between the two countries – trade, industry, energy, transport, communications, whatever might affect not just individual companies but industries and the wider economy. I gathered those articles into a thin photocopied stack. This package was then distributed around the Embassy by my own hand, and to key offices in Washington by facsimile machine, a technology that was the heart of the office in those pre-e-mail days.

THE FOREIGN-SERVICE FAMILY

Because our building at 100 Wellington Street was so small, many Embassy staff had their offices elsewhere and I rarely saw them. Squeezed with us into the Embassy's main place of business (archaically termed the Chancery) were employees of the US departments of commerce and agriculture, both of which had their own mini–Foreign Services plus their own locally hired Canadian staff. Employees in the consular, financial, and general-services offices, as well as those in the defence and law-enforcement agencies, worked in other buildings so we would see them only at training sessions, receptions, and social events.

Americans tend to be friendly, and top officers were inclined (or at least felt obliged) to host their closer colleagues in their homes a few times during a tour in Ottawa, sometimes inviting Canadian friends from outside the Embassy as well. They were generous about having me into their homes, where I soon felt comfortable and welcome. They invited me along to everything from golf to skating parties to motorcycle races. Drinks were abundant and conversation was wide-ranging. Foreign service is an entire lifestyle, much more than a job, and my colleagues were open about discussing their families' lives and challenges. I noticed that there was little inhibition about criticizing the US government as long as it was done within our own circle (rather than in front of Canadians, where, of course, our mission was to defend and advance the government's work and maintain a respectful relationship).

My American co-workers seemed to be more natural in their socializing, and certainly having more fun, than many in the diplomatic crowd, with the possible exception of the British, who also knew how to loosen up. While the US Embassy had a small liquor store on its ground floor, so the accredited diplomats could easily take their favourite products home, the UK High Commission actually had a bar installed at one end of its main meeting space in its building on Elgin Street.

The US Embassy had a Community Liaison Office that organized many broadly based events to bring the employee community together, particularly with families. While there could be some artificiality – people were deliberately going out of their way to build a transitory community to compensate for the absence of extended families and long-term neighbours – the result was many good friendships, genuine camaraderie, and a devotion to helping each other live well in an often isolating expatriate lifestyle. It took some colleagues weeks or months to notice – if it even mattered – that I was an LES, rather than an FSO.

I was invited to many formal receptions in the Chancery or at the more spacious ambassador's residence in the Rockcliffe Park neighbourhood. As time went on I also attended outside receptions, lunches, dinners, and other events on the Embassy's behalf, with or without Embassy colleagues. As well as giving me a wonderful seat in Ottawa's public-policy community, and a window on diplomatic life at an interesting time, it was a great honour to be trusted with representing our organization in this way. I generally felt valued within the US Mission and the State Department – certainly at least as much as anywhere else I've worked. Few societies can embrace outsiders so well.

INSTITUTIONAL KNOWLEDGE

Apart from exchanging stories about previous postings and State Department gossip, my colleagues' conversation often involved travel, culture, and languages, topics in which I was very interested. They asked me frequently about Canadian society and institutions as they tried to understand their temporary home's peculiarities. Why did some Quebecers want to leave Canada? Who was the Governor in Council? (It's an archaic euphemism for the cabinet.) Why did so many Ottawa couples live together for years and have children without getting legally married? Why was the Industry Department's headquarters named after C.D. Howe? These were the sorts of questions I fielded.

Over time I came to several realizations about the diplomatic world I was working in. For one thing, as my colleagues put it, the US Foreign Service really did look more or less like America. The FSOs came from diverse backgrounds in all parts of the country. They had worked as teachers, journalists, missionaries, soldiers, or even white-water rafting guides before joining the service. For another thing, contrary to newspapers' ignorant clichés about people with striped trousers attending posh receptions, diplomatic life was not necessarily all that comfortable or even pleasant. My colleagues had all the problems of ordinary people, like getting their children into suitable schools, finding health care, setting up their homes, making friends they could trust and count on, visiting aging parents, wrangling with teenagers, keeping their careers on track, fighting illness, and saving enough for retirement. But they had to manage all these problems discreetly and politely under many organizational constraints, without becoming news in the local paper, in a foreign environment (even if only mildly foreign), and they had to sort it all out again in three or four years' time, over and over again. It could be hard.

A breakthrough insight for me was that my youthful notion, back in the 1980s, that an FSO career would be a great way to travel the world safely and for free was very mistaken. Certainly, FSOs often got to see a bit of the world – but it wasn't safe or free. Many spent years in places they were challenged to enjoy. Although it was unlikely, they might be killed in a bombing in Baghdad or Benghazi, shot while waiting at a traffic light, or abducted. They might fly over and over half-way around the world – itself an uncomfortable experience – to spend a week at a pointless negotiation in a windowless hotel conference room. They might be left heartbroken and bankrupt after marriages that couldn't stand the strain of expatriate life.

By contrast, personal travel was getting cheaper all the time for all of us. Many Canadians with healthy salaries could, with a bit of planning, vacation almost anywhere they wanted, and work their way down their own bucket list of dream experiences. Meanwhile, while I lacked the prestige of diplomatic status, and my own personal life certainly had its own tumults, I was rooted in family and community, in a town where I belonged and felt at home, in houses where I became deeply settled. I might have envied my FSO colleagues some of their professional opportunities, but never their stretched-thin private lives.

EXECUTIVE LEADERSHIP

At the top of our own pyramid in 1990–91 was Ambassador Edward Ney, who had previously been chief executive of Young and Rubicam, the New York advertising firm. On my daily journeys downstairs and through the second floor to distribute the press clippings, I began to cross paths with the officers of the Political Section, and once during my first week, passing the executive offices, I caught a glimpse of Ambassador Ney: a trim, white-haired, sharp-eyed gentleman in a perfect blue suit.

When he and I were introduced and had a chance to chat for the first time at a reception a week or so after my arrival, we got talking about the Canadian media. He said he found it depressing to read so many newspapers. I remarked that the antidote was to read fiction. He said with a wink: "Like the *Toronto Star*." (The *Star* in those days was the leading anti-free trade and anti-American editorial voice in the country.) He was right, in that much of the anti-free-trade rhetoric spouted by the *Star* was a wilful distortion; the same was true, I would learn, of the rest of the Canadian media.

I had almost no prior experience dealing with executive decision makers. The head of the small high-technology company where I had started my professional life was a detail-focused engineer who liked to micromanage. Perhaps based on this, I innocently expected that the ambassador would be thoroughly conversant with all the files that the Economic Section worked on, and when asked to prepare briefing materials for him, I delved into detail. My FSO colleagues set me straight: particularly in Ambassador Ney's case, briefings were to be kept general, at least until we were asked for more.

I soon learned that the mentality of political-level leadership is qualitatively different from that of working-level policy types. Details matter relatively less to most political leaders; general perceptions and trends of feeling matter more. They care less about the trees or the landscape than about which way the wind is blowing right now. My presumption that our briefs to the executive office should be lengthy, analytical, and detailed was dead wrong. I learned to keep briefings at a high level of generality – making careful decisions about what to include and what to leave out.

REPORTING TO WASHINGTON

Later in a typical working day, after monitoring the media and handling the shorter-term tasks, I would pursue some research or reporting project suggested by conversations with the economic officers or by my own curiosity. The results were usually issued either as an internal memo or as a diplomatic telegram (a "cable").[18] In the first few months I mostly wrote factual reports containing little analysis. I would summarize some note-worthy development, perhaps adding a bit of context and commentary that might not have been understood by casual readers of press reports. The very first outgoing cable I wrote, for example, was a one-paragraph note informing Washington that the Supreme Court of Canada had confirmed that integrated circuit designs were protected by the Copyright Act. This would have been of interest to officials with interests in intellectual property rights (IPR) protection, which was then and is today a high priority in US trade policy.

Being a quick researcher and writer, after a year or so I was doing a substantial amount of our section's routine, factual reporting, particularly on trade policy. We often focused on areas where Canada had laws and regulations that were discriminatory, restricting foreign-based firms more than domestic ones. The Embassy was most interested in areas where those measures worked to the disadvantage of important US industries, especially when those industries took the trouble to complain to their government representatives.

One example was the pharmaceuticals business, where major drug firms – both US and European – were very dissatisfied with the patent protection they received in Canada. This was my first in-depth exposure, not just to intellectual property laws, but also to Canada's health-care sector, which would become a preoccupation of the Canadian public under the Jean Chrétien and Paul Martin governments from 1993 to 2006.

Pharmaceutical issues were also complex and interesting because the United States had mixed motives. On the one hand, the United States was home base for a number of global pharmaceutical firms, and the government thus had a strong interest in protecting those firms' rights to the new products which their research generated. That meant seeking stronger and longer protection for patents, and other advantages for the large, brand-name drug companies. On the other hand, health-care costs, and drug costs in particular, were a growing concern for the US public and their congressional representatives, which meant that politicians tended to want to keep pharmaceutical costs down in any way they could. This kind of conflict of interest can create awkward compromises in government.

I quickly adopted the standard State Department report-writing style, and my officer colleagues coached me to refine it. Its features were plain, straightforward English; active rather than passive voice; clarity and readability; leading with facts and stating them objectively; structuring the early paragraphs so they give the full story in brief; avoiding value-laden words and phrases; offering concise but insightful analysis; and explaining why the information mattered to US foreign relations. Each cable had a half-page or so of header indicating the cable's post of origin, date, sequential reference number, names of drafting and approving officers (sometimes the same person), and addressee offices and posts.

The usual addressee offices in Washington were the State Department's Canada Desk (more formally the Office of Canadian Affairs), which was a cluster of five or so people who were at that time part of the State Department's European Bureau (thus known as EUR/CAN); the Office of the US Trade Representative (USTR), which typically had one person chiefly assigned to Canadian trade affairs, plus various subject-matter specialists; and a person who followed Canadian issues in the US Department of Commerce's International Trade Administration (USDOC/ITA), which also had specialists in various topics. Any of a large number of other offices and/or foreign posts might be added to this list.

After the mid-1990s my cables became longer and sometimes deeply analytical, including historical context that I thought readers needed to comprehend an issue fully. Around 1995 I was given the authority to send cables on my own, though with the understanding that I would always seek appropriate input and clearances.

THE TEAM

The officers I worked with were the section head (minister-counsellor for economic affairs), a Treasury Department attaché with a supporting State Department officer, a trade-policy officer (my main co-worker in the early years and my supervisor after 1991; this job was soon upgraded to economic counsellor), an energy officer, and an officer responsible for transportation, communications, and border issues. The science portfolio was transferred to us from the Political Section and turned into an environmental-affairs role in the early 1990s. There was also a function that encompassed Canadian labour unions and the New Democratic Party (NDP) and that straddled the economic and political sections.

The US Embassy's Political Section, then as now, was smaller than its Economic Section and did not employ any permanent Canadian staff in those years. As Canada posed few political risks to US interests, and as the process of implementing (or arguing about) the Free Trade Agreement was mostly the preserve of the economic officers, the Political Section's main preoccupation was Quebec separatism and the impasse brought about by former prime minister Pierre Trudeau's patriation of the constitution in 1982.

Since I saw little of what the Political Section did, its work held a certain mystique for me. I assumed that what they did must be much more interesting and important than our seemingly drudging toil of implementing the FTA, managing the border, and generally pushing forward ways to make North America's economy more productive. It took a few years – including being told so by people at the top – to realize that our jobs in ECON were truly the heart of the action in that Embassy. While the political officers kept themselves busy enough, our work was much more diverse and dynamic than theirs.

Just a few feet from my own desk was a mysterious, locked suite that people entered and left but that nobody ever talked about. It was officially called "Political Liaison" and was, in reality, the Central Intelligence Agency (CIA) station. Eventually I would pick up a derisive, eye-rolling attitude from my State Department colleagues toward "the Agency" – typical of the common us-and-them mindset that one finds among bureaucratic clans. In 1996, at a time when I was working on aerospace-industry issues, I wrote to myself:

Last week [the transportation officer] brought one of the CIA officers into my office looking for information on Bombardier. He had obviously received some sort of tasking, probably associated with the possible rescue of Fokker in the Netherlands. I gave him Bombardier's annual report and my (still unreleased) report on the industry. [The transportation officer] came back in afterward and advised me to get my report out as soon as possible so CIA could not get away too easily with passing off my data as secret intelligence. He said he'd had that kind of experience in Moscow, and called them a "useless organization." [The trade officer], whom I mentioned this to when I took her the cable for clearance, also said they plagiarize open sources and pass it off as their own stuff.[19]

The Embassy in itself was a very complex, multi-stakeholder environment before we even went outside to deal with Canadians. The US federal government is decentralized. Departments and agencies have distinctive histories, logos, traditions, and cultures. I worked directly for the Department of State, the main foreign-affairs agency, which accounted for some 60–70 per cent of the Mission's organization and provided administrative services to the rest. State itself was a very complex system, with geographic, functional, and administrative bureaus. But by the time I left the Embassy there were some thirty other US government departments and agencies somehow represented under our roof. Often we had to take US state governments into account too, notably the border or "northern tier" states, on trans-boundary issues like water or transport. I had a good mind for this multi-stakeholder environment; I learned well how to keep people in the loop and develop consensus so we could move things forward.

Part of this was a constructive cynicism that I learned from my American colleagues. One of the most useful tips was their consistent advice that, when in doubt about whether an action was permissible or not, it was usually best to just press ahead and see if anyone complained. "Better to beg forgiveness than be denied permission" was an unofficial but time-tested motto that we relied on. Presented with a unique or unusual request, bureaucrats might have little to gain from saying yes and would prefer the safety of saying no. If you bypassed them, there was a good chance they wouldn't notice at all.

Then there was Canada: federal departments, agencies, boards, and corporations, all replicated ten or more times at the provincial and territorial level. A US ambassador could spend his three or four years just crossing the country, meeting these people and understanding what they did. Then there were third-country representatives (Mexican, British, or European, for example) and international organizations (to name only two, Canada hosted the International Civil Aviation Organization and the NAFTA Commission for Environmental Cooperation, both based in Montreal) that could come into play in what might seem at first like just a bilateral issue.

STAFFERS

Being the US ambassador to Canada (or chargé d'affaires for many months, as both Tom Weston and Terry Breese were) is, if properly understood, a very complex job. At the simplest level, an ambassador is the president's personal representative and tries to implement what the president wants. But this generally has to be done through a three-dimensional chess game with many organizations on the US side, many more on the Canadian side, and many issues in play, all at the same time – and while also serving as the chief executive of one of those organizations, an Embassy with hundreds of employees and six or seven regional offices.

I watched eight or nine people in this role during my time inside the Embassy, but as a bit player I cannot render judgment on how they played the chess game. From the sidelines, you notice just a few aspects of a leader's performance in a job that large. You notice whether they look and play the part; whether they seem engaged and attentive to the complexities, or detached; whether your own office gets informed and included in processes and decisions, or not.

I can say that the number and role of political office staff – people the leader brings with him into the job, who assist and control his interaction with the permanent organization – made a great difference. Some ambassadors brought no staff, managing with just the help of a career Foreign Service secretary. Some drafted a junior officer from the Embassy ranks to serve as executive assistant. And some brought in one or two staffers from outside the Foreign Service.

Staffers could make a dramatic difference in relations with Embassy officers who had to work the key issues, and with outsiders. I saw it as a source of downside risks to the organization. Even when staffers did not understand the three-dimensional chess game, they might do fine if they had clearly defined roles and respectful attitudes. But they also might obstruct or filter the flow of important information, meddle in the substance of issues (they generally had narrow knowledge of issues), breach political neutrality (they generally had party loyalties), or be gauche or bossy toward senior people. The role of staffers in executive offices has grown across Ottawa; we must hope the value they add offsets these hazards.

DIPLOMACY AND POLICY

Our office windows looked eastward across a small square (left vacant when the Rideau Club had burned in 1979) to the smoky-yellow sandstone of the Langevin Block, at the corner of Metcalfe and Wellington streets. Here we could see the third-floor office windows of Prime Minister Brian Mulroney and, on the floor below, the office of his communications adviser, then Norman Spector. Around the corner on the north side of our building, other offices looked directly across Wellington Street to the Centennial Flame, the Centre Block of Parliament, and the Peace Tower.

It was a great view on a clear day. During the height of the tourist season, the Changing of the Guard ceremony took place beneath our windows – with the drums and horns heard at nearly full volume through the loose, single-paned glass. We also saw all the political demonstrations on the lawn. It could be quite entertaining. At times, stepping out onto the sidewalk for my lunchtime walk, I would hear passersby complaining about our building's in-your-face position, nose-to-nose with Parliament; but it was a great spot to have an office.[20]

From some perspectives, US Mission Canada was almost too good at its job. When I was first interviewed at the Embassy in 1990 and I asked a question about policy making, the answer was: "We don't do policy here. That's Washington's job. We just communicate." This was correct in theory. But the Embassy, and particularly the Economic Section, grew very strong during the FTA and NAFTA years, partly because of my own work.

In July 1997, while I was visiting the State Department's Economic Bureau, a colleague told me: "Tokyo and Ottawa are unusual in that they are quasi-autonomous embassies. They do complete Ambassadorial briefers with no input from us" – briefers that, he noted, were "much better than anything the Canada Desk has." He went on to complain that the Economic Section in Ottawa was too big and that it competed with Washington offices to influence policy making.[21]

The Economic Section's size was not the source of this alleged problem. With just six or seven economic officers, Ottawa was less well staffed than embassies in several European capitals whose economic ties with the United States were much less significant. Rather, Ottawa's strength lay in a combination of factors. First, there was the high quality of the officers whom our section (and other posts such as Toronto) attracted. Ottawa offered not just a comfortable and secure North American living situation but also interesting and dynamic work in a big, active economic relationship, so great officers wanted to work there. In addition, there was the strong local professional staff, strengthened by the ways that our colleagues and the department empowered us in the 1990s to contribute to our full potential.

Moreover, in Ottawa there was the near-total absence of language and cultural barriers between the capitals, and this was further helped by Ottawa's proximity to Washington. We were in the same time zone, making phone communications easy, and officials could make short-notice day trips from one capital to the other when needed. As far as I could see, our engagement in the policy process was not a problem at all; it was valuable for both countries and an asset for Canada. To some extent it reflected weakness in the Canada Desk at State, which did not always have the kind of talent or leadership our Embassy could attract. Perhaps we could have managed this disparity better by talking to the desk more often to reduce duplicated or conflicting efforts and to find ways to help strengthen them.

RECATEGORIZING CANADA

The winding down of the Cold War contributed to the State Department's unusual decision in the later 1990s to shift relations with Canada out of one of its geographic bureaus and into another. Canada had traditionally been handled through EUR, the European Bureau, which was regarded as the senior and most important of the geographic bureaus. It was now to be part of Western Hemisphere Affairs (WHA).

While Canada's original placement in the European Bureau seemed a bit anomalous at first glance given its location on the western side of the Atlantic, handling Canadian affairs from EUR had made sense in the nineteenth and early twentieth centuries since Canada's foreign policy and defence were then still linked to Britain's. It continued to make sense until at least the 1990s for several reasons: Canada was a player in the Second World War transatlantic alliance, was a founding member of the North Atlantic Treaty Organization (NATO), and had substantial forces in Europe through the 1950s, 1960s, and 1970s. Outside of its integration with the United States, the strongest of Canada's trade, commercial, family, and social ties were with Britain and Europe. Its economic development was at a comparable level, its policy concerns tended to be similar, and it belonged to many Eurocentric international organizations and groupings.

But by 1998 much had changed. The post-war era had more or less ended with the breakup of the Soviet Union, the reunification of Germany, and the end of the Cold War. Canada was much more diverse and less British than it had been even as recently as the 1960s. It had withdrawn the last of its combat forces from Europe and closed most of its establishment there around 1993. Japan, not Europe or Britain, was Canada's second-largest trading partner after the United States. Moreover, Latin American countries had made great strides toward democratization and openness; Canada and Mexico had joined the United States in a trilateral free-trade agreement, and an effort was underway to liberalize trade on a hemispheric basis. Finally, Canada was eager to identify itself economically as a "Pacific Rim" nation, a group that included many Central and South American countries, and Canada hosted some of these at the summit of Asia-Pacific Economic Cooperation (APEC) leaders in Vancouver in November 1997.[22]

The idea that Canada should be treated as a "Western Hemisphere" country seemed like a consensus on investing in the future. If the Canadian side resisted, they did it quietly. Diplomats on both sides interpreted Canada's moves to open up its trade with Latin America as a positive step.. In September 1997 some rough notes from two of my colleagues informally reported how one of International Trade Minister Sergio Marchi's key aides had sketched out the picture over lunch. "Trade in Asia is extremely competitive, Canada won't become major. Europe is a mature market. The U.S is important but where is the next expansion? Good time for Canada to move vigorously in Latin America. Canada gets approaches from various countries who need to balance Brazil [the biggest regional power] and want to talk seriously. Add in U.S. interest in Latin America and there's an opportunity to get ahead of the train. Clearly, Canada wants the U.S. to move forward quickly on Free Trade Agreement of the Americas, but it won't sit and wait. Marchi believes Canada's actions vis-à-vis Chile and other steps will spur the U.S. to movement."[23]

One top officer at the Canadian Embassy in Washington told me: "Latin America is big enough for both of us. Let's work together, not dick each other around." A senior US diplomat with long Latin American experience remarked that "we play good gringo, bad gringo in Latin America. [The Canadians] push lots of issues that the U.S. can't – and they come out on our side in the end."[24]

In June 1998 the State Department announced that the creation of the Western Hemisphere Affairs Bureau, which would combine the existing Latin American bureau (ARA) with the Canada Desk. The official line was that the new bureau reflected "our intention to continue and deepen political and economic integration in our hemisphere ... By having Canada within a Western Hemispheric Affairs Bureau we should be able to deepen our cooperation in the Americas ... Indeed, it is impossible ... to conceive of hemispheric integration without Canada playing a strong and guiding role."

David T. Jones, a former Political Section head, writing in the Canadian press, painted the move as a demotion for Canada:

It is a fundamental reorientation of where the United States places Canada in its global view ... In effect, the United States has recognized that Canada is both unwilling and uninterested in sustaining its former commitments in Europe. The end of the Cold War has largely eliminated the need for another counterweight on the "western" side of the scale and Canada can opt out ... the transfer will mean even less high-level attention to Canadian issues. Although there are some outstanding, dedicated professionals in the Latin American Bureau, it is a distinctly second-tier bureau, behind the "mother bureau" EUR ... [Canada in WHA] will have a "culture problem" ... the Latin American bureau is geared to the issues of Spanish culture, development economics, political crisis and political-military arrangements. Dropping Canada into this mix is equivalent to wearing a three-piece suit to a mardi gras party in Rio.[25]

There was a grain of truth in this, but the conclusion that the move downgraded Canada was not fair. First, if Canada had let its NATO participation atrophy, even if it really had "opted out" of Europe, if it was choosing to look south and west more than east, and if this seemed to put it into new international company, none of this was the United States' fault. Canada's role as a close NATO ally had been waning since the Second World War and its spending on defence fell steeply during the 1990s (from 1.9 per cent of GDP in 1990 to 1.2 per cent by 1997). One of the perennial (and mostly futile) duties of the ambassadors I worked for was to implore Canadians to invest more in their own defence.[26] Jones's criticism saw the international landscape as it had been, not as it was becoming.

It might have been fairer to critique the way in which the decision to change bureaus was executed. Announced in mid-1998, but then delayed in various ways by Washington's bureaucracy, it did not become official until the fall of 2000. Meanwhile, the Canada Desk went without a director for a crucial period of about six months during the transition, during which a key opportunity to request new resources was missed (the "new" Canada Desk had the same funding, computers, and premises as the "old" one). The Desk also thereby missed an opportunity to use its arrival in WHA to educate other offices about Canada's importance and relevance. When an office director finally did arrive in WHA/CAN, he observed that Canadian news was completely absent from the daily briefers sent to assistant and deputy assistant secretaries of state. For a WHA country, it was considered particularly important to be present in the daily briefers because these senior officials in WHA did not see nearly as much telegram traffic as their EUR counterparts. This meant that daily briefers were the main place where a country desk's work got seen by the higher-ups.

"Canada hands" in our mission and on the Canada Desk became eager to highlight any links Canada might be developing with Latin America. To take just one small example, the WHA/CAN director heard in late 1999 that the government of Quebec was planning to open new offices in Buenos Aires and Rio de Janeiro, and he wanted someone in our mission to report it. This led to a difference of views between the Embassy and our post in Quebec City, since the latter (a bit like Quebec itself) tended to be Europhile and didn't welcome being directed from Ottawa.[27]

CANADIAN FEDERALISM
AND CONSTITUTIONAL NEGOTIATIONS

In its first five years, Brian Mulroney's Conservative federal government (1984–93) had already succeeded with major elements of its economic agenda (tax reform and Canada-US free trade). The political and constitutional side of the government's agenda faced more difficulty. Canada's constitution, like Britain's but unlike America's, is not enshrined in a single, central text; rather, it is a set of documents and conventions that has evolved and grown over time. Quebec had had a substantial separatist movement for at least a century, and a separatist provincial government from 1976 to 1985 under Premier René Lévesque.[28] That government held a province-wide referendum in May 1980 seeking a mandate to negotiate independence from Canada, which was rejected by 60 per cent of voters. The separatist (or "sovereigntist") movement remained strong through the 1980s and 1990s.

In the mid- to late 1980s Mulroney and his ministers led the provincial leaders through negotiation of a set of proposed amendments to the constitution. These amendments were intended to reconcile the government of French-speaking Quebec to the constitutional package passed by Pierre Trudeau's Liberal government in the early 1980s – which Quebec had never fully endorsed. Mulroney's negotiated effort to solve this problem – an effort that concluded in 1990 – was known as the Meech Lake Accord. Soon, however, the accord was under attack by a wide array of critics, including some more recently elected provincial governments as well as Aboriginal groups.

After lunch on my first day of work in the Embassy, someone encouraged me to join a small crowd that was gathered in the main conference room. This was a not-so-large, pine-panelled space on the second floor that had a television in one corner. Ten or fifteen of us sat, stood, or perched around it, watching a voting process in Manitoba's provincial legislature. We were waiting to see what Elijah Harper would do. On that day, 22 June 1990, Manitoba's Legislative Assembly was scheduled to vote on the Meech Lake Accord. Harper, the assembly's lone Aboriginal representative, held a deciding ballot. We all watched while he sat with an eagle feather in his hand and said no to Meech Lake.

The Meech Lake Accord's demise led to the resignation of Lucien Bouchard, the senior Quebec minister in the government, and his creation the following year of the Bloc Québécois (BQ), which would only ever contest seats in one province and was dedicated to removing Quebec from the federation. Meanwhile, Mulroney led his provincial counterparts into a further effort to bring Quebec inside the constitutional tent – and to a further agreement known as the Charlottetown Accord.

As a result of this long period of constitutional discussions, economic literature was accumulating on the benefits of Canada's federation and on the possible economic impact of some sort of renegotiated arrangement with Quebec. Nobody in the United States government seemed to be looking closely at all this economic work, so at the end of 1992 I took the lead in putting together a survey of it. This was my first serious step toward providing Washington with analysis of the economic and fiscal dimensions of Canadian federalism, an area in which I became the Embassy's expert and worked periodically until 2008.

STRESSES IN THE FEDERATION

Quebec sovereigntists were mainly driven by non-economic motives and were not eager to discuss economic implications of their proposals for changing the province's relationship with Canada. Some economists' pessimistic predictions about Quebec separation, and even attempts to focus on these questions, were decried as federalist "scare tactics." [29]

All Canadian provinces benefited to some extent from fiscal payments from the federal government known as "transfers," which are mostly intended to defray provinces' health and education costs. Since Quebec's income per person is below the national average, it also receives "equalization payments," which are intended to help poorer provinces provide comparable public services to those available in richer provinces. Advocates of Quebec's separation from Canada claimed that the federal system was wasteful – giving them at least one viewpoint in common with many conservatives in other provinces. They suggested that a separate Quebec could implement more effective policies, the greater efficiency of which would offset the loss of these federal payments and even make Quebecers better off as citizens of a separate country than under federalism.

An Alberta politician named Preston Manning had created the Reform Party, a breakaway group of Conservatives who were alienated from the broad nationwide party that Mulroney had assembled. The Reformers' chief complaint against Mulroney's government was that it had not done enough to downsize the federal government's role in the economy – as partly evidenced by the mounting fiscal deficit. But Manning also had a list of longer-standing grievances about the federal system, from bilingualism to abortion to the dysfunctionality of Parliament. Ultimately, it was and remained a populist movement. "We elect good people to Parliament," he said. "But after a while they stop being our representatives to Ottawa, and they become Ottawa's representatives to us."

The Mulroney team's hopes for successful constitutional reform were more or less finished off in the summer of 1992 by the rejection of the Charlottetown Accord in a national referendum. These constitutional struggles increasingly drained the political capital and momentum of the government under both Mulroney and his Liberal Party successor as prime minister, Jean Chrétien, in the 1990s, until Chretien wisely vowed to set constitutional issues aside and focus on the economy.

CANADA'S 1993 CONVULSION

The Mulroney coalition of political forces had governed for nine years, had done excellent work on the economic front, and had cultivated Canada's relationship with the Reagan and Bush administrations, but it disintegrated almost totally in 1991–93. When the dust cleared after the November 1993 election, the remains of the Progressive Conservative Party were reduced to just two seats in the 295–seat House of Commons. While Mulroney's economic agenda was a lasting success, his constitutional efforts were in ruins.

To no one's surprise, the Liberals under Jean Chrétien had won a large majority with 177 seats. The BQ, a party that had existed for less than two years and was ostensibly dedicated to splitting Canada apart, was suddenly the Official Opposition with 54 seats. Reform – which was not far behind, having won 52 seats – had also seemingly come from almost nowhere. Like the Bloc, Reform seemed (at least as it was portrayed in the establishment Toronto-Montreal-Ottawa media) to have a divisive, regionally based agenda for national politics.[30]

Our Embassy had the job of analyzing, reporting, and explaining all this to a Washington that didn't know much about Canadian politics but suddenly found the country more interesting than usual, not only because of the political turbulence, but also because of the intense focus on healthcare reform in Washington; the Canadian health-funding model was presented distortedly by both sides as an example of what good or evil might flow from changes to the US health-care system.

In retrospect, the creation of the Bloc Québécois looks like the turning point when a previously sincere Québécois independence movement began to become co-opted into the Canadian federal system. More than twenty years later, the BQ was still in Parliament, openly peddling its support to a minority Conservative Party government in return for cash for Quebec. Dependence on this flow of cash, ironically, keeps the Bloc established in Ottawa (though in the 2015 election it was reduced to a mere ten seats) and Quebec more or less reliant on the federal government. Canada is more secure from separatism today than it was in 1992, thanks in no small part, in this view, to the creation of the Bloc Québécois.

LIBERATING CANADIANS?

Quebec separatists very much wanted the US government's recognition and support, and through the years they were inclined to hope that the United States' origins in a revolution against empire would give Americans a natural sympathy with their movement.[31]

Just as Jefferson Davis, president of the Confederate States, had persistent and vain fantasies of France or Spain coming to the Confederacy's aid during the US Civil War, Bloc Québécois founder Lucien Bouchard and other Quebec separatists were powerfully attracted to the delusion that the United States covertly sympathized with them and might grant Quebec diplomatic recognition soon after independence.

But the US Civil War (1861–65) had mostly negative lessons for Americans. It had at least as deep an influence, perhaps deeper, on the American psyche, and is much fresher in Americans' collective cultural memory than the 1776 Declaration of Independence from Britain.[32] News of the Bloc Québécois's new status as Official Opposition in Canada's Parliament was met with disbelief in the US administration and in Congress as well as among ordinary Americans, who had very little inclination to be sympathetic to the separatist cause. To start with, Quebec simply did not appear to any outsider to be an oppressed society in need of liberation.[33] And more importantly, when Americans looked at Quebec separatism, they first remembered, not the courageous endeavour of 1776, but the ruinous split of 1861–65.[34]

QUEBEC AND INTERNATIONAL ENGAGEMENT

Quebec's separatist Parti Québécois (PQ) Premier, Jacques Parizeau, had told US Ambassador James Blanchard when the two men first met in October 1993 that he believed Quebec would accede easily to key treaties such as the North Atlantic Treaty Organization, the North American Air Defence Command (NORAD), and NAFTA. Blanchard (who had previously been governor of a large state, Michigan) objected immediately that Quebec could accede to NAFTA only after a couple of years of negotiating, which would require the participation of Canada. While this would be a crucial economic issue for Quebec in a real-life separation scenario, it took nearly two years to surface in public discussion.[35]

In 1994–95 Parizeau was the only provincial premier who was not on board the "Team Canada" trade-promotion missions led by Chrétien to China and Latin America. Parizeau chose to visit France instead. Presumably Parizeau, who was planning to hold a province-wide referendum on sovereignty in late 1995, wanted to avoid acknowledging his province's participation in anything positive about Canada; some thought he also enjoyed raining on any parade Jean Chrétien was leading. At any rate, his refusal to join the rest of the premiers seemed juvenile to many observers. Chrétien papered over the premier's absence with his Chinese and Latin American hosts by saying that he himself represented the province of Quebec on "Team Canada." While this was a bit awkward, Chrétien ended up getting the best of Parizeau in the optics of the affair, portraying the premier as an obsessive hermit.

Chrétien shrewdly took things a step further in February 1995. The prime minister chose a Montreal conference on trade with China to underline the links between federalism and an outward-looking economic policy. His emphasis on the benefits of Canada, rather than on the costs of separatism, was a significant change of tactic: it cast federalists in a much more positive role that that offered by the earlier argument that separation was, in essence, just bad. "For a country like Canada, jobs and growth mean trade ... Last November, I had the honor of leading the Team Canada trade mission to China ... Nine provincial Premiers helped lead the group. We were hoping for all ten but, unfortunately, M. Parizeau could not join us – he was too busy planning his trip to Paris ... While Quebec business joined forces with companies from all across this country to bring home jobs from Latin America, M. Parizeau was pursuing his agenda of separation in Paris." The prime minister then dove into the question that had been simmering but had not yet boiled: the accession of a separate Quebec to international treaties and agreements.

Two weeks ago, the American ambassador to Canada said that a separate Quebec would not automatically belong to NAFTA, and that a separate negotiation would be long and complicated. It will be for the advocates of separation to show how Quebec gains by having to negotiate a separate accession ... Last Sunday, M. Parizeau described a "no" vote as a vote for nothing. What is M. Parizeau's definition of "nothing"? ... Is NAFTA nothing? ... As a unified country, we were able to negotiate a deal that promotes the broadest possible range of Canadian interests. Is that nothing? We won access for a broad range of Canadian goods and services, while maintaining protection for key areas such as dairy production, cultural industries and procurement by provincial government departments and agencies like Hydro-Quebec. Is that nothing? M. Parizeau says Quebecers should not vote for "nothing." I say Quebecers should settle for nothing less.[36]

Our Embassy's report to Washington on Chrétien's speech included this comment:

Economic analysts have observed for years that two key economic obstacles to Quebec independence are the economic and financial dislocation associated with the transition to sovereignty, and an independent Quebec's status with respect to major trade agreements ... However, in public debate, federalists who emphasize transition costs risk a backlash, as they are invariably accused of "fear-mongering" by separatists. PM Chretien has chosen a safer and more positive course by stressing the economic benefits of being part of Canada ... Parizeau's argument that Quebec's accession to NAFTA would be virtually automatic is under attack.[37]

In his 1998 book, *Behind the Embassy Door*, Ambassador James Blanchard tells the story of how the Clinton administration's stance on Quebec developed. He observes that discussions of Quebec's possible separation from Canada always put the United States in an uncomfortable situation. Simple neutrality – "it's up to Canadians to decide" – was disingenuous and inadequate, because nobody would believe that the US government simply didn't care one way or the other about the constitutional fate of a major ally, leading economic partner, and close neighbour. And even this seemingly neutral position was loaded: saying "Canadians" rather than "Quebecers" implicitly reinforced the fact that Quebecers were Canadians and it also implicitly asserted that Canadians outside Quebec had a say in the matter.

THE RISKS AND COSTS OF SEPARATION

There were many costs and risks associated with the possible transition to Quebec's independence: maintaining investor confidence, dividing up public assets and liabilities (deciding what federal buildings, land, and organizations should be transferred to Quebec and how much they were worth), establishing some kind of monetary system or monetary union with Canada, surviving an initial recession (which looked almost inevitable), and maintaining trade relations. A Czech-Slovak style "velvet divorce," with Quebec and Canada cooperating to manage the transition smoothly, could solve some, but by no means all, of these problems.

As a result, it did not look as if the government of Quebec would enjoy an increase in its de facto sovereignty – its real-world ability to exercise free and independent policies – for perhaps three to five years after a split from Canada. On the contrary, in the meanwhile it would encounter a set of new or tightened constraints on its freedom of action with respect to spending, monetary policy, and trade policy. Some of these constraints would be long-lasting, such as the requirement for the Quebec government to open its purchasing opportunities to firms from the United States and the rest of Canada (from which it was exempt as a province but to which it would be subject as a NAFTA party). Others would affect crucial political concerns, such as whether it would have the freedom and funds to subsidize the aircraft industry or the cultural sector.

As planned, Parizeau's government held its province-wide referendum vote on separation in the fall of 1995. The question on the ballot was not very straightforward; it asked if Quebec should become sovereign after having made an offer to Canada for a new economic and political partnership. In the referendum campaign, there were two main economic issues: a separate Quebec's continued access to the benefits of the two big trade arrangements – the World Trade Organization (WTO) and especially

NAFTA – and the willingness or ability of the rest of Canada to negotiate an "economic partnership" with a sovereign Quebec.

Obviously, these were not the only possible questions to be explored; there was also the matter of other treaties and agreements and what currency an independent Quebec would use. Discussing these issues would presumably have made separation look even less straightforward and riskier. But they did not receive as much attention in the campaign as the federalist side had hoped, because federalists were reluctant to be the ones to bring them up lest their campaign appear to be negative and fear-based.

THE REFERENDUM CAMPAIGN

Until mid-campaign, federalists' treatment of the economic issues was low-key, stressing the positive benefits of membership in Canada. The federalists resorted to discussing the costs of separation, specifically job losses, only in the second half of the campaign as their poll numbers weakened.

Generally, the separatists avoided or downplayed the economic issues. They assured individual audiences – each group or constituency on the campaign trail – that their particular firms, jobs, or markets would be protected and secure if they voted "yes" to separation. Less frequently, they warned that a "no" vote would pave the road politically for budget cuts in Ottawa (which were in fact already, inevitably, on the way). According to a vague warning from Parizeau, saying "no" would also lead to continued exploitation of Quebec by large corporations. The separatist movement had been helped historically by Quebecers' resentment of their province's domination by an English-speaking investor class, and though this relationship had shifted toward much greater Québécois ownership and control by 1995, the warning about corporate domination still resonated.

The referendum on 30 October 1995 was a near miss for the separatists. In a high-turnout vote, 49.42 per cent of ballots were for separating. Parizeau had not quite obtained the mandate to negotiate, and he resigned as premier.

SUCCESSOR STATES AND TREATIES

How Canada's pre-existing international treaties and agreements would apply to an independent Quebec is an interesting question that – despite its importance – was not mentioned enough, much less answered satisfactorily, in the 1995 referendum campaign. The answer depended partly on what legal precedents existed. How had Washington handled its treaty relationships with other entities that emerged from a breakup or change of regime? These problems were familiar to some who worked on relationships in Europe and the former Soviet regions, of course, but not to anyone in Mission Canada. We had focused on the future of NAFTA during the referendum campaign, but there were dozens, perhaps hundreds, of other accords whose validity might come into question if Quebec moved to separate from Canada.

In fact, the US government applied a "presumption of succession" rule: successor states were usually presumed to keep the rights and obligations conferred by the pre-existing state's treaties and agreements.[38] After Quebec's secession, the "presumption of succession" process would have called for a case-by-case review of bilateral treaties and agreements, in order to decide which should continue and which should be revisited. The United States went through this process with Ukraine and Russia in the 1990s. With so many new states having been created, such large states were higher priorities, and small ones tended to have to wait longer.

Most relevant to Canada was the admirably well-managed Czech-Slovak breakup in 1993. State Department experts told me that the Slovaks had had good legal representation and that they acted pre-emptively, before the split and with cooperation from Czechoslovak government officials, to accede to membership in nearly all of the international organizations to which Czechoslovakia had belonged.

QUEBEC'S FOREIGN POLICY

The government of Quebec should have been doing its best to emulate this model, with primary attention to staying engaged with its main economic partners – Ontario and the United States. But in fact Quebec was taking a different path. Its surprisingly large "foreign ministry" was and apparently always had been preoccupied with France, and on obtaining diplomatic recognition starting with France in the event of secession.[39]

During the 1990s, the pre-eminence of the relationship with France began to be re-examined by academics and practitioners who noted that France was, after all, only the province's fifth-largest trading partner (its trade with Quebec was about one-sixteenth of Quebec-US trade). Quebec's real economic and social needs – the need to reduce unemployment, control public-sector deficits, and fund its social and cultural programs – would depend mainly on relations with Ontario and the United States, not with France.

But France provided powerful, and desperately desired, symbolic legitimacy and ego gratification to Quebec separatists. Quebec's Paris representatives (about twice as many staff as the Quebec offices in New York and Washington put together) received the same access to French government officials as Canada's diplomats. When the Quebec premier visited France, he would be greeted as a head of state and received by the president, and the French Consulate in Quebec City reported directly to the foreign ministry in Paris (rather than through the Embassy in Ottawa as would have been normal).

About a year after the referendum, Ottawa's local newspaper reported, "Foreign Diplomats Ordered to Report Contacts with Quebec." The *Ottawa Citizen* claimed that some diplomatic posts in town were being told to notify Canada's Department of Foreign Affairs and International Trade (DFAIT) when senior officials from provincial governments visited other countries and when diplomats or officials from other countries visited provincial officials. This was the first the US Embassy had heard of such a requirement.

It turned out that DFAIT had sent out a formal diplomatic note to this effect on 11 October 1996. The US Embassy must have overlooked the note (diplomatic note traffic did not make interesting reading). Apparently, the story broke only when several dozen diplomats were invited to a lunch with Bloc Québécois members of Parliament, because some diplomats, particularly from smaller countries, did notice the note and were reluctant to attend the lunch after they received it. One diplomat reported receiving a phone call from a DFAIT official questioning why he was attending the BQ lunch.

People in our building initially had difficulty believing that DFAIT would impose such a requirement. Provincial government officials visited Washington (and numerous other parts of the United States) frequently, and of course US officials, not only from our Mission but also from all sorts of offices in the United States, visited nearly every part of Canada. We considered ourselves free to interact with Canadians, and Canadians to be free to interact with us. Indeed, a request from other Canadian departments or offices that we approach them through DFAIT was usually a polite but clear way of resisting cooperation with us.

The diplomatic note actually read, "The attention of diplomatic missions is drawn to Article 41.2 of the Vienna Convention on Diplomatic Relations, which stipulates: 'All official business ... shall be conducted with or through the Ministry for Foreign Affairs of the receiving State.'" Copies were distributed through our section with a comment from the section head: *"For all – Shades of the old* USSR. POL *[The Political Section] is working to kill this."* While the United States would have been the foreign country most affected by this request by Canada, presumably other embassies objected as well, and to my knowledge it was not raised again.

THE 1995 SOVEREIGNTY REFERENDUM IN HINDSIGHT

In 1998, as key officers of our consulates in Quebec City and Montreal were preparing to leave Canada for other assignments, they provided a collective "out-briefing" for Ambassador Gordon Giffin. Most of these officers had been at post in Canada during the referendum period. As they reported it, the situation in Quebec remained volatile and dynamic in the spring of 1998, with strongly nationalist feelings on display. The Parti Québécois appeared well organized and electorally astute, and another term in office was possible. Meanwhile, Chrétien's Ottawa seemed to have a do-nothing approach to national unity.

In the longer run, though, demographics were working against the separatist old guard, essentially a generation of 1960s leftists, compared to whom younger Québécois were more technology-savvy, more business- and market-friendly, and more open to the economic and practical advantages of staying within Canada. The heart of the PQ was an older generation who remembered a time when Quebec had really consisted of a French Canadian working class dominated by an English-speaking proprietor class, and who were steeped in anti-capitalist and anti-colonial ideology. The younger generation saw fewer constraints on their own opportunities in a united Canada and a world of open borders.

The paramount analytical question posed to our Quebec experts in 1998 was whether the 1995 referendum had been separatism's high-water mark. The outgoing consul general (CG) in Quebec City, who had the leading responsibility for political reporting and analysis, thought that the peak had been reached, though nationalism would remain a strong force. His Montreal colleagues, who led on economic reporting from the province, were more inclined to think that another referendum was possible in the PQ's next term in government (that is, around 2000) and could possibly be won by them if the federalists' errors of the past were repeated. The outgoing CG in Montreal argued that the federal system inevitably would fail to satisfy Quebec's aspirations and that separation was just a matter of time. Her economic officer took an in-between view, saying that 1995 was a warning: if Ottawa continued to blunder, then the right combination of factors – perhaps including some perceived insult to Quebec – could push a vote over the top.

We knew that the Business Council on National Issues, which was the Ottawa-based policy voice for corporate Canada, was having trouble mobilizing executives on the national-unity file, and Ambassador Giffin found that business executives seemed unwilling to confront the Quebec government on anything. Federalists kept asking Giffin to encourage a more active US role in the debate. It was certainly too late to plead neutrality, since the Clinton administration's pro-federalist tilt during the 1995 campaign had made it clear that the United States was *not* neutral.

My American colleagues concluded that in the circumstances, as diplomats with a pro-Canada leaning, the best we could do was to avoid opening up specific issues (such as treaty succession) that might foster any sense that a transition toward separation might be underway. And we continued to hope that to the extent that there was an ongoing discussion about federalism, the business community, not just in Quebec but also in the rest of Canada, would become more engaged.

In retrospect, while the United States and Canada naturally had ongoing bilateral issues and differences in the 1990s, the United States took a generally favourable view of Canada's political and economic status quo. Quebec separatist leaders failed to give US policy makers confidence that the independent state they envisioned would be similarly amenable to US interests.

The transition costs that would be incurred during a shift by Quebec to sovereign status were likely to be large and, again, separatist leaders inspired little confidence that they had a plan to manage those costs. On the contrary, they seemed to disdain and avoid discussion of the whole economic aspect of the sovereignty project. This was in a decade when economic policy tended to be at the forefront of international public-policy debate, and when the general direction in many countries was toward improving macro-economic management. Premier Parizeau had done little to win the confidence of leaders and officials on the US side, and indeed had put them off further by engaging in some anti-corporate rhetoric during the referendum campaign.

CLINTON ON FEDERALISM

President Bill Clinton's speech on federalism at Mont-Tremblant, Quebec, in October 1999 was arguably the most important single event in Canada's relations with the United States in the 1990s. It helped to bring three or four decades of struggle over Canadian federalism to a close. Clinton set aside a prepared text and instead wove together his own experience in US state and federal politics, the powerful lessons from the disintegration of the former Yugoslavia, and other world events into a persuasive defence of federalism.

It was a long speech, but in a key section that in the official transcript is subtitled "How to Judge Independence Claims in Current Context," the president said:

> The suggestion that a people of a given ethnic group or tribal group or religious group can only have a meaningful communal existence if they are an independent nation – not if there is no oppression, not if they have genuine autonomy, but they must be actually independent – is a questionable assertion in a global economy where cooperation pays greater benefits ...
>
> I think when a people thinks it should be independent in order to have a meaningful political existence, serious questions should be asked: Is there an abuse of human rights? Is there a way people can get along if they come from different heritages? Are minority rights, as well majority rights, respected? What is in the long-term economic and security interests of our people? How are we going to cooperate with our neighbors? Will it be better or worse if we are independent, or if we have a federalist system?
>
> I personally believe that you will see more federalism rather than less in the years ahead ... And where there are dissatisfied groups and sections of countries, we should be looking for ways to satisfy anxieties and legitimate complaints without disintegration.

President Clinton closed his speech with this line: "I think more and more and more people will say, this federalism, it's not such a bad idea.[40]

The head of our Embassy's Political Section later told me that he was watching Quebec premier (and Parti Québécois leader) Lucien Bouchard's face as the president's speech ended, and that the impact was visible – Bouchard "looked utterly crestfallen." In our next staff meeting, one of our public-affairs colleagues wondered aloud whether we should say anything, publicly or privately, to soften the blow. Ambassador Giffin refused, stating: "Our chief executive came up here and made a statement. He gets to do that."

AFTER MONT-TREMBLANT

The Mont-Tremblant speech cleared the way for US representatives to give open expression to critical views on Quebec sovereignty, views they had held more privately four years earlier during the referendum campaign. It thus pushed separatists into a more defensive posture. The following month, former Ambassador Blanchard told a forum on Canada-US relations: "If Quebec separates, will it automatically be part of NAFTA? That's what their leaders are telling them. No, not necessarily, not at all ... Quebec politicians would be on their knees in Ottawa [for help in renegotiating access to all of Canada's international treaties and agreements]. That's not sovereignty. That's almost losing sovereignty." He added: "We are going to be much more supportive of federalism. We'll be much tougher on separatist movements in the future ... Why would we let ethnic tribalism break out in America?"[41]

Some Quebecers became more eager than ever to make their points. In early December, the US Council of State Governments – of which Quebec was the only non-US member – met in Quebec City, an event that five years (or even one year) earlier might have provided the PQ with a fabulous propaganda opportunity. Quebec Liberal Party leader Jean Charest, Premier Lucien Bouchard, and Deputy Premier Bernard Landry all spoke at length. The US Consulate reported that the Quebec politicians essentially abused the conference to carry on their own internal debate at the expense of American attendees, rushing out to speak to the press after each of their speeches. They were more eager, of course, to impress the Quebec public than their North American neighbours.

Fortunately for all North Americans, 1999–2000 was a period of technology-led economic boom and vigorous job growth. Montreal saw greater employment, increasing construction, a return of convention traffic, and a renewal of US investment. When the PQ cited all this, and an American officer colleague asked me about it, I told him that the provincial government "mistakes a high continental economic tide for a home-grown policy success! But I don't begrudge them the prosperity." I could have been much less charitable. If Montreal was recovering a little from decades of decline, it could be more reasonably ascribed to the PQ's political failure – its failure to win independence – than to its economic management.

My feeling, and that of many American friends of Canada, was that it was high time the sovereignty debate faded from the scene and that Quebecers – like other Canadians – focused on their economic future within Canada and North America. As former Ambassador Blanchard said, "Canadians are nitpickers that nitpick each other to death, and that's what has happened with this Quebec issue."[42] It was time to move on, and most of us did.[43] Federalism, and international integration, looked like the road to a better future.

2

Our Continental Economy:
Half Built before the Storm

In the early 1990s, with the great geopolitical struggle against communism being over and market economies seemingly victorious, economic interests became ascendant in the US administration. The Department of State vowed "to re-adjust its cold-war priorities toward greater emphasis on trade and investment issues" – this set our Economic Section's course for the duration of the Clinton years – "and toward nontraditional areas of diplomacy, such as the environment, human rights and humanitarian needs, narcotics, population, nonproliferation, refugees, and terrorism." This list foreshadowed the priorities of the early twenty-first century.

Canada and United States had the largest bilateral economic relationship in the world. For this reason alone, trade issues were sure to provide the core of the Embassy's economic work. The passage in 1988 and implementation starting in 1989 of the pioneering Free Trade Agreement further intensified this trade focus. The Embassy's top assignment when I arrived in 1990 was the selling and implementation of the FTA. It had been the biggest issue in the country during the preceding few years, and in the early 1990s it had survived the key political hurdles of an election and passage through Parliament, but it was still controversial and had to be defended, explained, applied, and interpreted.

CANADA IN NORTH AMERICA'S ECONOMIC ASCENT

Three generations earlier, Liberal prime minister Wilfrid Laurier ended his long career by staking the 1911 election on a deal that moderately liberalized trade with the United States. He lost to Sir Robert Borden's Conservatives, who advocated preferential trade within the British Empire. (As Conrad Black notes, "such was the suspicion of the United States in [Parliament] that it was assumed something reprehensible must be behind the Americans' sudden rush of apparent reasonableness" in agreeing to reduce tariffs with Canada.)[1] Although Laurier's government was fifteen years old and thus due to lose an election, the fact that a trade deal with the United States was the key issue of that campaign became the basis of a viewpoint that freer trade with the allegedly sharp-dealing Uncle Sam[2] was a losing platform in Canadian politics.

Borden's victory notwithstanding, British imperial solidarity gradually weakened. The United States became Canada's leading economic partner after the First World War, and by riding two great forces – the rise of the United States' immense economy, plus well-managed immigration – Canada grew quickly into an advanced industrial country.

In 1940–41, as the United States leaned toward supporting Britain's war effort as much as President Franklin D. Roosevelt could without actually entering the conflict, there was a perceived need for greater Canadian industrial integration with the United States, which led to the 1940 Ogdensburg Agreement establishing a Permanent Joint Board on Defence and then, in 1941, the Hyde Park Declaration on Co-operation in War Production. In 1956 the latter was transformed into the Defence Production Sharing Agreement. Given the threats to the continent and European allies during the 1940s and 1950s – first Germany and the Axis, then the USSR and communism – rationalizing defence production on a continental basis made some sense regardless of whether one was a Canadian nationalist, a continental integrationist, or a British Empire loyalist, so it had cross-party support.

TOWARD CONTINENTAL FREE TRADE

By the 1960s, the automotive sector led North American industry in its size and its sophistication. Canada had a long record of developing good auto products, but it was obvious that its market was too small for the efficient scale of that vast, complex industry. Manufacturers that thrived in Canada were those that integrated with US partners. Moreover, there was clear evidence of the payoff from liberalizing trade: reduction of many countries' trade barriers through the General Agreement on Tariffs and Trade (GATT) was boosting world economic growth, a very noticeable contrast to the ruin caused during the Great Depression when countries had raised tariff walls and growth stagnated.

For Canadian companies and plants to be more competitive in the 1960s, their market apparently had to get bigger and so barriers had to come down. A logical place to start was a Canada-US free-trade arrangement in autos and parts. The 1965 "Auto Pact," which removed tariffs on autos and parts between the two countries, helped to drive Canada's economic growth for the next two decades. That agreement led to hundreds of thousands of highly paid, high-skilled jobs, billions in research and development spending, and a very successful export record for Canada.

Liberalized Canada-US trade in defence and in autos had clearly worked. Economists pointed out that the same approach should work across the economy. After the Auto Pact, there was a sustained constituency for a broader free-trade agreement among economically conscious Canadians. An influential 1967 book by Ronald and Paul Wonnacott[3] advanced the theoretical understanding of the issue, fostering thorough study and modelling by academics and governments that lasted more than two decades. Those were times when, despite the lack of computing power, policy analysis was sometimes done more methodically than it is now; governments had internal capacity for data collection, modelling, literature surveys, and other research that today is purchased from consultants or, more often, not done at all.

But Canadians were understandably concerned about getting closer to the United States, a country that had been viewed with suspicion in Canada ever since the American Revolution. Many Canadians wanted to keep an independent cultural identity, maintain control of their own economic direction, and retain corporate head offices, designers, research and development, and other functions. There was concern about foreign control, as well as the possibility that free trade might go further than it should in some areas.

GOVERNMENT IN THE ECONOMY

The political pendulum was swinging in an anti-business direction and toward government intervention during the 1960s, particularly after 1968 under Prime Minister Pierre Trudeau. To the extent that it was implemented in policy, this often hurt investment and growth. After the oil shock in 1973, international economic turbulence made matters worse for growth and incomes, often then driving further attempts at government control. Under Trudeau, in the decade after 1973, Canada attempted wage-and-price controls, foreign-investment controls, and massive intervention in the energy sector through the National Energy Program (NEP). By the early 1980s, the economy was a shambles.

These policies not only hurt Canada, they also hurt and irritated our neighbours. A briefing to President Ronald Reagan prior to an early meeting with Trudeau in July 1981 advised the president to

> raise the issue of Canada's discriminatory investment policies with the Prime Minister ... Canadian investment policies, particularly those of the National Energy Program, are having an increasingly detrimental impact on the overall U.S.-Canada relationship. Canada's policies have had a serious impact on a number of American firms ... measures being proposed to implement the National Energy Program ... significantly depart from accepted international principles of fair and equitable treatment of foreign investments ... As a result, U.S. firms would likely be forced to sell certain assets, at depressed rates, to Canadian interests in order to remain competitive.
>
> The Canadian Foreign Investment Review Agency (FIRA) was established in 1973 to increase Canadian control and ownership of investment in Canada and to ensure benefits for Canadian firms from such investment. While we do not challenge either FIRA's existence or its screening of new foreign investment, we do find its administration objectionable. Particularly troublesome are the legally enforceable commitments extracted by FIRA from firms investing in Canada, such as specifying when firms must purchase Canadian goods and/or requiring firms to export a specific share of Canadian production. In addition, FIRA's veto power over the transfer of Canadian assets from one U.S. owner to another is unacceptable.
>
> The result of these practices has been a distortion of trade and investment flow. Many U.S. firms have been thwarted in their efforts to invest in Canada by the unreasonable and sometimes uneconomic commitments exacted by FIRA.[4]

An update to the president a few months later assessed what the United States could do:

> Canada is in the midst of efforts to enhance its national identity and the role of Canadian enterprise in its economy. While we respect these efforts, we must insist that they be pursued in a non-discriminatory manner, consistent with Canada's international commitments ...
>
> These policies currently being pursued by Canada: (1) are to a degree expropriatory; (2) force businesses to make uneconomic decisions, increasing costs and hurting consumers; (3) are contrary to the

letter and spirit of international obligations; (4) nullify some of the benefits of previous trade concessions; and (5) interfere with trade and investment flows. These policies also undercut U.S. efforts to persuade other countries to move away from such policies. Finally, Canadian investment policies increase pressures, especially in the Congress, for the United States to adopt similar policies – to the detriment of the United States, Canada, and the world trading system.

... It is important to note that sympathetic Canadian officials have privately urged us to pursue our rights under the General Agreement on Trade and Tariffs in order to strengthen their internal efforts to change Canadian policies they too find objectionable.[5]

Little wonder that in 1982 Canada's economy was in its worst shape since the Great Depression (inflation and unemployment were both around 11 per cent and growth was negative); nor is it surprising that some Canadian officials apparently were even less enthusiastic about Trudeau's economic policies than their American counterparts.

To his credit, Trudeau could admit that a rethink was due. He asked a former finance minister, Donald S. Macdonald, to head a royal commission that would take a thorough look at Canada's economic situation and prospects.

THE FREE-TRADE VISION

When it reported in 1985 to a new prime minister (Brian Mulroney of the Progressive Conservative Party, which had won a majority of seats in Parliament in the 1984 election), Macdonald's royal commission recommended fundamental policy changes. One of them was that Canada negotiate a free-trade agreement with the United States. Few now recall that the FTA was not Brian Mulroney's personal idea, nor necessarily his party's idea.[6] But just as Trudeau deserves credit for launching the economic rethink, Mulroney deserves credit for deciding that his government could bring a free-trade agreement to realization.

Mulroney courageously staked the prime minister's job on his belief that the Canadian electorate was ready for big changes in economic policy, including a comprehensive trade agreement with the United States. And he succeeded, with a great deal of help from business leaders and many others – including unintentionally from Pierre Trudeau, whose interventionist policies, by being sustained for too long and failing, prepared Canadians for a fundamental change in direction.

In the 1988 election campaign, both sides oversold their arguments on free trade. To win the election, Mulroney (whose arguments were backed by many large businesses) notoriously promised "jobs, jobs, jobs," while his opponents (including then Liberal Party leader John Turner, Council of Canadians leader Maude Barlow, and Canadian Auto Workers president Bob White) forecast Canada's economic and cultural destruction. Sadly, many Canadians were still ready to be convinced that their own country's largest and most successful companies, in backing free trade, somehow didn't know what they were doing and were only being lured down the throats of their bigger American competitors.

From an economist's point of view, the "for" argument in favour of free trade was solidly based in theory and practice, and net gains could safely be expected for both countries from the FTA. But those gains would not be all that dramatic, since trade in goods between Canada and the United States was already relatively free of barriers, at least by the standards of most countries, partly thanks to the work already done by the Auto Pact a generation earlier. Also, framing the argument (as Mulroney did) around job creation, while it reflected the way economic news was usually cast at the time, was misleading. The gains from free trade come from cheaper imports and greater productivity, not from more jobs; the number of jobs is determined more by demographics and technology and by the quality of government economic management. The FTA had a ten-year phase-in period, so the process of reducing most of the already modest tariffs to zero would not be completed until 1998, stretching the period of adjustment.

The economic adjustment involved for Canada was less significant than the change required in Canadians' political world view. Canada was a relatively small part of a big, evolving world economy; rather than taking prosperity for granted, Canadians had to understand what their relative pluses and minuses were in that world, and it would be good to have sound strategies for managing them.

When it came to selling the FTA to the broad Canadian public – which was part of the US Embassy's mission when I came on board in mid-1990 – much of that was being done by Canada's government and business leaders. The Embassy did not have the resources to influence the opinions of millions of Canadians; we could only really reach the few people we came into direct contact with, only some of whom were receptive to what we had to say. The FTA had formally been Canada's initiative; Canadians had come to Washington and asked for it. It was really up to Canadians to decide among themselves whether or not they had made the right choice.[7] With free trade's opponents being many, active, strident, and loose with the truth, including more than a few in the Canadian media establishment, the Embassy had plenty of work just to correct distortions, misquotes, or errors of plain fact about the United States and its policies in the mainstream media, think-tanks, and academic institutions.

IMPLEMENTING THE FTA

In what was quite a breakthrough for the time, the Canada-US Free Trade Agreement contained a binding dispute-settlement mechanism, under which persistent problems could be referred to quasi-judicial panels made up of trade-law experts from both countries. The panelists would hear arguments, debate the merits among themselves, and write an opinion by which the two governments were supposed to abide but for which there was no enforcement. (There was also a mechanism for investment disputes, to protect business investments from being harmed arbitrarily by government actions.)

By mid-1990, the first trade disputes were already working their way through the new panel system. This was quite a precedent for international trade deals at any level, and thus it attracted the interest of the worldwide trade-law community. In fact, the dispute-settlement mechanism came to be viewed as a considerable step forward in the trade-policy world. A version of the Canada-US model would be adopted in the North American free-trade agreement in 1994 and would help to shape the new World Trade Organization in 1995. This made Ottawa in the early 1990s, in a modest way, an exciting place and time to be involved in international trade-policy discussions.

When Julius Katz, who previously had a long career as a State Department economic official and was now deputy US trade representative, made a brief visit to Ottawa during my first year or so at the Embassy, he took time to join a discussion panel with a large audience at the University of Ottawa's Faculty of Law. It impressed me how comfortably a government economic official could blend such quasi-academic activity into his job. Intellectual engagement was woven into the fabric of US government, especially in the State Department.[8] Katz, and other US government officials I watched in similar settings, spoke with a confidence and relative independence one seldom saw in Canadian officials in those days, and even less so today.

Among our specific trade issues during the early years of FTA implementation, we had some complex arguments with Canadian federal officials about how American alcoholic beverages – mainly wine and beer – were treated by Canadian provincial liquor authorities. Monopolistic government-owned liquor control boards and distribution systems protected wine and beer made in-province by finding many ways to promote them over goods from outside. American goods that managed to be admitted into the province at all had to pay more mark-up margins and service fees than Canadian products, yet they were given poorer retail shelf space and no product promotion.

While Canadians may have thought this sounded like fair game – why not support the home product? – the whole point of international trade policy is that too much of this kind of thing coddles inferior products and services and cheats consumers. It restrains economic growth and ultimately depresses ordinary people's living standards.[9]

While exposing, criticizing, and reducing trade barriers was complex and daunting work, I embraced it not just because it was my job but also because it was consistent with the principles of my economic education as well as with my personal support for the FTA two years earlier. My colleagues and I had no trouble aligning our day-to-day work with both theoretical and practical economics.

CONTEMPLATING NAFTA

Beginning around 1990–91, Canada, the United States, and Mexico were consulting each other and their businesses and publics on the idea of a three-way North American free-trade agreement modelled on the FTA.

Mexico had initiated the idea. The government of the day under President Carlos Salinas de Gortari was interested in advancing market-oriented economic reform. Mexico had to accelerate job creation to a pace that would keep employment ahead of the country's high birth rate. Also, as was true of Canada, Mexico's economy depended on the health of its trade and investment relationship with the United States; access to the US market had to be maintained to protect Mexican living standards.[10]

In the 1990s I made regular visits to the Press Club building, just a few doors down Wellington Street from the Embassy, to monitor what was going on around Parliament Hill. The Press Club had bulletin boards and display tables filled with paper copies of notices, releases, studies, schedules, and so on. The small theatre on the ground floor provided the backdrop for various photo opportunities, press conferences and announcements. Of course, I did not have press credentials, but I usually managed to slip in.

One day in my early months at the Embassy, I went there to hear Prime Minister Mulroney's international trade minister, John Crosbie, and his two opposition party critics give their political parties' answers to some key questions about possible negotiations with Mexico. It became a lesson in finding the real story underneath what babbled into the microphones.

Would the bilateral FTA be reopened, potentially reversing some of Canada's gains from the 1988 FTA talks? Crosbie promised that it wouldn't. Would a new trilateral deal replace the FTA? Crosbie avoided the question. (In fact, the FTA was suspended in 1994 to make way for the North American Free Trade Agreement, with the proviso that, if NAFTA ever ceased to apply, the FTA would resume.)

Wouldn't Canada be overwhelmed by low-wage Mexican products? Crosbie pointed out that most Mexican exports to Canada were already free of duties, yet Mexican goods made up only about 1.3 per cent of Canada's imports. Did Canadians support talks with Mexico? The government admitted that there was bound to be some opposition. That was a mild way of saying that the coalition of groups that had fought the FTA was still active and determined.

Back at the Embassy, I told my boss, the trade officer, that the Liberal Party's official critic, Roy MacLaren, had not answered Crosbie with a prepared statement but merely invited questions. My colleague said, "There's your story! The Liberals are split on free trade, or else they would have had a statement." He was right. MacLaren – who would later be international trade minister – was trying to ease his party away from the hard anti-FTA position it had taken in the election campaign in 1988, which it had lost. With MacLaren's help, soon the Liberals would again take the more free-trading stance that they had held eighty years earlier under Wilfrid Laurier, and that they continue to hold more than two decades later.

NDP trade critic Dave Barrett had a firmer position. He told the press conference that Mexicans were exploited for sixty cents an hour in jobs transplanted from the United States and Canada that were not tied to the indigenous market. Like most in his party, Barrett spoke as though the basic argument in favour of liberalizing trade – which is about as close to a scientific truth as economics can offer – either did not exist or was mere corporate propaganda that did not warrant answering. His position was that Canada should not enter the negotiations until the government showed how Canada could benefit from them.

This put the cart before the horse. It was a pretty safe expectation that we would have net gains as a country if we genuinely and substantially liberalized our international trade. Over the one hundred and eighty years since the theory had first been worked out by David Ricardo, this had been shown over and over again by experience (including specifically to Canadians through the Auto Pact), and was further validated by the latest research on economic growth.[11]

The task ahead of countries that might want to negotiate a trade-liberalizing treaty was to find out what specific gains and sensitivities their political stakeholders faced, how much liberalization they could actually accomplish given all the political realities, and how to compensate the minority of stakeholders who were likely to lose out. It was not about whether to try, but about how much liberalization could be achieved in the circumstances. This was what the NAFTA consultations and negotiations needed to do.

Barrett and other free-trade opponents were in just the situation I had predicted when I had applied for my position and was asked to write a short essay on political reactions to a North American free-trade agreement. In the debate over the FTA in 1988, the opposition's argument to Canadians had essentially been that "big powerful efficient American companies will take your jobs" – even though it was Canadian businesses that were pushing for the FTA. Just two and a half years later, it was the Mexicans who wanted to be part of a tariff-free area, and suddenly the opposition's argument had to become, "Low-wage, environmentally dirty Mexicans will take your jobs." A narrative could have been constructed that united these two perspectives, but in fear-mongering, simplicity is desirable.

The opposition's argument was further contorted by claims that, while poor Mexicans were going to take all the jobs, this was somehow going to be bad for Mexicans. The way for the NDP and the Council of Canadians to square this awkward circle was to argue that when corporations did well in Mexico – creating jobs and building infrastructure – ordinary people somehow lost out, through destruction of their environment, of their traditional cultures, and so on. This was an early rumbling of the anti-corporate, anti-globalization messages that would become no more logical but that would be heard much more often in the 1990s and early 2000s.[12]

CHRÉTIEN AND HARPER

Jean Chrétien, a well-liked and respected Trudeau-era minister who had first been elected to Parliament in 1963, had taken over the leadership of the Liberal Party after its defeat by Mulroney's Conservatives in the 1988 election campaign on free trade. As leader of the opposition, Chretien was keeping a low profile in the early 1990s, quietly rebuilding his party and letting Mulroney's problems, scandals, and enemies accumulate – as do those of almost any government that is well into its second term.

One summer evening in 1991 as I walked home down Wellington Street, I noticed Chrétien posing for a photo with some businesspeople in front of the Château Laurier hotel. Catching a glimpse of NDP leader Audrey McLaughlin passing a few steps away, he teasingly called her to join in, but she walked off. Chrétien fell in with me, we began strolling together, and he joked with me about McLaughlin's humourlessness. For the next forty minutes, as his car and Royal Canadian Mounted Police (RCMP) driver slowly tailed us toward Stornoway, the opposition leader's official residence in Rockcliffe Park, we walked and talked together.

Chrétien asked me what impression his strong accent made. I told him that people viewed it as a sign of authenticity – a contrast, I gently noted, to the popular image of Mulroney. Chretien said, "It's true what they say about Brian – he's packaged." At the first opportunity, I disclosed where I worked, since Chrétien had a right to know that I was liable to share things he might say with my Embassy colleagues. I could see that this information gave him momentary pause, but the conversation quickly warmed up again.

It was wide-ranging, and the opposition leader encouraged me to ask questions. I focused mainly on drier topics such as macroeconomics and trade policy. Toward the end of our walk, he opined that freer trade and more open markets were just the way things were going everywhere. I thought this was revealing, suggesting that a free-trade policy on his part would reflect less intellectual commitment than trend-following. A few years later, after more encounters with politicians, I would not have been surprised by such a comment. It was not theories or economic principles, nor even party ideology, that mattered to a career politician like Chrétien. He cared mainly about where public opinion was going. This was good in the circumstances, insofar as he was not necessarily wedded to the economic legacy of his years on Trudeau's team. Jean Chrétien would soon lead one of the more pro-free-trade governments in Canada's history.

At that time, in 1991, the Mulroney government was still hoping to get re-elected on a record of successful constitutional reform as well as economic reform. But Canadian voters in 1991–93 were sick and tired of constitutional issues and had come to see the economy as the major problem facing themselves and the country. Many in the opposing Liberal Party, which was far ahead in the polls, thought the focus should be on the recession and the budget deficit, issues they could accuse Mulroney of neglecting.

On trade, Chrétien's Liberal team softened its previously anti-free-trade position and adopted the language of markets and international competitiveness – while saying that the Liberal Party wanted to renegotiate at least parts of the FTA and proceed with caution on NAFTA. The party was using this nuanced stance to straddle a wide field of opinion in its ranks, from cultural nationalists to big business. It still had a strong left-nationalist wing (typified by Sheila Copps, Lloyd Axworthy, and Brian Tobin) that mostly opposed the FTA, but it also had people with strong corporate connections who strongly favoured the agreement.

Because of this wide base, the Liberals were also vague on fiscal policy – specifically whether and how they would tackle the government's very difficult debt-and-deficit crisis. Anyway, they did not really need a clear platform in the circumstances: opposition parties do not win elections so much as governments lose them. The Conservatives certainly looked to be on a losing track and the Liberals really just had to look like a government in waiting.

Of course, there were other parties on the federal scene, and one with clear views on economic issues was the populist Reform Party, which had arisen in western Canada but was planning a national campaign in the 1993 election. I telephoned the party's headquarters and asked for someone to talk to about Reform's economic platform. Even with its geographically confined base, in the province of Alberta, Reform was drawing 15 per cent support in nationwide polls – already about even with Mulroney's flagging Conservatives – and the party was rapidly organizing in Ontario, which would help it gain momentum. Initially, the Reform officials I talked to suggested I contact Tom Flanagan, the University of Calgary academic who had been Reform's intellectual mentor. But then they called back to let me know that their chief policy officer, Stephen Harper, would be in Ottawa a few days later and could come by to see us.

Harper, who would later be Canada's prime minister from 2006 to 2015, was a reserved, well-spoken man in his mid-thirties who described himself as a fiscal economist. He came upstairs into our very unglamorous offices and talked with the Embassy's trade officer and me for an hour or so.

Harper said he did not believe in discretionary fiscal management and was convinced that it was politically easier to cut spending massively than incrementally. As he listed them, Reform's priorities for spending reductions reflected the party's grievances against the federal system, which were as deep as those of the other upstart party that had cut into Mulroney's support, the Bloc Québécois (though a bit more clearly articulated). Harper wanted to cut funding to parliamentary institutions and party caucuses; "thick layers of middle management" in government; bilingualism, multiculturalism, and government advertising; grants to interest groups for lobbying purposes; foreign aid; subsidies and tax concessions to businesses; and what Reformers called "universal and bureaucratic social policy."

Harper admitted that Reform was internally split on the Goods and Services Tax (GST), which Mulroney's government had introduced in 1989 as a centerpiece of its tax reforms. Reform Party leader Preston Manning, like much of the economics profession, approved of the GST on grounds of efficiency (since it replaced a less-well-designed sales tax), but the rank and file disliked taxes in general and so the party said it was examining other tax-reform options.

Reform's views were also split on free trade. Harper thought the party's next policy convention would favour the FTA but would resolve to make it "work better" – the kind of position you take when you like something but want to mollify its critics.[13]

SEEING THE ECONOMY

My role in the Economic Section gave me responsibility for following all aspects of the Canadian economy except agriculture, transport, and the financial sector. That left a broad and interesting field that included manufacturing, mining, energy, cultural industries, health care, and technology. Our section had a travel budget that, as I eventually discovered, few of my colleagues wanted to use. Most of them had already spent enough of their lives in airports and hotels, and wanted some peace between moving in and moving out of Ottawa. I liked travel, it was easy to get permission to do it, and I learn well visually, so I got to know Canada's economy by seeing it for myself. Most industries were willing to host an interested visitor. I also attended conferences where I could meet and learn from industry experts. Normally, I followed up my trips, even those to relatively dull conferences, with written reports that organized and analyzed the information I had collected, and this process reinforced and deepened my knowledge.

Much manufacturing, such as automotive, was already thoroughly documented and could be studied fairly well from Ottawa and from our Consulate in Toronto. I went to see industries and plants of special interest, especially in Quebec: a pharmaceutical factory in Montreal, Bombardier's executive-jet assembly facility in Dorval, textile plants in the Eastern Townships. Technology was interesting and trendy enough, and cultural industries sufficiently sensitive politically, that officer colleagues would come along with me on trips to see enterprises in these sectors: the nuclear laboratories in Chalk River, medical-products and telecom systems in the Ottawa region, publishing and advertising groups in Toronto.

But it was the natural-resource-based industries – energy, mines, forestry, and fisheries – that gave me the best reason to utilize the travel budget and explore my country. I saw ocean experts in Newfoundland and Nova Scotia, a nuclear-power plant in New Brunswick, the immense La Grande 2 hydro facility in northern Quebec, an electric-power-system control centre in southern Ontario, the oil sands in northern Alberta, oil wells in the Northwest Territories's Mackenzie River valley, a gas well in Inuvik, a fish ladder in Whitehorse, sawmills and aquaculture on Vancouver Island. I even went to Winnipeg and talked to the Canadian Wheat Board and the Aboriginal Peoples Television Network. It was a wonderful economic education spread over twenty years, one that delivered real, comprehensive knowledge of how Canada's – and to a great extent North America's – sectors and regions were knitted together and were changing.

ASSESSING NAFTA

In the fall of 1992, around the time of the US election that brought the Democratic nominee Bill Clinton to the White House, the Embassy hosted a team of investigators from the US General Accounting Office studying (in advance) various aspects of North American free trade in order to make a public report on the subject to US Congress. I helped to organize the visit and accompanied the team as it met with Canadian federal trade officials, opposition politicians, business and labour groups, and academics.

Certain points were made consistently by the Canadian experts. First, they expected that NAFTA's impact on Canada would be felt mainly through the agreement's effects on the US economy, rather than through Mexico or Mexico-Canada trade. This was because Canada's trade and investment links with Mexico were so weak and those with the United States so strong.

The second key point the experts made was that, while access to Mexican markets was a modest but worthwhile goal, Canada had actually entered the negotiations for primarily defensive reasons: to protect the gains it had made in the US market through the FTA. A third point was that, now that the negotiations were finished, the government of Canada viewed NAFTA as a substantial improvement on the FTA and believed that its negotiators had defended Canadian interests very successfully.

Democrat Bill Clinton and Liberal Jean Chrétien both appealed to groups, such as unionized workers, that were skeptical about trade liberalization. Both expressed doubts about the trade agreement with Mexico during their respective successful 1992 and 1993 election campaigns, and vowed to make it "work better." Both were sensitive to the left wings of their parties. But once they were in office, both, after a show of resistance (and the addition of "supplemental agreements" to strengthen enforcement of the three countries' own labour and environmental laws), eventually announced in late 1993 that they could accept NAFTA.

Canadian observers were able to enjoy the US domestic debate on NAFTA during 1993 with amusement and some sympathy given their own agonies over the FTA in 1988. They generally liked Vice-President Al Gore's performance in his televised debate with the former third-party presidential candidate and strident NAFTA critic, Ross Perot. Open markets began to look more like something an educated, progressive liberal (such as Gore and Clinton) could endorse. Canadian free traders' concern about the risk of NAFTA being killed in the new Congress was tempered by some speculation about the opportunity that outcome might create for Canada to offer itself as a free-trade partner for Latin America.

THE LIBERALS BEND

At the time of Canada's November 1993 federal election, NAFTA was set to enter into force in just a few weeks, at the start of 1994. The rhetorical excesses of NAFTA critics had made such an impact on ordinary Canadians' minds that 63 per cent of those questioned in an Angus Reid poll thought Canada had more to lose from NAFTA than either Mexico or the United States did. Even so, nearly as many Canadians supported the agreement as opposed it.

The new Liberal government led by Prime Minister Jean Chrétien at last clarified its position on the deal in the days after winning the election. The new team said it wanted to renegotiate the FTA and NAFTA in order to obtain changes to trade-remedy laws, which were the subsidy and dumping rules that allowed companies in the United States and Canada to ask courts for special taxes on foreign products. Defending against these measures in the courts was very burdensome, so just bringing a legal action might be enough to drive a foreign competitor out of the accuser's market, even if the accuser had a weak case. Reforming these laws had been urged by many economists and anticipated in the FTA, but never achieved, making it a key piece of unfinished business.

Chrétien's fledgling government also said that it wanted the same exemption for its energy sector that Mexico had obtained in the NAFTA negotiations: Mexico's oil and gas sector was largely nationalized under a state company called Pemex, and Mexico wanted it to stay that way. Roy MacLaren, now the minister for international trade, announced these reservations about NAFTA to the Canadian public in very general terms, emphasizing that talks were underway with both the United States and Mexico.

There was not much room, or time, for renegotiation at that point, and in fact none really occurred. Our Economic Section reported to Washington that, since the text of NAFTA had already been approved by the US Congress, and since (in reality, as opposed to Canadians' imaginations) Canada was by far the country least affected by the agreement,

> Canadian observers are realistic about the scarcity of time and leverage available to the new Liberal government to win further adjustments to NAFTA. Most commentators recognize reform of trade remedy laws as a worthwhile goal which may be pursued after NAFTA is implemented January 1. Influential groups have called on the Liberal government to implement NAFTA ...
>
> There is some skepticism about Prime Minister Chretien's vow to renegotiate the energy provisions of the FTA and NAFTA, though this rarely shows up in media reports. The Liberals' professed dissatisfaction on energy puzzles most informed observers, and changes would require altering the original agreement (as opposed to merely negotiating a side letter or other understanding).[14]

In the end, as a result of domestic pressure on the Clinton administration, two side letters were negotiated, and on 2 December 1993 Chrétien turned his party's awkward corner on trade policy (and, to some extent, on energy policy too) by announcing his intention to proclaim NAFTA on 1 January 1994.

Mexico actually had fairly sound environmental- and labour-protection laws on its books – but its governments often did not enforce them. The 1993 "side letter" agreements on the environment and labour created trilateral commissions which would hear complaints of cases where a NAFTA member government was alleged not to be living up to its own country's laws in those areas.

The side letters helped to assuage some of the North American public's concern about the agreement triggering an industrial "race to the bottom," meaning the fear that, as tariffs came down, Canada and the United

States might compete with Mexico to attract investment and jobs by lowering their regulatory standards.

THE CRITICS

It was easy for opponents of the FTA and NAFTA to stir up public anxiety, both before and after the agreements came into effect. Canadians' support for the specific agreements tended to be weaker than their support for the general concept of freer trade, because the agreements were attacked almost daily in the Canadian media.

Statements made by FTA and NAFTA critics, which are on the parliamentary record, are interesting to review today. In November 1992 the Trade Subcommittee of the House of Commons heard testimony from the Action Canada Network, led by Tony Clarke, who informed members that the FTA (then four years old) had hurt the economic, social, and political life of Canada, eroded its sovereignty, and transferred powers to transnational corporations and technocratic elites. NAFTA would further weaken democracy in Canada by replacing legislative decisions with what Clarke called "technocratic committees operating under a North American constitution administered from Washington." By the latter, Clarke presumably meant dispute-settlement panels and/or the commissions on environmental and labour cooperation.

This was the kind of "information" that Clarke and other leading opponents of trade liberalization contributed to the public discussion. It was so exaggerated as to give the listener no sense at all of the actual terms of the agreements. The distorted language was crafted to exploit Canadian irritability and insecurity wherever possible, in this case about constitutional issues. The New Democratic Party continued for months to claim that NAFTA would "rewrite Canada's economic constitution."[15] Canada's free-trade critics offered almost no explanation of exactly how such evils could flow from a treaty whose main purpose was to reduce barriers to merchandise trade.[16]

In the end, of course, none of those evils materialized, or at least not as a result of NAFTA. Unrelated forces such as technological change and the unique rise of China as an economic power would have warranted more fretting than NAFTA did, but human beings have a way of disregarding real threats while obsessing about false ones.

The distortions peddled by the NDP and the Action Canada Network over the years on the subject of NAFTA were not just wild as rhetoric; they also turned out to be wild as economic forecasts. Canada's economic performance in the late 1990s and early 2000s was terrific, and all the credible studies showed that trade and investment liberalization had delivered great benefits. For all the accusations that free trade would "hollow out corporate Canada," in 2006 Canada had more than twice as many world-leading companies as it had in 1985, and their annual revenue had grown by over 80 per cent in real terms.[17]

Yet most writing about NAFTA and the FTA obscures this and makes the record sound much more ambiguous. In 2014 a relatively knowledgeable fellow citizen asked me whether free trade had in fact been good or bad for Canada. He had no idea what the answer was. All that had stuck in his mind from twenty years earlier was the apocalyptic scaremongering, and he honestly wanted to know whether that had come to pass or not.

LATER ASSESSMENTS OF FREE TRADE

In the first half of 1997, with NAFTA now three years old, US economic officials did some stock-taking. Unfortunately, and despite some good efforts, the once widely anticipated push for freer trade across the western hemisphere had not gained momentum. While there had been bold pronouncements and high-profile trade missions (such as Brazilian President Henrique Cardoso's visit to Canada in April 1997), the scale of the obstacles was becoming clear. Examples were Brazil-US differences on agricultural products such as oranges, and Canada's intensifying dispute with Brazil over subsidies to aircraft manufacturers.

Still, for its own part, NAFTA was doing just fine, particularly as seen from Canada. An analysis we produced in the spring of 1997 concluded:

> Most Canadians seem to have put the core issue (free trade versus protection) behind them. Consistent strong export growth and record merchandise trade surpluses have virtually silenced FTA/NAFTA opponents. Academic and think-tank assessments of the agreements' impacts on Canada are all positive. NAFTA was a non-issue in the June 1997 Canadian federal election ...
>
> The government's emphasis on high-profile trade promotion efforts, its signing of the Canada-Chile and Canada-Israel preferential trade agreements, Canada's current chairing of the Asia-Pacific Economic Cooperation forum, and its interest in pursuing a trade agreement with [the South American trade bloc] Mercosur all appear to Canadians to cast their government in the role of a free trader, and this role is acceptable to the majority.[18]

In late June 1997 another General Accounting Office team visited Ottawa, this time to research the actual effects of NAFTA (versus predictions about it). It had become clear that the last-minute addition of "side letters" on labour and the environment was symbolic, serving essentially to smooth Chrétien's and Clinton's public shifts toward endorsing NAFTA. The monitoring offices were understaffed and underfunded, and the issues they were supposed to address were largely under the jurisdiction of states and provinces, rather than of the federal governments that were NAFTA's signatories, so little could really be done under the side letters to address those issues.

While the growth of trade flows among the NAFTA countries was clearly raising real incomes after three and a half years of implementation, the effect on jobs was less clear. This is consistent with economic theory, which predicts that trade liberalization will reduce costs and thus lead to higher real incomes, but not necessarily to higher nominal wages, nor necessarily more jobs. Manufacturing productivity in Canada was lagging that in the United States – which suggested that Canada's export gains were being built more on its depreciated dollar than on efficiency gains. Even workers in sectors that were doing well under NAFTA were not yet seeing higher nominal wages.

Canadian experts concluded that Canada had done well in the NAFTA negotiations: it had protected its gains from the FTA and built effective dispute-settlement systems. But the ongoing failure to eliminate trade-remedy laws within the free-trade area was a serious shortfall. Former FTA negotiator Michael Hart, of the Centre for Trade Policy and Law, argued that, within a free-trade area, anti-dumping law was nothing but a way to harass your competitors (some might say that the same had been true before free trade). Hart said the US-Canada softwood-lumber dispute provided "a perfect example of what not to do" with trade-remedy instruments.

Jagdish Bhagwati, a leading international trade economist, passed through Ottawa in 1997 and he offered both praise and criticism for NAFTA. He agreed that keeping the anti-dumping regimes had been a particularly bad decision. They were too easy and cheap for companies to wield, and aimed too specifically at individual countries and industries. The NAFTA labour and environment side agreements were also unhelpful; these were examples of a new trend to intrusive trade policies, which were largely meant to force the developed world's idea of reforms on less developed countries. Environmental and labour standards certainly ought to be addressed – Bhagwati noted that the United States itself had cases of bonded workers and garment-industry sweatshops – but trade agreements were not the way to accomplish this.

It is important to note that these were and are criticisms of the NAFTA's negotiators' inescapable political compromises, not of their underlying effort to liberalize trade. Bhagwati argued that there was no race to the bottom in environmental and labour standards, a race that NAFTA critics had warned of. Most firms, especially the big ones, cared about their reputations and valued their quality controls, and they would not be attracted to low technology or to low standards. Nor was it likely true, Bhagwati argued, that trade with developing countries would depress wages in the United States or Canada.

After 1997, the trade-policy discussion in Ottawa circles moved beyond NAFTA. There was a wave of post-FTA/NAFTA initiatives, including the Free Trade Agreement of the Americas (FTAA) and the Multilateral Agreement on Investment (MAI), along with, unfortunately, an intensified and misdirected discussion in Canada of the interplay of trade policy with culture.

The FTAA and MAI initiatives faded away in 1997–98 for political reasons. But, while there was just not enough support for more trade agreements, there also remained, or should have remained, no question that the FTA and NAFTA were positive lessons for all countries to follow and for the western hemisphere to build on.

In May 1999 US trade-policy expert Jeffrey Schott, who was then with the Institute for International Economics, visited Ottawa at the Canadian government's invitation. In a speech he delivered a rather pessimistic tour of the policy landscape. The Clinton administration, he said, was being timid in trade negotiations and had failed to defend trade agreements from critics in the Democratic Party, the same critics who had caused the labour and environment side letters to be bolted onto NAFTA. Europe and Japan were doing no better, leaving a leadership vacuum that was affecting the whole international trading system. Schott was right, and, in contrast, Canada's political shift in the same years toward favouring open trade and investment reflects its arrival as an economically successful country and policy leader.

It is usually the rising and leading economic powers (like Canada at the time) that most seek to free up trade, transportation, and investment. But there was also a trend in this direction at the time among the small- to medium-sized economies. It seemed that smaller countries from Eastern Europe to Latin America to Asia had learned the clear economic lesson of the post-war era – that openness succeeds and isolation fails. And smaller countries also were often better able to implement those lessons than the big ones. This was partly because they were motivated to grow and to catch up with the economic leaders, and partly because they could often achieve national policy consensus more easily. Over the generation ahead, Canada would come to advocate maintaining and strengthening international economic integration even more than the United States.

SUMMITRY AND PROTESTS

The Summit of the Americas, held in Quebec City in April 2001, was in retrospect not the ideal backdrop for Canada's first top-level meetings with the incoming George W. Bush administration that had just taken over in Washington. The Summit was a multilateral setting for meetings with an administration that had, it would turn out, little interest in multilateralism. The Canada-US meetings on its margins mainly had to tackle a bilateral agenda (oil and gas, softwood lumber, telecommunications), not a multilateral one. The Summit set multilateral goals that in the end would fail: to complete FTAA negotiations by early 2005 and implement an agreement in 2006.

And, moreover, Quebec City was one of a decade-long series of summits, several of them hosted by Canada and which I directly witnessed – from APEC Vancouver in 1997 to the G20 in Toronto in 2008, and including President Bush's visit to Ottawa in late 2004 – that played into the hands of aggressive protesters. Over and over, protests and security dominated the logistics for these events and the media around them. The protests were great successes for radical groups and fiascos for summit diplomacy. Protesters got tremendous media coverage, inflated summit costs, created legal and image problems for police forces and governments, impeded the substantive agendas of the meetings, and tainted legitimate international negotiating processes (APEC, MAI, FTAA) in the public mind. This tainting of diplomatic process – rather than democratizing or informing it – may or may not have been a strategic goal of the anti-trade crowd who showed up for the protests, but it was certainly their legacy. (Something similar occurred with Canada's energy regulatory processes a few years later. To stop specific projects, activists took to attacking the whole process and suing the regulators. This not only killed the projects, it also undermined the legitimacy and efficiency of independent regulators, throwing everything into the political arena – a huge loss to good public policy in Canada.)

On 26 January 2001 federal New Democratic Party leader Alexa McDonough announced that her party opposed the very *holding* of the Summit of the Americas, saying it was a risk to democracy in the western hemisphere and that the NDP would stand "shoulder to shoulder" with Canadian groups

protesting against the event. Our Embassy commented to Washington that
we were surprised a national party leader would oppose Canadian leadership in a multilateral summit that had noble objectives, such as advancing
democracy and human rights in the hemisphere, and that was mainly composed of developing states. It was a low point for the NDP.[19]

During President Bush's late 2004 visit to Canada, I watched a confrontation between protesters and police in downtown Ottawa from a
perfect vantage point, the front window of the lounge just off the lobby
of the Château Laurier hotel. On that day I came to the realization that
these so-called demonstrations were little more than organized, premedi-
tated, aggravated assaults on police. They did nothing to promote mean-
ingful discussion about trade policy or globalization, and their aims (to
the extent they were articulated) could have been promoted better and
with far less effort by other means. Since protesters seven years earlier in
Vancouver had managed to hijack permanently the Canadian media's
coverage of the 1997 APEC summit to focus it on their own activities, followed up by the protests around the WTO ministerial meeting in Seattle in
1999, such assaults had tended to become a narrow, self-perpetuating sub-
culture among people who seemed more interested in media exhibition-
ism than in foreign policy.

The failure to reach agreement at the WTO ministerial meeting in Cancun, Mexico, in mid-September 2003 generated a large volume of public
comment in Canadian media. Canada's international trade minister,
Pierre Pettigrew, was consistently statesmanlike, refraining from assigning
blame for the Cancun failure. Outgoing prime minister Chrétien, in what
seemed to be unscripted remarks, appeared to blame farm interests in the
United States and European Union, but Pettigrew was quick to defend US
efforts in the negotiations. Our Embassy took greater interest in Pettigrew's comments, since he was likely to remain a player in an anticipated
government led by Liberal Party leader-in-waiting Paul Martin, after Chrétien retired from the scene.

Some media commentators offered long-overdue analysis of the positions of Canadian critics of the WTO and/or globalization. One observed
that these critics "have subtly shifted their position in the past few years,
so that they now implicitly support the free-trade agenda ... In the past,
[Maude Barlow of the Council of Canadians] has been an outspoken supporter of [developed country] farm subsidies ... Yet by the time she got to
Cancun, Barlow ... was full of sympathy for Mexican farmers, who were
out throwing rocks at police." The writer noted one of the logical traps
that Barlow and others had gotten into more than a decade earlier, when

they opposed two very similar trade agreements (the Canada-US FTA and NAFTA) with very different arguments. "By opposing trade, Western anti-globalization protesters essentially put themselves into a direct conflict with precisely the constituency whose interests they claimed to be representing. One could see this tension emerging quite clearly during the protests against the [2001] Summit of the Americas in Quebec City ... Since then, a number of prominent spokespeople have begun inching away from the anti-trade position ... But this move poses a very important question. If you are no longer opposed to trade, but merely to the terms of trade, then why oppose the WTO?"[20]

Another columnist wrote on the same day in a different Canadian newspaper that "the success of the numerous anti-free trade groups in legitimizing the concept of 'fair trade' over 'free trade' ... guarantees a heightened level of political and bureaucratic meddling [and] the failure of future trade talks. If you're not sure of the self-serving abuse inherent in such an approach, go and ask the over 16,000 British Columbians who have lost their jobs in the forest industry as a result of the American softwood lumber producers' pursuit of 'fair trade.'"[21]

ECONOMIC PERFORMANCE IN PERSPECTIVE

In January 2000 our section offered Washington a historical retrospective on Canada's economic performance that looked back half a century. It noted that our two countries' economic histories had a great deal in common, strengthened by Canada's openness to trade, investment, and immigration and by its efforts throughout the twentieth century to integrate with the United States. These trends had accelerated during the 1990s, and by 2000 they were widely accepted politically. But Canada's economic performance, while good, had not kept up with that of the United States, and so in 2000 the country had less relative stature as an economic (and political) power than might have been hoped by Canadian leaders of 1950 – and certainly less than predicted by Sir Wilfrid Laurier, prime minister in 1900, who famously said that the twentieth century would belong to Canada.

The relative size of Canadian government had peaked in 1991–93 and had declined markedly since then, and social expectations of what government could and should deliver had been scaled back. And Canada had become a net international investor – meaning that Canadians owned more assets abroad than foreigners owned in Canada. This was a shift from earlier decades of development based on Canada being an investment host, attracting British and American capital into Canadian industries. The bottom line was that Canada had matured into a fully developed economy in the 1990s, in no small part thanks to the FTA and NAFTA.

The Canadian economy changed direction after the bursting of the technology-driven asset bubble around 2001. In 2001–02 there was a general decline in world trade volumes from their peak in 2000. This was very unusual, partly explained by the crash in information technology and telecommunications stocks, which affected the whole financial system for a time. Canada-US trade in computers, electronic components, and telecom equipment collapsed by 47 per cent from 2000 to 2002. Performance of the Canadian economy was not at fault: it outgrew the US economy each year from 1998 to 2002, averaging 3.7 per cent in annual real growth.

In retrospect, what was really happening was the beginning of a decline in manufacturing's share of GDP and a partial reversion to an economy dominated more by natural-resource extraction. In the Embassy team's analysis at the time, part of the problem in the early 2000s was that the Chrétien government was not tackling the remaining hard economic-policy challenges. "The Chretien government's unfinished economic business includes: Rebuilding health care ... [which] has been damaged by long-term financial starvation ... [increasing] competition [in telecommunications, airlines, newspapers, bookstores and financial services] and ... [liberalizing] internal markets [i.e., interprovincial trade] ... Observers expect little progress in these areas ... the constraints of leadership politics, budget commitments, and federal-provincial relations will make it difficult for them to deliver real substance in what remains of their third term."[22]

The Chrétien government was not just getting old, and concerned about its re-election prospects; on trade and economic policy it was also getting worn down and intimidated by the militant anti-liberalization backlash.

TIME FOR A NEW ECONOMIC AGENDA

When Paul Martin took over the Liberal Party leadership in January 2004 and brought in his new cabinet team, we surveyed the bilateral trade-policy outlook. The main theme was how much less promising the scene was than it had been a few years earlier.

Trade policy has been pushed down the national agendas of both Canada and its main trading partner, the United States, since 9/11. The pre-Seattle era of multiple new FTA negotiations/agreements and rapid trade growth seems to have ended ... Perennial disputes with the United States (along with a major new problem – BSE [a disease that interrupted the cattle and beef trade for more than a year]) appear likely to dominate the new [trade] Minister's agenda. And increasingly, the government's critics complain that dispute settlement panels – the face of the "rules based trading system" which previous trade ministers touted as the key to protecting Canada's economic interests in the world – are viewed as ineffective in resolving these disputes ... [SARS, a virus outbreak that particularly affected the Toronto area, and BSE] served not just to dent cross-border goods and services trade, but also to keep politicians, officials and the public focused on safety and protection, rather than the 1990s themes of efficiency and openness ...

[There is] an apparent emerging consensus in Canadian policy circles that, fifteen years after the FTA and a decade after NAFTA, it is time for a new "big deal" on North American integration. While there are arguments to the contrary – some experts make the case that useful harmonization/liberalization can best be achieved on a more incremental basis – we increasingly hear key Canadian players in business, government and academia calling for bold new initiatives. A daunting aspect for the Trade Minister, however, is that these proposals often go well beyond trade or even economics into a wide range of issues touching on the security of North Americans, from public health to missile defense.[23]

Keeping the border both working and secure was a very large piece of the Canadian agenda. Border traffic had been disrupted by measures taken after the terrorist attacks in the United States on 11 September 2001. Since then the bilateral trade-liberalization process had struggled; on the US side, security concerns tended to override trade, but, on the other hand, the collaborative response by Canadian deputy prime minister John Manley and US homeland security secretary Tom Ridge had done a good job of restoring stability and addressing problems at the end of 2001 and for some time thereafter. Canadian industry minister David Emerson, a former corporate CEO and business-school professor, offered this practical commercial perspective on the border in his first major speech as minister, in September 2004:

From my experience, there is often more cost embedded outside the factory gate than inside it. It means we need to focus on far more than plant efficiency. The Canada-U.S. border has never been a seamless, costless or invisible divide between our two countries but its significance faded significantly in the 80s and 90s. Since 9/11, the border has

become a significantly greater cost and risk point as we work through
Canadian and American security issues. Add to this the variety of
trade frictions such as softwood lumber, BSE, and the relatively wide
exchange rate swings of the past few years, and you start to realize that
"border risk," as I like to call it, has become a critical challenge for
Canada. In other words, the border is back with a vengeance ...

Think about total supply chain disruption and all the consequent
costs. We need a broad-based, frontal assault on border risk ... If we are
the most trade-dependent of the major countries, we had better be the
best at it, or we are vulnerable.[24]

In early 2005 an Embassy colleague and I met with a senior business
association representative who had one of the best perspectives on how
the border affected North America's economy. He outlined the argument
for a North American approach to enforcing trade rules on counterfeit
products, intellectual property, subsidies, and dumping. His argument
went like this: Canadian authorities had been taking resources away from
port and border enforcement. This allowed more rule-breaking of various
kinds, notably Asian-made counterfeit products leaking from Canada into
the United States. This would soon drive the United States to step up
enforcement at the northern border, aggravating the very "thickening" of
the border that Canadians were already complaining about.

A media storm in the United States over counterfeit products – such as
Indian-made pharmaceuticals – coming in from Canada could produce a
US reaction that would create still more major problems for cross-border
trade. As our business contact said, "we can't talk perimeter security
together if we can't police our borders. Even just a bit more effort by Customs at the Port of Vancouver would help a lot. Once bad products are in
the country, it's too late."[25]

A NEW WAVE OF BILATERAL ISSUES

New things were happening in North American trade in the 1990s and
early 2000s that made the FTA and NAFTA look like just the beginnings of
a collaborative process – not its fulfillment. Novel issues were popping
up, things that neither Embassy – ours on Wellington Street in Ottawa
and the Canadian Embassy on Pennsylvania Avenue in Washington – had
dealt with before. The Internet drove many of these. A major example was
Americans buying prescription medications through Canada-based websites and warehouses that could be cheaper sources of needed drugs but

that avoided various health regulations and quality controls. This was a problem, not only because US patients were dodging their own country's regulations, but also because while they thought they were buying from a Canadian supply chain, this was not always assured.

There was also a growing complex of problems around intellectual property rights – an area where the US government was a leading advocate for better international rules, because the United States has been home to so much inventive and creative activity. For example, while creators and rights owners had found ways to prevent their products from being stolen by companies, this was much harder to do when the violators were individuals – and file-sharing websites were paving the road for those individuals to share products en masse. Because Canada had less-well-developed protection of IPR than the United States, rights owners thought the country could easily become a base for widespread IPR evasion. Early in 2004 we reported:

> In a surprise decision the Federal Court of Canada ruled last week that downloading music from the Internet using peer-to-peer software does not constitute copyright infringement. The ruling, which denied a motion to compel Internet service providers to disclose the identity of 29 alleged file-swappers, built on earlier court decisions that have expanded user "authorization rights" in Canada. Although the recording industry plans to appeal the decision, the ultimate solution lies in the government moving forward with copyright legislation and ratification of the WIPO [World Intellectual Property Organization] "Internet treaties." We plan to raise our concerns with Canadian officials ...
>
> Both the March 31 Federal Court decision and the December Copyright Board ruling have explicitly noted that Canada's copyright legislation does not adequately address new and complex digital copyright issues ... Copyright reform finally needs to move out of the courts and into the legislature. This decision puts to rest our Government of Canada interlocutors' oft-repeated argument that a "rush to reform" is unnecessary since the Copyright Act adequately addresses digital issues. WIPO ratification has moved from being an irritant to an urgent issue that must be solved by the Parliament.[26]

For this and many other reasons, in the early 2000s many of us in Canada-US policy circles wondered whether there should be a new "big deal" in continental relations. This could mean a high-profile agreement, with a top-level political push behind it, not only to further open up trade and investment, but also to resolve a variety of leftover and/or emerging issues, either bilaterally between Canada and the United States or trilaterally including Mexico. The debate was not so much over whether there was progress still to be made, including unfinished business from NAFTA; clearly there was. The question at the bureaucratic level was whether a higher-profile "big deal" would work better than a quieter, more incremental approach. At the political level, it was whether there was enough appetite to take on another big push for North American integration and win voters over to it.

We all knew there were problems to fix, but, unfortunately, many of the problems were either big and highly politically charged (like softwood lumber and BSE), with dynamics of their own, that a new initiative could not resolve. Or they were old problems that had withstood earlier efforts at repair, suggesting that tackling them meant a lot of hard work without near prospect of success (such as trying to repeal the trade-remedy laws).

While visiting Idaho in July 2004, Prime Minister Paul Martin told Americans that NAFTA needed work, and he called specifically for more leadership on respecting the results of dispute-settlement processes. Speaking to reporters, he emphasized the need for the North American economy as a whole to grow more efficient to meet challenges from emerging Asian economies.[27]

A NEW NORTH AMERICAN INITIATIVE (NAI)

Players on the US side were open to ideas, and many were discussed. The hypothetical next step was tentatively dubbed the North American Initiative, or NAI. The mainstream thinking was that NAI would have to take an incremental approach because there was not enough appetite at the political level for selling a big deal to the public. As a result, senior officials wanted low-hanging fruit: easily achievable goals where much of the groundwork already existed or could be completed without much legal fuss. They hoped to develop an agenda of reforms that would be substantial yet not so politically difficult as to put off policy makers, legislators, or the public. Because of the difficulties of getting a trade deal through the US Congress, this came to mean that the NAI should not require US legislation.

Senior bureaucrats wanted the NAI process to be managed centrally, but they also wanted to present it as being driven by the private sector. These two goals were hard to reconcile; the practical result was that there was too little private-sector input into developing the NAI concept.[28]

The Smart Border Action Plan, launched under the Smart Border Accord in December 2001,[29] had succeeded because there had been so many issues that were unaddressed on the security and border-management side of the relationship. These were non-economic undertakings that the FTA and NAFTA had not even tried to fix, plus newly emerged problems brought about by the growth in traffic that those agreements' success had generated, combined with reactions to the September 2001 terrorist attacks that were slowing and disrupting commerce. When officials wondered if the success of the Smart Border Action Plan could be reproduced a few years later on the trade and economic side of the relationship, they failed to realize that there really wasn't any low-hanging fruit on the economic side. Most of what was left was high and tough to pick.

By late 2004, the best prospects seemed to be mainly work to remove regulatory barriers (along the same lines suggested by Canada's External Advisory Committee on Smart Regulation in September 2004) and to promote short shipping routes on the coasts and the Great Lakes (such as the idea of a new fast ferry from Toronto, Ontario, to Rochester, New York) as a way of relieving congestion at land-border crossings.

A related question at the Embassy was whether we should encourage a presidential visit to Canada soon after the November 2004 US elections, to kick off the political push for NAI talks. One objection was that a presidential visit might serve only to highlight the big unresolved issues like softwood lumber and BSE, and these would overshadow the comparatively modest agenda now being suggested for NAI. The media story would become, "So how is NAI going to fix softwood lumber?" An even bigger problem was that, while all three national leaders informally agreed to move forward on some form of NAI, there was a mismatch of agendas. Canada and Mexico were focused on NAI and economic policy, while the George W. Bush White House wanted the main focus to be on border security and military cooperation.[30]

This clash of priorities troubled us in the weeks around the visit, so I tried to strengthen the NAI's appeal to the White House through an eight-paragraph analysis that presented it as part of the long-term economic-policy story that had been unfolding in North America for decades. This short document, which was read and appreciated by senior Washington officials, argued that the US government could develop and promote the security side of NAI using the same framework of economic benefits that underpinned the Auto Pact, the FTA, and NAFTA:

The economic payoff of a prospective North American initiative – in terms of higher incomes and greater competitiveness – is available, but its size and timing are unpredictable, so it should not be oversold. Still, a respectable economic case has been made for such an initiative ...

Past integration (not just NAFTA but also many bilateral and unilateral steps) has increased trade, economic growth, and productivity. Studies suggest that border efficiency and transportation improvements (such as the lower cost and increased use of air freight) have been a huge part of this picture. Indeed, they may have been more important to our growing prosperity over the past decade than NAFTA's tariff reductions. Freight and passenger aviation are critically important to our continent's competitiveness, and businesses are very sensitive to the timing, security, and reliability of deliveries – hence the "border risk" which so concerns Canadian policymakers.

A stronger continental "security perimeter" can strengthen economic performance, mainly by improving efficiency at land borders and airports. It could also facilitate future steps toward trilateral economic integration, such as a common external tariff or a customs union, if and when our three countries chose to pursue them. Paradoxically, the security and law enforcement aspects of the envisaged initiative could hold as much – or more – potential for broad economic benefits than the economic dimension.

Some international economic initiatives (such as free trade agreements) produce across-the-board measures that generate broad benefits for a country's industries and consumers on a known time-line. This was true of NAFTA but it is less likely to be true of the economic aspects of the NAI. Non-tariff barriers such as standards and regulations generally must be tackled one-by-one. This is a piecemeal process and the ratio of payoff to effort is likely to be lower than with across-the-board measures. Governments naturally focus on resolving the problems which their firms or citizens bring to their attention. While this approach has merits, it tends to deliver the payoffs toward particular interests. If there are hidden costs, there might be little impact on national performance ...

In contrast, cooperative measures on the "security" side, a critical focus of current bilateral efforts, can deliver substantial, early, and widespread economic benefits. Security and law enforcement within North America have evolved rapidly since 9/11, leading to many less-than-perfect processes for handling legitimate international traffic. Collaboration to improve these processes could yield efficiency improvements which would automatically be spread widely across the economy, leading to general gains in trade, productivity, and incomes.[31]

STALLED

While President George W. Bush's protest-plagued December 2004 visit to Ottawa was not quite the fresh start in the US-Canada relationship that many of us were looking for, it did focus the White House briefly on Canadian affairs. Encouragement came in early January 2005 as we received signals that Canada's new ambassador in Washington would be former New Brunswick Premier Frank McKenna, an appointment that drew widespread approval. McKenna, a business Liberal, had successfully marketed his province's bilingual workforce to investors, energizing its economy. Since leaving politics seven years earlier, after a decade as premier, he had been in the corporate world and was liked and respected on all sides.

NDP Leader Alexa McDonough probably did not intend to compliment McKenna when she said, "He is clearly an integrationist in his view of the Canada-U.S. relationship. He has enormous corporate connections. He'd be there as a very eloquent spokesman for corporate Canada." But to many of us working on the bilateral relationship, that sounded pretty good, particularly when initiatives like NAI hadn't had as much private-sector input as they needed, and the fact is that McKenna was a great choice for ambassador. Even Conservative MP Jason Kenney thought so: "I think there's a broad consensus that we need to reboot the Canada-U.S. relationship and a senior Canadian political and business figure like Mr. McKenna would be well-suited."

By 2005, eleven years after NAFTA, all of our extensive thinking and talk about bilateral integration post-NAFTA had mainly led in two directions: on the security front, to the Smart Border Accord and initiatives related to or descended from it, and, on the economic front, to the push for regulatory reform and cooperation. The latter was a repeat of many earlier efforts but differed in that it had a summit commitment backing it after Bush's December 2004 visit.

What had not happened was a new round of formal, systematic efforts to improve the US-Canada trading area: to eliminate the use of trade-remedy laws within the free-trade area (continued use of which economists and trade experts all said made no sense), to strengthen our pioneering trade-dispute settlement system (which, while useful, could be better, as the lumber experience showed), and/or to move toward a customs union (which the Canadian business sector wanted, whether or not we called it by that name). In fact, by 2005, the Embassy economic staff had trouble remembering the last time a senior US economic-policy official had come to Canada to discuss and promote the trade side of the relationship.

Two to four years after 9/11, what might be called "straight economic" issues (versus security or security-driven matters) were regaining their weight in the business being conducted on the Embassy's top floor, meaning they were taking up roughly half of our agenda. But that agenda was moving slowly, blocked by major disputes or irritants that were very hard to solve, such as intellectual-property issues, cattle and beef (BSE), and lumber. One of my senior colleagues summarized the bilateral economic situation this way in September 2004: "Our relatively few economic problems are stuck somewhere in the middle of briar patches of narrow self-interests. On the US side, solutions to softwood lumber and BSE are largely held hostage to single-issue groups. On the Canadian side, restrictions in wheat or dairy markets are done to protect some small segment of Canada. Unraveling these thorny branches consumes most of our time and to be perfectly honest, our efforts do not bear much fruit ... The largest successes have been in keeping new border initiatives from interfering with honest commerce. Changes and modifications to the Bioterrorism Act are good cases in point."[32]

THE PACIFIC:
A NEW FRAME FOR THE COMPETITIVENESS DEBATE

The Internet and security issues were not the only big forces changing Canada's trade and investment landscape in the early 2000s. A macroeconomic tilt by Canada away from manufacturing and back toward resource processing seemed to be starting around that time. Looking at Canada's trade with East Asia in March 2004, we found that

China overtook Japan last year as Canada's largest trading partner in the region ... The share of Canada's global imports supplied by East Asia rose sharply during this period, from 12.9 percent in 1999 to 15.7 percent [in 2003]. Meanwhile, the share supplied by the United States slid from 67.3 percent to 60.6 percent (though the U.S. continues to receive a steady 86–87 percent of Canada's exports) ...

Existing trade likely understates the value-added in Canadian exports to China, by failing to reflect Canadian content in many U.S.

manufactured exports ... Canadian manufactures are increasingly rout-
ed through the United States for reshipment or further processing
before arriving at their final destination.

Canadian businesses share most of the problems of their U.S.-based
counterparts (indeed, in many cases they are the same corporate entities and/or Canadian content is trans-shipped through U.S. firms).
Canadian officials appear ready to view these trade relations in a continental framework: they are considering "reaching out to corporate
America and helping them market North America across the Pacific."[33]

The FTA and NAFTA had come just in time to prepare North Americans
to meet this challenge, both by making the industrial structure more competitive and by reorienting thinking about the continental economy's
position in the world. Former US Trade Representative Charlene Barshefsky told a think-tank in February 2005 that China presented the United
States with an economic challenge that was fundamentally different than
that posed by other countries, and that to compete with China, America
"must do more than try and manipulate competitiveness through trade
policy – we must actually become more competitive."[34] NAFTA had already
done a great deal to help this.

My own conversations with Canadian business leaders and economists
found them much more comfortable with international outsourcing than
the general North American public.

In their view, Canada's economy has been a major beneficiary during
the past decade of outsourcing from firms based in the U.S., Europe
and even India. They see China and India inevitably hosting a global
manufacturing shop-floor which can help to sustain high-value-added
jobs in North America, and even "help North America to move up the
value-added chain" – a long-standing preoccupation in Canada's traditionally resource-based economy. Moreover, they dispute the breadth
of the front on which outsourcing affects North American firms – citing large sectors in the Canadian economy (energy, minerals, chemi-
cals, many services) which cannot participate because their supply
chains are entirely on this continent.[35]

Unfortunately, these open and pro-competitive attitudes, which were
very helpful psychologically and politically for businesses in facing the
rise of East Asia, were exactly opposite to much of the thinking about
international trade in the halls of the US Congress in the 2000s. A senior

officer from the Department of Commerce vented to a few of his Embassy colleagues in mid-2006:

> We have Congressional Representatives who don't even know what "export" means – they think it means "exporting jobs," and will launch into a diatribe about how evil exporting is. Even the smarter ones don't get foreign investment. Unfortunately, neither side of the political aisle in the U.S. has been willing to bring sanity into this discussion. During the last election, both parties were railing against foreign investment, and even against exporting. Internationalism is at a low ebb ... We will have problems with anything we attempt to do that smacks of us promoting foreign investment ... We are not allowed to directly encourage any foreign company to invest in the U.S. ...
>
> A colleague of ours ... in New York attended a meeting at which foreign investment was discussed, and a day later, his name appeared in the New York Times, under the heading "USDOC official encourages exporting jobs." Two days later, the Secretary of Commerce got a tongue lashing by a congressional committee on the action of one of his employees ...
>
> I even worry when the Ambassador talks to companies considering an investment here [in Canada]. For example, Dell invited him to the launch of a local call center expansion. This is harmless enough, but all that has to happen is some U.S. press guy asking why the Ambassador is attending a meeting in which American jobs are being destroyed. Of course the reality of it is that INDIAN jobs are being destroyed, since most of the new call centers are in India. But, that is logical. Here's how bad it gets. While I was in Germany, our Chargé d'Affaires was flayed in the Wall Street Journal because he attended the opening of a McDonald's. I don't know how something like that becomes national news for the WSJ, but it did.[36]

THE SECURITY AND PROSPERITY PARTNERSHIP (SPP) INITIATIVE

While the Bush White House had a firm ideological commitment to pro-market international-trade policy, those sentiments were very difficult to put into practice during the president's second term. In the first half of March 2005, word came around that the North American Initiative was now to be called the Continental Security and Prosperity Framework (CSPF). This would soon change to Security and Prosperity Partnership.

The defence and security side of the deal was still more or less as conceived in 2004, but the economic and commercial side, while it outlined in general language many desirable areas for collaboration, was limited to a regulatory-reform effort. Some language on environmental cooperation would also be included.

Our Embassy's senior officers soon grew cynical about the whole NAI/CSPF effort, particularly its lack of substance and Washington's management of it. One suggested we call it "North American Strategy for Advancing Legal Dialogue on Regulatory Integration Policies," or NASALDRIP. Another wrote, "I have been appalled all along in this process at the lack of private sector or stakeholder input in this – I will resist commenting on the childish behavior of those close to the center of power who want to control such a venture over every other consideration ... despite my admiration for many of my colleagues on our desk, the Western Hemisphere Affairs front office just does not 'get' Canada – we do not fit into the WHA mold."

The big, persistent bilateral disputes – softwood, BSE, intellectual property – were also very serious obstacles. Yet another senior officer commented, "Major problem is that [NAI/CSPF/SPP] ignores the bilateral issues that dominate public discourse here right now ... the document provides a great framework for dealing with those bilateral issues (except softwood) but then ignores them. That makes the document an easy target for the general skeptics (as well as the knee jerk anti-American, anti-globalization crowd) without giving any material (or even cover) to the Canadians who want further integration ... This does not look like an easy or automatic sell, even though it should be."[37]

One of my senior colleagues observed that, on the environmental side, the initiative simply recited areas in which Canada and the United States were already cooperating well, without addressing conspicuous problems that had been hard to fix (such as Devils Lake in North Dakota, where the state's plans to construct an outflow were opposed by neighbours in Minnesota and the province of Manitoba, or the problem of pollutants in the upper Columbia River). Nor did it mention climate change, where Canada wanted to have a dialogue (the Kyoto Protocol entered into force in 2005, but the Bush administration had no intention of ratifying it, so Canada needed to broker a new approach on which the two countries could align).

Making matters worse, reaction to the US government's Western Hemisphere Travel Initiative (WHTI), which would soon require passports for all people entering into the United States including Canadians, had made the atmosphere for discussion very difficult. Canada would eventually have to live with the WHTI, but it was a material new barrier to the cross-border movement of people, one that was visible and irritating to millions of Canadians.[38]

The lengthy effort to launch a post-NAFTA integration initiative was, at least on the Canada-US front, more like a collision with reality. The NAI/CSPF/SPP initiative reflected an authentic desire in the Bush administration to do something big and positive in the relationship, but it ended up trying to do this without private-sector championing, without US legislative action, and while bypassing major contradictory circumstances – namely, the wave of antipathy over softwood, BSE, the war in Iraq, missile defence, the WHTI, and the Bush administration's impatient, anti-diplomatic mentality in general. It was not working and it was not going to work.

In early May 2005 Bush administration officials offered a briefing to the US legislative branch on the SPP. A report of the ensuing exchange sheds light on how Congress looked at North American integration three and a half years after the 9/11 attacks and well into the Iraq War.

> State, Commerce and Department of Homeland Security met with about 20 House staffers (Reps. Norwood, Reichart, Tancredo, Inglis and others). Questions from House staffers focused exclusively on security issues. One staffer asked whether the SPP was an effort to circumvent Congress. He stressed that the U.S. Government should make securing the border and law enforcement our focus. Another staffer asserted that the border does not exist at the moment, and that the U.S. Government should use "this negotiation" to secure the borders. He added that, in a balance between commerce and security, we should err on the side of security. A third staffer noted that while most Members of Congress support efforts to balance security and legitimate travel and trade, illegal immigration on the southern border is the 800 pound gorilla in the SPP. She commented that we should be turning our attention to the real issue of illegal immigration, corruption and narcotrafficking in Mexico.[39]

SPP had started life as an initiative to fill some important gaps in continental economic integration; it evolved into a package that was mostly about security and borders, with a bit of regulatory reform, but a package that was still intended to deepen and improve NAFTA; and in the end it was sunk by congressional suspicion, within an enduring post-2001 emphasis in Washington on security, crime, and immigration control. The liberal economic-policy assumptions of the 1990s were disappearing.

NAFTA IN RETROSPECT

In the first decade of NAFTA, Canada's merchandise trade with Mexico grew by a factor of more than four – much faster than Canada's trade with Europe or Japan, or than Canada's overall international trade, though, of course, from a very low starting point. The agreement helped Canada toward one of its own long-standing economic-development goals, which was to expand value-added exports, meaning manufactured products that were presumed to embody more technology and education, as opposed to raw or semi-processed resource-based commodities. Also, exports of Canadian telecommunications products, aircraft, and energy technologies to Mexico contributed to Mexico's capital investment base, making Mexico's economy more productive and efficient and the whole North American manufacturing economy stronger and more competitive.

In addition to reducing barriers with Mexico, NAFTA had a psychological benefit in waking up Canadian businesspeople to the development and commercial possibilities in the western hemisphere. NAFTA participation also made Canada more present and engaged in the hemisphere's diplomacy. Canada had moved ahead to negotiate closer trade relationships with other Latin American partners (Chile and Costa Rica) and had become a player in the Free Trade Agreement of the Americas process while it lasted.

While the FTA/NAFTA dispute-settlement system was an important innovation, it was only one dimension of a broad, brave trade-liberalizing push that had driven healthy economic growth for more than fifteen years. Even if the vaunted dispute-settlement mechanism really had failed completely – which was far from the case – the agreements would still have been very successful for both countries.

Asked in February 2008 by Ambassador David Wilkins's office to state the concise case for NAFTA, I answered this way:

North America either succeeds or fails as a single economy. Much of what people don't like about trade is not NAFTA's fault; it is more recent developments (last 5–7 years) and more global in nature (China). Trade with Canada and Mexico has strengthened the U.S. manufacturing and export economy into a continental economy, by supplying resources that made our industries more competitive on a world scale. A 2008 model pickup truck that incorporates metals from Canada and wiring harnesses from Mexico can be more competitive against trucks from overseas.

Those who opposed NAFTA fifteen years ago predicted not just job losses, but massive job losses. They predicted not just income losses, but massive income losses. The United States (and Canada) have had not just job gains, but huge job gains, over the past fourteen years. We have had not just income gains, but huge income gains. NAFTA's opponents were massively wrong on both these counts.

Now, because world trade patterns have been shifting strongly over the past 5 to 10 years due to globalization, the same people have a new chance to blame NAFTA. They are shooting at the wrong target. NAFTA has strengthened North America's manufacturing and export economy, making us far better able to cope with the rise of big emerging economies.

Reopening NAFTA will only risk turning back the clock, making us less competitive against global forces and less able to defend the jobs and prosperity we have built in North America.[40]

I would stand by this assessment today.

THE CRITICS AGAIN

The Security and Prosperity Partnership failed to advance and deepen NAFTA as it should have. Instead, it only gave NAFTA's critics another turn at the media megaphone. This was unfortunate because the New Democratic Party and others continued to put forward shallow, fallacious arguments that the trade agreements had hurt the majority of Canadians. To informed watchers of economic policy making, the NDP had lost all credibility on the subject of the impact of trade agreements, mainly because its trade critic spouted factual untruths, such as asserting that 80 per cent of Canadian families earned less in real terms in 2007 than they did in 1989. (Canadian real household income grew by a healthy 2.5 per cent average from 1984 to 2007.)[41]

These arguments were easy to rebut, something I undertook myself in a lengthy open letter in mid-2007, but inevitably the lies got more media space than the truth and so filled up the public conversation on the subject. NAFTA's critics blamed NAFTA for assorted problems that either didn't exist or whose causes had little plausible connection to NAFTA. To NDP eyes, examples of NAFTA's supposed evils were stagnating incomes of poorer households (Statistics Canada analysis said this was due primarily to cuts in employment insurance, welfare, and so on), more Canadians working overtime (only an NDP politician would make this out to be a problem), young people using their earnings to pay down student debt rather than buying new vehicles (how was student debt worse than vehicle debt, and, in any case, what did this have to do with NAFTA?), and the high cost of energy (NAFTA had zero effect on the cost of energy to a Canadian household).

The factual truth was that Canada's unemployment rate had fallen from 11.4 per cent in 1993, which was the year before NAFTA was implemented, to 6.1 per cent in 2007 – the lowest in *over thirty years* – while real income per worker was up by about 20 per cent. As far as public opinion went, polling in September 2007 – twenty years after the national debate on free trade – found that 57 per cent of Canadians thought they would be worse off without the FTA, 64 per cent supported enhancing the free movement of people between Canada and the United States, and 72 per cent supported building a more integrated rail-, highway-, and air-transportation infrastructure between the two countries. Americans generally agreed.[42]

Maude Barlow, chair of the Council of Canadians, preposterously said that SPP "is quite literally about eliminating Canada's ability to determine independent regulatory standards, environmental protections, energy security, foreign, military, immigration and other policies," and that it "renders Canada not only unwilling but unable to provide for the energy needs of its citizens – now and in the future."[43]

While she occupied roughly the same part of the political spectrum as Barlow, Green Party leader Elizabeth May was far more sensible than Barlow's group about SPP. May identified two concerns with the SPP process: border security, and a failure to recognize climate change as the continent's major security problem.[44] She told us in a 2007 meeting at the Embassy that thickening of the border caused Canadians to feel "cheated" about NAFTA, which they had been told would secure their access to US markets. She suggested that a serious Canada-US effort to collaborate on climate change could help to dispel suspicion of the SPP and help transform perceptions of SPP as a "sinister agenda" into a "sensible agenda."[45] May's not unreasonable input contrasted sharply with the unwillingness of the NDP, the Council of Canadians, and other groups to consider taking any future role in the SPP process or even to view it in a balanced and factual way.

Like May, the Canadian Centre for Policy Alternatives steered a fairly reasonable course, saying that "Canadians are richer, but they feel less secure and families need to run harder to stay in place," and that "SPP contains much that could be useful, but risks putting private before public interest."[46]

THE ANTI-NAFTA BACKLASH
IN THE UNITED STATES

In the United States, distortions about SPP were even wilder than those we heard in Canada. Echoing the "North American constitution" fear-mongering we had heard in Canada fifteen years earlier, some American critics of the SPP characterized it as a secret plan to integrate North America, allegedly featuring a single currency. When a senior US diplomat (with Canadian experience, but then serving in Europe) asked me to put this in context for him, I explained:

> Of course the SPP exists as a public, trilateral initiative, but it is a very far cry from an integration plan. The truth is quite the contrary – as citizens, we should count ourselves lucky if even a few of the SPP's modest and sensible objectives get realized. The conspiracy "evidence" is highly developed, a remarkable testament to the power of current media. For example, someone designed hypothetical "Amero" coinage and paid to have samples made at a private mint. Then they advertised those discs for sale on the internet; so then of course the conspiracy kooks reproduced these images of the coins and represented them as if they were a government-minted currency-in-waiting. Generally this stuff does not get picked up in Canada.

One of my colleagues observed, "I cannot believe anyone in his right mind would categorize the SPP as a plan for unification. My God these journalists are idiots ... I remember one day we were laughing on the phone because we were both reading the same SPP document, which was so timid it was ridiculous – maybe, if we were very careful, we could agree on what day of the week it was."[47]

Some of the crazy anti-SPP rhetoric was, of course, driven by 2008 being a US election year. Both of the leading Democratic presidential contenders – Hillary Clinton and Barack Obama – had bowed to protectionists in their party by taking the position, particularly in their televised debate on 26 February, that NAFTA "was oversold" (Obama) or had "not lived up to its promises" (Clinton) and had to be "fixed so it works for American workers" (Obama) in a way that "addresses its shortcomings and brings it up to date" (Clinton).[48]

These statements troubled many in the Canadian policy establishment, who saw a risk of Canada being sideswiped by a US political backlash against imports from countries such as Mexico and China. Tom d'Aquino, president of the Canadian Council of Chief Executives (CCCE) and an original promoter of the Canada-US Free Trade Agreement, made a formal statement in response: "I have observed many American elections and realize that in the run-up to a national vote, candidates sometimes appeal to the more extreme voices in their constituencies. But I detect more than rhetoric at work here. Protectionists in many cases are attacking the fundamentals of liberal economics, which have long been proven to offer the greatest benefits in terms of growth, job creation and improvements in quality of life ... The vibrant and progressive Canada-United States relationship, which has served as a model to the world, now more than ever needs allies and friends on both sides of the border to speak up in its defence."[49]

I pointed out to my colleagues that, in the unlikely event that a new president were to abrogate NAFTA (even if en route to renegotiating it), the 1989 Canada-US Free Trade Agreement would automatically come back into force. A senior colleague who was an expert on the FTA agreed: "There was a conscious decision to put the FTA into a state of suspended animation as NAFTA came into force so that our FTA would not be put at risk by any adverse political upheaval in Mexico. Who knew it would be the U.S. that would some buyer's remorse?"[50]

Even Ontario Premier Dalton McGuinty – whose province, and party, were not the greatest defenders of open markets – published an opinion piece defending NAFTA.[51]

FROM BUSH TO OBAMA

Of the Democratic presidential candidates in 2008, Jagdish Bhagwati, a top academic expert on international trade, wrote that

> no Democratic candidate during the primaries can be anything but a protectionist. ... [In recent years] the antiwar groups that have helped lift the party's fortunes also overlap often with anti-globalisation and hence anti-trade groups, so the party tends to be propelled into an anti-trade position willy-nilly ... [but] whereas Mr. Obama's economist is Austan Goolsbee, a brilliant Massachusetts Institute of Technology PhD at Chicago Business School and a valuable source of free-trade advice over almost a decade, Mrs. Clinton's campaign boasts of no

professional economist of high repute. Instead, her trade advisers are reputed to be largely from the pro-union, anti-globalisation Economic Policy Institute and the AFL-CIO union federation.[52]

In fact, back in February 2008, staff at Canada's Consulate in Chicago had met with Goolsbee. As the Consulate reported to Ottawa, Goolsbee

was frank in saying that the primary campaign had been necessarily domestically focused, particularly in the Midwest, and that much of the rhetoric that may be perceived to be protectionist is more reflective of political maneuvering than policy. On NAFTA, Goolsbee suggested that Obama is less about fundamentally changing the agreement and more in favour of strengthening/clarifying language on labour mobility and environment ...

Noting anxiety among many U.S. domestic audiences about the U.S. economic outlook, Goolsbee candidly acknowledged the protectionist sentiment that has emerged [and] cautioned that this messaging should not be taken out of context ... He also suggested that of the Democratic candidates, Obama has been the least protectionist ...

On the subject of the border, he confirmed much of the current debate is focused on the southern border and in the context of immigration policy ...

When asked about Obama's statements and position on NAFTA, Goolsbee was quick to indicate that [Senator Obama] is less interested in fundamental changes to the agreement and more looking at clarifying language on labour mobility and environmental standards. Again stating that he was not an expert on the agreement, he suggested Obama wanted to work with Canada and Mexico to make labour and the environment more core to the agreement. He again cautioned that much of the current conversation in the U.S. about the negative impact of free trade is not aimed at Canada. He said the "blood bath" is over expanding free trade to countries like Peru and Korea ...

As Obama continues to court the economic populist vote, particularly in upcoming contests like Ohio, we are likely to see a continuation of some of the messaging that hasn't played in Canada's favour, but this should continue to be viewed in the context in which it is delivered.[53]

Our Embassy followed up in mid-March with an analysis of informed Canadian perspectives on NAFTA:

Where it exists, Canadian discontent with NAFTA (and earlier, the FTA) focuses on the continued use of trade remedy (anti-dumping and countervailing duty) laws, a related lack of effectiveness in dispute settlement reflected in over-use of the "extraordinary challenge" procedures (notably in pork, swine and lumber), and a clause (NAFTA Article 605) that prevents parties from voluntarily restricting their exports of energy. Any return by the United States to the NAFTA negotiating table would likely see Canada present a well-prepared agenda aimed at making progress in these areas, which are well understood and discussed in Canadian trade policy circles ...

No significant part of the NAFTA can be renegotiated without reopening the agreement in its entirety. In that event, Canada would have a negotiating agenda of its own. Key features of the Canadian agenda would be to seek new rules constraining the use of countervail and anti-dumping laws between/among the parties; to strengthen dispute settlement mechanisms in ways that would enforce more lasting U.S. compliance; to possibly eliminate the investor-state dispute mechanism (NAFTA Chapter 11); and to possibly eliminate the article constraining export restrictions on energy products.

Indeed, Canada could pursue major improvements to the bilateral trade regime, even if NAFTA remains in place. One eminent Canadian trade policy expert and veteran negotiator has proposed that Canada do just that. He is currently advocating that Canada spend the remainder of 2008 developing a "constructive agenda" to be pitched to the next U.S. Administration. That proposed "constructive agenda" would feature a major effort to address the security and regulatory dimensions of the bilateral trade relationship.[54]

The George W. Bush administration, to its credit, remained firmly and openly pro-trade to the end. At a multilateral meeting in Latin America in January 2008, Daniel S. Sullivan, the assistant secretary of state for economic affairs, informally

suggested the establishment of an association of free trade partners in the hemisphere, committed to democracy, the rule of law, and open market policies, the primary purpose of which would be to work together to promote competitiveness and ensure the benefits of trade liberalization were spread as widely as possible in all our societies, especially to small businesses, farmers, and others who had not yet directly benefited from free trade. Such an association could have strong links to the private sector and could include initiatives, such as the U.S. Treasury's program to enhance access to financing for small and medium enterprises ... [and] knitting together the different hemispheric trade agreements – possibly harmonizing issues like customs procedures, rules of origin, intellectual property rights, etc. ... increasing competitiveness and social cohesion in the Western Hemisphere.[55]

Sullivan's words, in my view, pointed the right way forward – then and now. But in less than a year the Bush administration would be gone, and I would be working outside of trade policy.

3

From Erasing the Border
to the Global War on Terror

On 2 August 1990 – in my sixth week with the US government – Iraqi forces invaded and swiftly occupied the neighbouring state of Kuwait. The latter was a US ally, but Iraq claimed it as a lost province. The United States needed to turn this back but, lacking a suitable regional ally that could fight the battle with Iraq, would have to do the bulk of the job itself. The head of US Embassy Ottawa's Political Section, a speaker of Arabic who had lengthy experience in Middle Eastern posts, soon disappeared from our building for temporary duty elsewhere – as I was told, a task force in Washington.

I had a dark moment one evening about a week into the US military operation, when Iraq's Scud missiles began exploding on Israeli territory. I feared that the conflict would widen, and this revived ingrained fears from my Cold War youth, with its images of widespread missile-borne destruction. But the worst did not happen.

DESERT STORM

The US action to retake Kuwait, Operation Desert Storm, involved sending half a million troops half-way around the world. America's first major foreign-policy crisis in the post–Cold War era turned into its first real, full-fledged military offensive since the Vietnam War. The combat phase, from mid-January to mid-February 1991, became a highly popular media event, thanks to satellite data transmission and to the exciting speed at which the war unfolded. CNN's round-the-clock news coverage set a new standard for merging mass journalism with entertainment.[1] Casualties were modest; Kuwait was retaken from the Iraqis; the troops of the US-led coalition did not march on to Baghdad but stopped more or less at the Iraqi border; the oil-field fires were extinguished; stability was restored.

Largely because it was over quickly, the war was also a military, financial, and political success. The US public and America's allies generally supported it. While wars are always expensive, this one was affordable because it was quick, because it used hardware that could be supplied out of existing inventory, and because much of the war's cost to the US government was spent on US-sourced goods and services. Most importantly, the war implemented and validated the "Powell doctrine" articulated by General Colin Powell, then chairman of the Joint Chiefs of Staff (and later secretary of state). That doctrine said that the United States should enter a war only if it set well-defined and limited objectives and used overwhelming force to achieve them.

VICTORY PRESIDENT

In April 1991 President George H.W. Bush included Ottawa on the itinerary of what was essentially a post-war victory tour.

As often happens on presidential visits, the White House team arranged for the president to appear briefly at the US Embassy building to greet the staff. When the hour came, we had a dense crowd in the small lobby of the Chancery at 100 Wellington Street, including numerous officers and other employees, their spouses and children, and an honour guard of US Marines by a podium on the staircase. It was my first experience of a formal appearance by a national leader.

After some waiting, Bush's arrival was announced and he swept in the door to a roar of applause, making his way around a clearing in the middle of the crowd. People crushed forward to shake his hand or stand near him, hoping to have their photos taken by colleagues or friends. I felt a surprise one commonly feels upon seeing a celebrity in real life. Though President Bush was a relatively tall man, I was struck by how small and ordinary he looked amid the crowd.

He made his way to the podium on the marble staircase and delivered a short speech containing what I would come to recognize as the standard elements of such an address: saying how good it is to be in Ottawa, what a great country and friend Canada is, and what a terrific team we have in the Foreign Service, and acknowledging and thanking the Embassy staff, Americans and Canadians, for their work on behalf of both countries. After that, it was a victory speech, reviewing the swift success of the Gulf War and declaring that "we've whipped the hell out of that Vietnam syndrome!" – to enthusiastic cheering.

The speech was followed by more jockeying among the spectators to shake the president's hand and be photographed with or near him. I chose to take it all in from the back of the room. Even before the visit, I had been amazed by the quasi-religious attitude of many of my American co-workers toward the presidency. The eagerness to get within touching distance, to be seen with or near the leader, to tell stories or display mementoes of this contact, seemed to have nothing to do with exercising influence or having social access to the leader or his circle. It was superstitious, an attitude one might expect from medieval society toward the pope but not from citizens of a technologically advanced republic in the late twentieth century.

NATIONAL CULTS

Countries (and some organizations and professions) have taken on the character of cults to hold themselves together. America's cult of itself is based in its foundation-story: the Revolutionary War, the Declaration of Independence, the constitution, and the presidency. While the presidency is central, America's relationship to other countries hardly figures at all in this cult. The cult's watchword is freedom, though this almost never specifically means freedom from Great Britain or from its monarch or its aristocracy, but rather freedom from government and oppression generally.

The America-cult is very well developed and was perhaps at a historical peak in the Reagan-Bush 41 years. Jingoistic, hero-worshipping media coverage of the First Gulf War and the American field commander, General Norman Schwarzkopf, and the demonization of Iraqi President Saddam Hussein produced a surge in the America-cult in 1990–91. In her book on the origins of war, American writer Barbara Ehrenreich remarks that the Iraq War reduced a sophisticated society of hundreds of millions to a collective bellicosity more appropriate to a band of thirty or forty people.[2]

While the success of that war produced a brief surge in the president-cult around the senior Bush, it was not durable enough to win him a second term, and it declined over the subsequent decades, in part because presidents Bill Clinton and George W. Bush embarrassed it in their different ways. The America-cult has declined for other reasons too, perhaps mainly related to the increasing fissions in national politics.

English-speaking Canada's cult of itself is very different from America's. Rooted in the Loyalist migrations northward after the American War of Independence, it is built largely around Canada's relationship to the United States. It is much less well developed than the America-cult and has

fewer visible symbols or historical touchstones. The office of prime minister plays little part in the Canada-cult, but the presence of the United
States is fundamental to it.

In the 1990s and into the early 2000s, the Canada-cult was juvenile, insecure, touchy, and resentful. The closer Canada got to the United States, the
more insufferable and petty the Canada-cult became – a bit like a difficult
fourteen-year-old forced to take a long vacation with his parents. (Paradoxically, one benefit of the two countries' divergence in the decade after
2001 is that it gave the Canada-cult some space to grow up and become
less US-obsessed.)[3]

ERASING THE BORDER

It may be difficult to believe now, but for five or six years from the mid-
1990s until 11 September 2001, US experts on Canada anticipated the
eventual fading, if not disappearance, of the US-Canada border – not as a
line between two sovereign authorities, of course, but rather as a barrier
to the movement of people, goods, and services. The US reaction to the
attacks of September 2001 killed that vision. That it had ever existed certainly seemed incredible when looking back from 2008, at the end of the
George W. Bush administration and in the seventh or eighth year of its so-
called Global War on Terror (GWOT) – the Bush team's concept for a multi-
faceted attack on terrorist organizations and their state sponsors.

The vision of a gradually erased Canada-US border was driven forward
through the 1990s by expanding trade volumes, which were making the
constraints at the border more and more troublesome. We had a decade
of successful experience of the FTA and NAFTA. Obviously before us was the
European example, where decades of integration had arrived at a seemingly successful customs union and an agenda to unify labour markets.

We had the apparent will of the political leadership in both countries
to make the border work more smoothly and reduce barriers to legitimate
traffic – efforts that, in spite of this willingness, had trouble keeping up
with the tremendous growth in traffic brought about by trade liberalization.[4] Canadian business was managing the adaptation from "country
mandates" to "product mandates" and was thriving in an increasingly
globalized economy.[5] In the eyes of American officials, the main resistance to erasing the border came from backward elements of political
opinion in Canada, which remained reflexively suspicious of the United
States and bitterly opposed to what they decried as the withering away of
Canada's capacity to set its own policies and determine its own destiny.[6]

In mid-2001 senior officials in parts of the two countries' federal governments were ready to start talking openly about more steps toward integration and the eventual erasing of the border. This conversation, which had "Canada-U.S. Partnership" or CUSP for a working title, was less about whether this should happen than how to give it enough momentum to overcome bureaucratic inertia. The border (unlike tariffs or investment rules) involved a particularly wide range of government departments and agencies, many of which had vested interests – employees, offices, and budgets – that depended on border barriers of various kinds, not to mention private interests that might also depend on keeping those barriers.

An early briefing paper to newly arrived Ambassador Paul Cellucci on 9 May 2001 was part of an effort to start building the necessary political-level support for overcoming these barriers. The border, we told the new ambassador, "is a multi-headed challenge where bureaucratic regulators are falling behind NAFTA's tremendous growth. Our attempt, through the Canada-U.S. Partnership (CUSP), to give policy coherence to 'stovepipe' parochial interests (e.g. Customs-to-Customs) badly needs political direction ... to give CUSP the political mandate it needs to cut through red tape ... True solutions must cut across departments, agencies, and levels of government. Few, if any, of our existing mechanisms pull together all pertinent players. CUSP was an attempt to do so but ... agencies outside DFAIT and State did not buy in."[7]

Few people, in Canada at least, appreciated that those months before 11 September 2001 were the best opportunity to seek such solutions that we had had for decades – or that we would have for many years to come, if ever. During those months the George W. Bush administration was trying to integrate more global economic thinking into the National Security Council and into foreign policy. Much of the administration would shift in the opposite direction in the years after the September 2001 attacks.[8]

THE PERIMETER CONCEPT

Former prime minister Brian Mulroney, who by 2001 had been seven years out of office, was one of the relatively few Canadian leaders at the time who could unapologetically promote an idea such as a customs union, since he did not need to court votes.[9] On 19 June 2001 Mulroney said publicly that a customs union should be the next big step forward in US-Canada relations. He also suggested that Canada should remove interprovincial barriers to trade, end or reduce corporate subsidies, and continue tax reform. Essentially, he was urging greater fulfillment of the economic program that he had pursued during his nine years in office.[10]

Mulroney noted that a customs union would require Canada and the United States to have common, jointly enforced rules on the entry of third-country goods (and people), and he applied the term "perimeter" to this regime. This implied greater integration of the continent's military and immigration services, as well as tariffs and other trade controls.

The "perimeter" term gave a name to measures that would have to exist to some extent in any customs union among allies. Our two countries were already in a close security alliance through NATO and NORAD – as we had been for sixty years. We already had an undefended border that was very porous to people, goods, and services. Naturally, we were already very sensitive to each other's openness to the continent from other parts of the world. A customs union would just need to formalize and further align the parts of this relationship dealing with goods. If we went one additional step and relaxed rules on cross-border movement of people – to some degree deepening the integration of our labour markets – then we would inevitably need to coordinate our rules on entries of people, as well as goods, from the rest of the world. Mulroney's term for this coordination, "perimeter," was a logical corollary of "thinning" the 8,900-kilometre (5,500-mile) border. If you have a pond and I have a pond, and we plan to widen the ditch that connects them, we should logically take more interest in what's happening on each other's shorelines and maybe even look at some shared best practices for managing runoff.

We were all groping for new visions of what we thought the border would become, and ways to explain what we were advocating. My Economic Section colleagues challenged me (as a Canadian with, presumably, a feel for what would work with the Canadian mindset) to come up with a vision and a name. My immediate reply was that whatever I came up with might not have the word "border" in it at all, and they seemed to like that. So I proposed *Main Street North America – a place where people meet, traffic moves and business gets done.* This vision had a fleeting public life in Ambassador Cellucci's speeches in July and August 2001.[11]

The ambassador emphasized that "to continue with the traditional border approach means we'll have to put a lot more people in facilities on the border to handle the volume to try to reduce the gridlock and the delays. That's a pretty monumental task." Borrowing Mulroney's terminology, he spoke of the "perimeter" approach as a better way to employ the same resources, concentrating law enforcement and intelligence staff on filtering entries from outside of North America while facilitating business between Canada and the United States.[12] The Canadian ambassador in

Washington, Michael Kergin, chimed in that "in many ways, the 20th century perception of the border is now obsolete."

Unfortunately, in 2001 Canadian reporters ignored the "Main Street North America" concept and seized on the less friendly sounding "perimeter" word. They knew this could trigger Canadian sensitivities about sovereignty and US control. Ambassador Cellucci was soon hit with persistent hostile questions – a minor feeding frenzy – about what exactly this "security perimeter" would entail. As a result, the narrative veered away from "working together to make the border easier" toward "the U.S. wants to put up a security perimeter around the continent." We had made the mistake of letting the initiative appear to be coming from the US side – which was guaranteed to make many Canadians distrust and fight it.

Canada's big-business lobby group, the Canadian Council of Chief Executives, had better success in 2002–03 pitching its well-thought-out proposal along the same lines, which they dubbed North American Security and Prosperity (NASP). It called for:

1. Reinventing the border – making it a "zone of cooperation," not a line – and focusing security efforts on the "approaches to North America." The border should become "an effective, shared checkpoint within an integrated economic space."

2. Regulatory integration on a "test it once" principle. Shared technical groups would work out details.

3. Ensuring resource security – building the energy relationship and finding permanent resolutions to disputes about how to price natural resources (natural gas, timber, water).

4. North American defense alliance. To keep our relationship a "community of sovereign nations," Canada must invest in its own homeland security capability, not as a concession to the U.S. but for its own benefit.

5. Twenty-first century institutions which are trilateral and "sovereign, not supranational," topped by a Treaty of North America which sets out broad shared objectives for U.S./Mexico/Canada but allows for flexibility in national approaches to achieving them. Plus joint commissions of experts on the International Joint Commission model.

Most interesting to me was CCCE President Tom d'Aquino's frank admission, under questioning by parliamentarians, that the CCCE really would have preferred a de facto US-Canada customs union. He said the CCCE

avoided advocating this because the phrase "customs union" was a political turn-off on both sides of the border. In fact, d'Aquino was very clear
that the NASP he was promoting would be neither a customs union, nor a
common market, nor a currency union, nor a merger of foreign and
defence policies – none of which would have been politically saleable
in Canada.[13]

After the full implementation post-2001 of GWOT security measures, this
vision articulated by Mulroney, Kergin, Cellucci, and d'Aquino would
have sounded like a good but no longer attainable dream to Canadians
with a stake in an open border. By the fall of 2003, 60 per cent of Canadians would say they supported a "common security perimeter" with the
United States.[14] But by then the opportunity was gone.

11 SEPTEMBER 2001

On the morning of Tuesday, 11 September, a few minutes before 9:00, I
was at my desk in the Embassy when word spread that an airplane had
struck one of the twin 110-storey towers of the World Trade Center in
New York. A few of us gathered in the top-floor conference room and
watched the disaster unfold on television. A second plane hit the other
tower just after 9:00 and we continued to watch – and consider the implications – as both towers burned. They collapsed later that morning.

The Embassy management soon sent most of us home, which irritated
me since I wanted to be at my desk where I might stay better informed
and possibly somehow be useful to the government. While the events
were obviously dramatic, I considered it unprofessional to be sucked into
the mass-hysterical grief and melodrama that was pouring through the
media. Wanting to think more coolly about the events, and wanting others to calm down, I downplayed the attacks a little in my own mind and
dismissed the media's dramatization of them. This threw off my perception of how much the attacks – and particularly the public reaction to
them – would matter for the world's future. As a result, later in the day
when a low-key, thoughtful neighbour said, "We could find ourselves living in a different world," I was initially surprised and puzzled about what
he meant. But I soon realized how right he was.

During the next few days I was appalled by those (such as a feminist law
professor in my neighbourhood) who expressed the view that "the U.S.
had it coming," that is, it had brought the attacks on itself by its own evil
conduct. I was disturbed, though not surprised, by how many people –
seemingly, in particular, urban left-wingers – took this perspective.

After puzzling for a while, I eventually decided this must be the juvenile bitterness of disappointed leftists who, a decade after the Cold War, couldn't accept that time wasn't proving them right, that history hasn't agreed with them. Put in this situation, people can become desperate for some sign that their favourite villain, be it the United States, capitalism, big government, or society at large, is finally about to get its overdue comeuppance. In this case my professor neighbour seemed to feel that her disapproval of US foreign policy was somehow being vindicated by militant Islamists' attacks on thousands of innocent civilians. Such an attitude ignored the fact that those victims were from many nationalities. Even if they had all been Americans, they were non-combatants who could hardly be held responsible for US foreign policy.[15]

THE WAR PARADIGM

In those first days after the attacks, as we groped for language to use in public communications, I came to be still more troubled by the administration's (and it seemed, nearly everyone else's) seemingly unhesitating adoption of "war" as the paradigm for what was happening. There were understandable triggers for calling it a "war," of course: there had been an organized violent attack on the United States, unfortunately reminiscent of the one made by Japanese forces on Pearl Harbor, Hawaii, in December 1941 that had brought the country into the Second World War.

At the same time, there were also serious problems with thinking of the 12 September situation as a war. The enemy was initially unidentified and might not be a state or government. On the contrary, the enemy turned out to be much more like an international criminal network. The attackers would presumably have intended to provoke a strong political reaction (this would be a likely result of such an attack, and it would raise the status and influence of the attackers and their creed), so it did not require much thought to see that calling it a war was probably playing into the attackers' hands.

Another problem with the "war" tag was that, while alternative paradigms – for example, Cold War-style geographical containment by building up US allies, or perhaps a global crackdown on what might be seen as a form of organized crime – might turn out to provide more effective models for fighting this enemy, these alternatives were quickly pushed off the table as we all got conditioned to the war language.[16] A third problem with the war paradigm was that America's being psychologically on a war footing was likely to – and eventually did – lead the country to compromise the very principles that America and the West represented to the attackers: openness and transparency, human rights, and democratic accountability.

Perhaps in the political circumstances the White House had no real choice but to declare the United States "at war." But I saw no sign at all that other options had been considered, nor that the war paradigm was soundly based. A page of "Key Words and Themes" from the president and the secretary of state, made available a few days after the attacks, led with the subheadline "War on Terrorism." Its sound bites declared that this was "unlike previous war" (without saying how) and that "we will stick with the campaign until we are successful" (without defining success). Its second line described the Islamic militant organization al-Qaeda as "a large 'terrorism' holding company with [11 September attack mastermind Osama] bin Laden as the 'CEO'" (without any effort to explain why the United States was declaring "war" on a corporate organization).[17]

Three days following the attacks there was to be a public memorial service for the victims (the final death toll was nearly three thousand) on Parliament Hill. The ambassador was to speak. I managed to make two insertions into his remarks. At the first use of the word "war" ("We are, as President George W. Bush said, facing a new kind of war"), I inserted: "It is not necessarily a war of violence. It is certainly a struggle of principles." And after the text called on Canada and the United States to "fight the evils of terrorism and protect our way of life on this shared continent," I inserted: "In doing so, we will respect every day the values that our attackers scorn – democracy, the rule of law, and individual freedom."[18] I wonder if this last promise would have made it into White House remarks. Nothing like it appeared on the page of "Key Words and Themes" that we received from the administration to guide our communications.

Five and a half years later, a senior fellow at the Council on Foreign Relations, Peter Beinart, critiqued President George W. Bush's use of the word "war" after 9/11:

> From the beginning it was designed to contrast with crime, which many Republicans said had been the Clinton administration's framework for fighting al Qaeda. Democrats allegedly saw anti-terrorism as police work ... If the real threat was not terrorist networks but governments, then of course war, rather than crime, was the correct prism ... In 2005, officials tried switching to the less felicitous "global struggle against violent extremism." President Bush quickly reinstated "war on terror" or "war on terrorism" after conservatives accused him of going soft ...

But in the American political lexicon, "war" also means something else ... something akin to national mobilization [and with the implication] that it would be America's top priority. In that way, too, however, "war" has become less apt. In October 2001, 46 percent of Americans, a massive plurality, told Gallup pollsters that terrorism was their No. 1 priority. On Election Day 2004, it was 19 percent. Today [2007] it is 5 percent ...

If "war" is increasingly problematic, "terror" is even worse. From the beginning, critics have noted that terror is a tactic and thus not America's real enemy ... over time the "terror" we're ostensibly battling has grown ... Conceptually, this is a mess ... [and] future officials may feel it limits their ability to make good policy.[19]

While the reaction to 11 September could have been even worse than it was, it nevertheless more or less lived up to what Conrad Black calls "the propensity of the Americans to rise to instantaneous bellicosity without an apparent thought to where it might lead."[20] I was later reminded of the GWOT rhetoric and mentality when reading one of the best memoirs of the First World War. Soldier Robert Graves, on leave from the useless slaughter of young men on both sides in the trenches in France, visited home in England, where people were nearly close enough to the front to hear the guns firing and yet were brainwashed with unrealistic propaganda about a national struggle to uphold civilization. "England looked strange to us returned soldiers. We could not understand the war madness that ran about everywhere ... The civilians talked a foreign language, and it was newspaper language. I found serious conversation with my parents all but impossible."[21]

To many, the war-on-terror concept was part of a serious wrong turn in US military policy in the longer run. This was a turn away from defence and deterrence as core principles, which had prevailed early in the Cold War, and toward war as a supposed preventive measure, which began to take hold in the 1980s and reached its apogee after 2001.[22]

CELLUCCI'S BALANCED ADVOCACY

Ambassador Cellucci happened to have a business meeting with Canadian International Trade Minister Pierre Pettigrew scheduled for 14 September 2001. The ambassador's keeping this appointment helped to signal continuity in the relationship and some degree of business as usual. International civilian aircraft had been prevented from landing in the United States during the intervening three days, and long lines of vehicles had formed on the Canadian side of border crossings as admissions to the United States greatly slowed, so there were many possible distractions, yet Cellucci and Pettigrew discussed a variety of topics, including softwood lumber and the desirability of facilitating aviation and border traffic. The ambassador reiterated his vision for the border, as we noted in a briefing note to the State Department: "We need to continue to work for a technologically smarter border and an effective perimeter strategy that will pick up criminals and terrorists on entry into North America, rather than attempting the nearly impossible task of intercepting them along a 4000-mile-plus border. Minister Pettigrew said he was a strong supporter of the measures the Ambassador had been raising. The Ambassador noted that, while 'business as usual' might be difficult, it would be important to do all we could to restore normalcy."[23]

The management of the border had challenges before September 2001, challenges that the ambassador had already studied and understood in his five months on the job, and wanted to help to fix. It is greatly to his credit that, just three days after the attacks, and on the very day that he gave an emotional speech to one of the largest crowds ever gathered on Parliament Hill, he also remained focused on the ongoing business of the bilateral economic relationship and on restoring our two countries' ability to get it done.

Ambassador Cellucci and some important Canadian players like Minister Pettigrew could see clearly that the economic aftershocks of the tragedy were likely to be damaging. Jayson Myers, chief economist of the Alliance of Canadian Manufacturers and Exporters, addressed this topic authoritatively in a speech on 21 September. Myers noted that there was both a sudden slump in demand and a sudden rise in costs – portending a compounded slump in economic output and trade. Additional shocks could well arrive from financial crises in other parts of the world. The US deficit, which had been eliminated under the Clinton administration, would return "at least as long as the war on terrorism lasts." US unemployment would rise, trade disputes would become harder to resolve, and multilateral trade and investment issues would slip lower on the US agenda. This forecast proved accurate.[24]

One of our Embassy's top practical concerns in the hours and days after the attacks was the chaos created by the grounding of over two hundred international flights in Canada. About five hundred international aircraft had been in the air and bound for US airports on 11 September but they found themselves unable to enter the United States owing to the closure of airspace after the attacks. Roughly half of them were diverted to Canadian airports – principally Gander and St John's, both in the province of Newfoundland, and Halifax in Nova Scotia. These diverted aircraft and passengers took several days to a week to clear away.[25]

Years later, an analysis commissioned for Transport Canada tallied the costs for Canada's transportation sector of post–11 September security measures. By this account, nearly all the impact was on the aviation and trucking industries (versus railways or port and marine organizations). The total annual toll on the country's transport sector from September 2001 to April 2005 was estimated at C\$315–549 million in direct and indirect operating costs (mostly paid by truckers through waiting times, paperwork, security surcharges, and added training). In addition, a cumulative C\$511–608 million in capital costs (such as computer-system improvements) were incurred over that forty-three-month period.[26]

In the weeks after the attacks, Ambassador Cellucci continued to provide a valuable voice for the two countries' shared economic as well as security interests. He spoke well and courageously for both Canada and the United States on 16 October when he appeared before the Immigration Subcommittee of the US Senate:

No other foreign relationship of the United States so directly affects the lives, work and well-being of Americans everywhere. Thirty-eight of our states have Canada as their number one trading partner ... We share a continent and we share an economy. Canada clearly must be part of any solution to the problem of American and ultimately North American security ... This means coordinating laws, policies and practices so that we have confidence in each other's ability to imply a diminution of either country's sovereignty.

Mr. Chairman, we also have learned since September 11 that our nation's security against terrorism goes hand-in-hand with North America's economic security. In the days following the tragedy, as customs and immigration monitoring tightened along the Northern Border, we experienced twenty-mile-long truck backups. The integrated American and Canadian auto industry, dependent on just-in-time deliveries, closed plants for lack of parts. Other manufacturing industries also suffered. Layoffs and hardship followed. The volume of U.S.-Canada trade dropped by as much as 40 percent in the week following September 11. It is only now recovering, thanks to increased staffing ... This surge ... cannot be the long-term solution ...

Under NAFTA, North American trade has grown 122 percent. This kind of growth, creating jobs for citizens and opportunities for companies, can only continue if our Northern Border works well ...

A smarter, more targeted approach would yield better security at a lower price. I am afraid that using the border to weed out that tiny percentage who pose a threat can only harm our economic security, while providing no assurance ... Let me propose that we put our resources into joint efforts with Canada "away from the border" by using technology, intelligence and information sharing ... better coordination with Canada of both countries' visa and asylum policies ... employing technology for a voluntary personal border crossing identification that is connected to a binational database. Several versions already exist ...

While more agents along the border will help, our best defense lies in increasing our intelligence and investigative capabilities and improving coordination and information flow among U.S. agencies and their Canadian counterparts ...

Improved cooperation should be linked to technology facilitating legitimate commerce. One example would be cross-border vehicle tracking and identification/computerized manifesting system connected to a binational database ... Combine automated manifesting with securing the cargo at point of departure, identifying the truck and its planned route, and certifying its arrival and unloading at the proper destination ...

Another example is random factory inspections. The idea here is, again, to move enforcement activities away from the border and obviate the need to construct or use border infrastructure for [enforcement].

Mr. Chairman, these ideas are just a beginning ... We cannot afford to jeopardize the North American economic machine that nourishes our freedoms. Economic security goes hand-in-hand with security against terrorism.[27]

There is good reason to cite Ambassador Cellucci's remarks during this important appearance at such length. Paul was later, until his untimely death, and even afterward, gratuitously painted in Canadian newspapers as an undiplomatic, tough-talking bully who thought he could push peaceful Canadians around, a mere henchman for a war-hawk president (who was similarly libelled, though with less injustice). Where does that (of course, imaginary) Paul Cellucci show himself in his words on the subcommittee record?

US diplomats are often criticized, especially by Republicans, for selling the United States short, neglecting their nation's security and promoting foreign interests to America, rather than promoting American interests abroad. In carrying these messages directly to Congress as he did, a politician like Paul Cellucci surely knew he was inviting such criticism, which could have been costly for him. Canadians were very fortunate to have a US ambassador with the courage and commitment to make the case for their economic interests in Washington, at his own risk and at a time when that city's mentality was "We're at war and under attack!"

BORDER AND PERIMETER

Unfortunately, the "perimeter" concept that former prime minister Mulroney had floated and that Ambassador Cellucci had tried to discuss with Canadians was being torn apart by Canadian media. Reporters and commentators revived worries about sovereignty, the vaguely defined bogeyman that so often haunts sensible efforts at international integration. Trade-policy expert Michael Hart observed at the time that the silliest attitudes toward sovereignty and nationhood were held by Canada's chattering classes, while ordinary Canadians had healthier and more pragmatic attitudes toward relations with the United States. Sovereignty, Hart rightly argued, was a nineteenth-century concept that should not get in the way of pursuing shared interests with another country.[28]

It was a myth that the perimeter idea was some sort of demand from the United States that required an imminent policy choice by Canada. Rather, it was a logical, even necessary, evolution of work we had been doing together for years. The integration choice, as Michael Hart pointed out, was largely made generations earlier during two world wars and through the Defense Production Sharing Agreement, NORAD, the Korean War, and NATO. These decades had left Canadians with a deep investment in sharing responsibility with the United States for the security of the North American continent. It was sixty years too late to say that Canadians did not want that responsibility.

Much of what kept both countries' officials so busy at the border could have been, but wasn't, swept away sooner – it was the unfinished business of the 1989 FTA and the 1994 NAFTA. The best solution to border problems in late 2001 would have been a whole new round of integration initiatives with the United States to fix the flaws and fill the gaps in that unfinished agenda.

The US government did not have very precise information about what was happening at and around the border with Canada, given the huge geographic area and many remote locations and the number of players and communities involved. We did not have much data at all on the extent of drug trafficking, unreported border crossings, or smuggling. For years after 2001, Canada continued to argue that police resources near the border were adequate, and the federal police force, the RCMP, was even looking to close some small posts to reallocate resources toward larger ones while also encouraging local authorities and residents to contribute more to border surveillance. It was easy enough for officials on the US side to say that more resources were needed, but much harder to determine how much illegal activity was occurring where, and therefore to make recommendations about which new resources would be most helpful.

Both Michael Hart and representatives of the Customs and Excise Union (CEU) (the association of Canadian border guards) told Parliament that, while Americans had suffered a great and sudden loss of confidence in the rest of the world on 11 September, Canada had slowly been losing their neighbours' confidence for years before that, through lack of investment in its military, police, and intelligence systems. As CEU officials put it, "Americans did not get the sense that Canada's security had been compromised from out of thin air." In the years before September 2001, the auditor general, the Canadian Security Intelligence Service (CSIS), the RCMP, and the Canadian Police Association had all expressed concerns about Canada's permeability through its borders.[29] Given how this perception interplayed with the new security paradigm in Washington, Canada's chance to launch a new post-NAFTA integration drive had not just been delayed by three or four years by the events of 9/11. More likely, it was lost for decades to come.

GETTING BACK ON TRACK

As the weeks of November 2001 went by, the political focus turned to the imminent US-led invasion of Afghanistan. By 23 November, there was a verbal agreement between US secretary of state Colin Powell and Canadian foreign minister John Manley that a Canadian infantry battalion would join the invading coalition. With both the security alert and the focus on line-ups at the border set to cool off a little, or so we hoped, the Embassy's Economic Section thought it was time to offer the US government a refreshed look at Canada's economy, one that would communicate that cross-border economic relations were still important to the United States and had to be accommodated and strengthened in the new circumstances.

I tried to draft something that would take our readership – perhaps just a dozen or so officials at the Canada Desk and in the Economic Bureau of the State Department – much deeper than the common notions, which were either the pre-September message that "more integration is inevitable" or the post-September one that "Canada is a vulnerability for America." Our fifteen-paragraph text led off with what made Canada's economy distinct within North America, different from a regional economy of the United States such as New York, the Pacific Northwest, or California (most notable were Canada's being a petroleum exporter, and also its independent dollar). The analysis then moved to the importance of border management for both countries:

> Any loss of efficiency at the U.S.-Canada border imposes a general cost increase and efficiency loss on Canadian industry, especially manufacturers. This adds a further degree of supply side shock to the demand slowdown, which will amplify the job losses, the decline in Canadian economic output, and thus the indirect costs to the U.S. economy (especially since many of the cross-border-integrated firms are substantially U.S.-owned) ...
>
> While bilateral collaboration is superb, amid ongoing expansion of cross-border trade and population mobility, the border was in danger of becoming a significant impediment to continental economic growth [prior to 11 September]. Events since then have swiftly and powerfully focused Government of Canada attention on this problem. This situation clearly creates previously unexpected opportunities for progress on advancing the bilateral security and economic agenda.[30]

This, along with Ambassador Cellucci's testimony to the Senate, captures the messages we were sending to Washington in late 2001. We urged the US government to keep US-Canada relations on their pre-September track – working to strengthen integration for the sake of our shared prosperity – or at least restore that track as soon as possible.

While many of us working in US-Canada relations had a forward-looking vision for North American integration (whether we were going to call it CUSP or NASP or NAI or CSPF or SPP), our arguments seemed in danger of becoming not proactive but reactive: a rearguard action, a losing battle, an echo of the 1990s when the policy establishment had seen economic liberalization and growth as being the path forward to global democracy and freedom, before the world changed colour on us.

The Border Security Agreement and Smart Border Declaration signed by the United States and Canada in December 2001 were partly based on work done prior to 9/11, but after the attacks this work was accelerated and enhanced with security measures that might not otherwise have been included. These arrangements widened and deepened coordination of law enforcement along the border, developed bilateral Integrated Border Enforcement Teams (IBETs), and initiated a new era of coordinated visa policies.

Six months later, mid-way through the tense and turbulent bilateral relationship of 2002, Canadian deputy prime minister John Manley and US homeland security secretary Tom Ridge were able to report solid progress in these and other areas. While the sudden advent of the new national security preoccupation in the United States could not easily disrupt the collaborative momentum with Canada that had been developed since long before 9/11, it certainly redirected it toward a more security-oriented agenda.[31]

About half of our time at regular weekly staff meetings on the fourth floor of the Embassy in the first quarter of 2002 was occupied with economic and border matters – a lower proportion than before September, but still large. We continued to rate our top economic priorities as being the lumber dispute, energy supply, and border management. GWOT-related issues (including the allied effort in Afghanistan, aviation security, visa issues, and terrorist financing) filled most of the rest of the agenda, and more regular political business (such as electoral observation, organized crime, narcotics control, and routine defence relations) accounted for relatively few items.

Notes I prepared for a talk by Ambassador Cellucci at Harvard University in Cambridge, Massachusetts, in early February opened with a paragraph called "The Struggle against Terrorism" yet managed to be almost entirely about economics.[32] On 14 February the two countries announced the relaunch of the in-transit passenger pre-clearance project at Vancouver airport, an important transportation improvement effort that had been sidelined in September but that was back on track six months after the attacks.[33]

CONTINENTAL SECURITY AND CRISIS SCENARIOS

As part of a new command structure, in early 2002 the United States announced the creation of a new Northern Command (USNORTHCOM) responsible for protecting all of continental North America, its surrounding waters, and parts of the Caribbean. Canada could have offered to integrate some of its forces with USNORTHCOM, or to join a possible "naval NORAD" (another continental-defence innovation being contemplated at the time), but did not do so, choosing instead to study the question.[34]

As a result of a wide-ranging brainstorming conversation in which I participated in May 2002, Embassy staff were asked to consider Canadian domestic-security scenarios that could lead to a US military presence being needed on Canadian territory. I was familiar with the main historical precedent, which occurred in 1941–42, so I summarized that experience for my colleagues' benefit. [35] During the Second World War, around ten thousand to twenty thousand military personnel occupied and developed a transport corridor from Edmonton, Alberta, through Whitehorse, Yukon, to Fairbanks, Alaska. The purpose was to enable the effective defence of Alaskan territory against Japan, particularly by building airfields. The US occupation of this corridor – which became the Alaska Highway – was tolerated by Canadian authorities though it had not been requested by Canada.

The situation came about because of wide gaps between Canadian and American perceptions of the threat to continental security. Canadians did not share Americans' sense of immediate threat from Japan and they were not prepared to commit major resources to defending the west coast of North America. Strong sentiment thus developed among some US politicians that Canada was the weak link in continental defence and that the very least Canada could do was stand aside while the United States did what it thought was necessary to defend the continent. Canada's minister of national defence for air, rather than arguing the project's military merits, just told Canadians that the strengthening of relations with the United States was strong and sufficient reason for it. There was no Canadian military liaison or joint-command apparatus (other than the high-level Permanent Joint Board on Defence), and it was not even clear whether the US forces would give up control of the facilities after the war ended.

The way this occupation came about – an experience that in 2002 was sixty years old and little known – provides a model for a similar scenario in the future. If a perceived urgent threat to our shared security was considered less grave by Canadians than by Americans, then hosting the US military or security response on Canadian territory could become, in effect, Canada's involuntary contribution to the "shared" continental-defence effort. A more modern scenario could involve a deployment in a more populous area of Canada, with more political impact and intergovernmental conflict. Long-term US military and political interventions in Middle Eastern and Latin American countries often started life as efforts to protect US citizens and commercial interests when the US government unilaterally decided that the host government was not up to the task.

An example, in miniature legal form, of this sort of problem was the initiative to put air marshals – armed law-enforcement officers – on selected passenger airline flights, including some cross-border flights. It illustrates how both countries' officials struggled for years to catch up with the reaction to the 2001 terrorist attacks. Our Embassy reported in November 2002:

> A Canadian interagency group is considering the basis for the legal authority, status, and liability of Canadian and U.S. air marshals who are in air space and territory that is not under the control of their respective governments. The Canadian government plans to engage us eventually in discussions that would lead to a reciprocal agreement on these issues. Canada is also looking at other situations in which the law enforcement personnel of one country might cross into the territory of the other ... In the absence of clear existing legal authority for armed U.S. marshals in Canadian air space ... specific questions under consideration include, but are not limited to: under what legal authorities do the marshals operate ... what is the status of the marshals when in and over the other country ... do they have diplomatic status? What is the liability of the sending government for accidental or other actions of its officers ...?
>
> Our [Canadian government] contact made clear that [the government] is strongly committed to the existing air marshal program. The Cabinet will pass an order that will authorize the presence in Canada of armed U.S. air marshals, probably before the end of this Parliamentary session. However, this authorization will not address the marshals' status or the liability question.[36]

Canadian officials were in the awkward position of pledging their commitment to a "joint" security program, even passing a cabinet order to authorize it (after it was already operating), while they were still asking basic questions about its legality. Such situations can easily arise again, perhaps on much larger scales.

The best way for Canada to mitigate the risk of this kind of predicament is to be generally perceived and trusted in the United States as a reliable ally and security partner, to be able to make a good show of responding to situations on its territory that Americans think put them at risk, and to avoid as much as possible the widespread perception among Americans that their border with Canada is a vulnerability.

AFGHANISTAN

While Canada would later keep its troops out of the Iraq conflict that started in 2003, it joined the allied military effort in Afghanistan that began in the months after the September 2001 attacks. In April 2002, in what became known as the Tarnak Farm friendly fire incident, the bilateral relationship on this mission suffered early collateral damage when four Canadian soldiers were killed accidentally by a bomb from a US plane. The US president said that he had

> immediately expressed to Prime Minister Chretien my deepest sorrow and sympathy at this tragic accident. Canada's fallen heroes and their families are in our hearts and prayers. Canada is a vital member of a mighty coalition against terrorism and hatred. It is shouldering great burdens and making tremendous sacrifices to make the world a safer place for all people. It is doing so in defense of the values that define the Canadian nation and that unite our two peoples. As I told the Prime Minister, we will work together with Canada in a thorough and timely investigation to determine exactly how yesterday's tragedy in Afghanistan occurred. We will draw every possible lesson from what happened and do everything we can to protect coalition forces engaged in this vitally important mission.[37]

Continuing the damage-control offensive, the president wrote to the next of kin of the soldiers killed, and Ambassador Cellucci, the American consuls general in six Canadian cities, and senior officers of the Embassy and consulates offered condolences to Canadian leaders. Canadian military commanders replied with comments such as that "between soldiers, there is no anger, but sadness for the people involved, including the F-16 pilot who committed the fatal error," that "this was a classic example of the fog and friction of war," and that they appreciated that a Canadian officer had been invited to sit on the US investigating panel. The American pilots were found to have contravened established procedures and to have caused the incident, and the pilot who dropped the bomb officially apologized. The aftermath was handled well, but it was still a tragic, embarrassing, and entirely avoidable loss.

An Ipsos-Reid poll of Canadian opinion later in April found, according to the *Globe and Mail* newspaper, that 86 per cent of respondents agreed that Canadians and Americans had one of the best relationships of any two countries in the world. Gratifyingly to those of us who had been working on the economic side for the preceding decade, 66 per cent of Canadians believed that the greater intertwining of the two economies through freer-trade mechanisms had been positive.[38] An Ekos poll a month later found that "Canadians feel more poised and confident today than at any time in the past 10 years – about our identity, about the economy, about our ability to handle change."[39]

But the way Canada's first deaths in a combat zone since the Korean War occurred contributed to the slow accumulation of negative Canadian public attitudes toward the US-led wars in both Afghanistan and Iraq. One radio talk-show listener called in angrily to say, "Stop saying they gave their lives for their country! Their lives were *taken* from them in a stupid accident."

In my own view, the incident indirectly fed an important undercurrent of sentiment in Canada that the threat from terrorism was partly driven by US policies, that the United States was over-responding to it, and that Canadians might do better to dissociate themselves from both the policies and the over-response than to be an accomplice to them.

EMOTIONAL DIVERGENCE

The tone of the reporting in Canadian newspapers until April 2002 conveys a sense of solidarity with America, of pride in being its closest neighbour and ally, of a desire to be helpful. After April, a kind of mild backlash appears: a disillusionment with the war rhetoric, and beneath it a building dislike of President Bush.

Distaste for the character and style of some of the top figures in the administration was strong among the better educated because George W. Bush, and to some degree key advisers like Vice-President Dick Cheney and Secretary of Defense Donald Rumsfeld, were perceived to be men who liked simple answers, a circle whose anti-intellectual propensities – rooted in and conditioned by American cultural traditions and Republican Party politics – had been showcased in Bush's election campaign against the more sophisticated Al Gore two years earlier. Knowing they were so disliked by foreign intelligentsia seemed to reinforce the administration's disregard for international criticism. In 2002 they imagined they had the means to impose America's will around the world. Foreigners were not going to vote in the 2002 or 2004 elections for which the Republican team in the White House was preparing, so they had little immediate reason to worry about what people outside the United States thought.

The president's "you're either with us or against us" rhetoric on terrorism was deeply harmful to respect for US diplomacy in the post-2001 period. It sounded like an explicit dismissal of any nuance in allies' positions, and indeed it could be interpreted as a dismissal of diplomacy generally. Bush was focused on two priorities, defending the homeland and winning coming US elections, in which diplomatic considerations carried little weight. As 2002 wore on, signals of this became as evident in his administration's economic policy (for example, the massive subsidies embodied in the 2002 US farm bill, which were strenuously protested by America's trading partners including Canada), as it was in the Global War on Terror.

WANTING DISTANCE

Many Canadians whose reaction to the 9/11 attacks would have stopped short of saying "America got what it deserved" nevertheless felt a well-justified instinct to keep their distance from the United States. This caution was well articulated by commentators such as University of Toronto professor Stephen Clarkson and also by former Liberal foreign affairs minister Lloyd Axworthy, the latter addressing the subject of the war in Afghanistan and the unified command under which it was being fought.[40] Axworthy warned against participation in the war as "the latest sacrifice being put on the altar of 'homeland security' ... [and] being complicit in Washington's flouting of the Geneva Conventions."[41] More than a decade later, as the US Senate Foreign Relations Committee reported on the Central Intelligence Agency's post-2001 use of torture, and as analyses of the US military and intelligence shortcomings in Iraq and Afghanistan accumulated, these warnings looked well founded.

A 2002 comment by Canada's pre-eminent military historian, J.L. Granatstein, placed Canada's defence predicament in historical context in a way that resonated with my own study of North America's continental-defence experience in the Second World War.

Homeland security is at the top of the U.S. agenda, and it will remain there for the foreseeable future ... This is not a new situation ... [In 1940] the United States wanted strategic and tactical control of Canadian forces ... [In 1941] the U.S. Navy took control of sea defences off

Newfoundland. And in 1942, the United States built the Alaska High-way over Canadian territory and had up to 15,000 troops in the Dominion.

After the war ... the United States and Canada both believed themselves vulnerable to a Soviet attack and, since the United States was determined to protect its people whether or not we went along, good sense demanded that Canada join in its own defence ... What did artificial concepts of sovereignty and independence mean in the face of such a threat? Coordination and mutual cooperation were the better way to achieve Canadian interests ...

To me, the Canadian national interest is as clear today as in 1940–41 and 1957–58 ... The federal government, fearful of interference with cross-border trade, scrambled after September 11 to bring Canadian border screening, immigration and refugee practices more into line with U.S. desires. If we go into a continental defence arrangement, we can expect renewed U.S. pressure to increase our military efforts.

Will this be another outrage, an affront to all nationalists? Only to those with their heads deep in the sand.[42]

Retired major-general Lewis MacKenzie echoed these comments in discussing the specific arrangements of the Afghanistan military effort:

Some commentators and politicians conveniently ignore the critical distinctions between the military terms "command" and "operational control" – thereby misleading the public. Once they depart Canadian airspace, our Canadian battle group will be under the operational control of the U.S. commander in Afghanistan. On their arrival in the region, the U.S. commander can only employ the unit within the parameters of a previously arranged "contract" between our two governments. The Canadian battle-group commanding officer will retain direct command over his troops ... We had similar arrangements ... in Somalia in 1992 ... a boringly common relationship within NATO ...

The United States has been attacked at home and is at war. It is committed to defending its citizens and naturally looks to its borders with its neighbours ... [Canada] has suddenly realized that the coinage of sovereignty is military power – but is so far behind that it will take years of catchup ...

The events of September 11 are generating a series of initiatives that will force us to live up to our obligations in areas where we have been found wanting. We would be a stronger, more sovereign nation as a result.[43]

These were defence-policy perspectives that, however true, had limited resonance with the broad Canadian public (fewer of whom have military experience, or follow military affairs, than Americans do). Deputy Prime Minister John Manley expressed a view that looks very balanced in historical perspective. Criticizing the US administration's overdone "axis of evil" rhetoric as being too belligerent, he added, "I think we should always be a bit preoccupied by the fact that the U.S., as the only superpower in the world, can act in a way that is a bit unilateral. But since September 11, we have to recognize that they have taken a multilateral approach that is positive."[44] "I don't think the war against terrorism should extend beyond what we see as being direct links to September 11 and, without a connection to that, I don't think that countries that are involved as part of that campaign are going to want to see it extended."[45]

Manley came to be highly respected and valued on the US side in the post–September 2001 era for this ability to voice such nuanced, balanced positions, as well as for his highly effective work on the Smart Border Declaration and Action Plan. This work served both Canada's agenda for a functional border and the US agenda for security.

Even Canadian Conservatives gave Manley due credit. Former Ontario Conservative premier Mike Harris, who was critical of the Chrétien government's "slow response" after September 2001 – saying it was a missed opportunity to gain credibility with the United States – privately called Manley the best of the Chrétien team. Harris told US officials that Manley understood the importance of mutual confidence and cooperation on security, and of framing the continental-security arguments in ways that advanced Canadian interests, but that Manley did not have sufficient mandate from Prime Minister Chrétien to carry this through.[46]

POLITICAL DIVERGENCE

Through the months following the September 2001 attacks, Canada was preparing to host a G-8 summit (a meeting of the leaders of the United States, Canada, Japan, the United Kingdom, France, Germany, Italy, and Russia with the purpose of coordinating economic policies) in the mountain town of Kananaskis, Alberta, in June 2002. Here and elsewhere in that difficult year, Canadian and other non-US political leaders had to work hard to keep the US administration's Global War on Terror from displacing everything else on the international agenda. Prime Minister Chretién's personal representative for the Summit (and also the PM's personal representative on Africa), Robert Fowler, maintained that an Africa Action Plan would be the centerpiece of the summit event. Chrétien and Fowler wanted to have terrorism issues addressed mostly at the level of the foreign ministers' meeting in Whistler, British Columbia, in mid-June, so that the leaders' Summit could focus on economic issues, its traditional object, including the Africa plan.

Chrétien wished to invite United Nations (UN) secretary general Kofi Annan and about half a dozen key African leaders to the summit. The participating countries agreed to the Africa agenda in advance. But a Canadian official was subsequently quoted venting anger at US officials' last-minute efforts to tilt the agenda toward other issues. "They wanted control of the sessions. They wanted to change the agenda. They just wanted to orchestrate everything."[47]

Around the time of the June 2002 Summit, Foreign Affairs Minister Bill Graham was reported to have said, "Immediately after September 11 there was a natural, tremendous rallying around the United States. But we've always said, 'We stand beside you, but we don't jump how high [you tell us] to jump.'" Noting that there was a "degree of anger and irritation" in Canada about some US measures with political implications, Graham cited the US farm bill (a very generous package of politically driven subsidies that ran against the spirit of trade agreements and would hurt other agricultural exporters, including Canada). He also cited what was seen as US protectionist behaviour in trade disputes over lumber and steel, and US decisions to withdraw from two important international arrangements, the Kyoto Accord on climate change and the International Criminal Court. The code word for all this was unilateralism – a perceived Bush administration attitude that the United States would do things it saw as being in its interest without needing to consult with anyone or even necessarily follow agreed-on rules, because it wanted to, had the muscle to do so, and was determined to pursue a certain course of action (some in the White House might have said "principles") regardless of what others might think. "We can help the United States by working with them," Graham said. "Yes, there's frustration over unilateralism and it's now coming back out. After September 11 we had to put it aside. Naturally when you are in a crisis you put aside differences. But the differences are differences in policy, not just personalities ... We can destroy the terrorist network in Afghanistan, but we're not going to destroy terrorism unless we do a lot of other things in Afghanistan in terms of the political climate there, dealing with the warlords and drugs ... I think the United States recognizes that as well, but there is a somewhat different approach ... I think they often look to military solutions to problems that we don't look to military solutions for."[48]

Graham was voicing a sentiment that would gradually take our two countries further apart as the US reactions to 9/11 played out during the remaining six and a half years of the Bush White House and as Canadians identified less and less with the US foreign-policy lines that were drawn in the process.

CANADA'S IMAGE IN WASHINGTON

A memo from the State Department's Canada Desk to the under-secretary for economic affairs complained around this time of "an on-going Canadian tendency to emphasize expediting of cross-border trade rather than increasing border security," and noted that "it is important not to divert resources and political will to additional goals that are not clearly focused on border security concerns."[49]

By the end of 2002, at least one respected Canadian media commentator sensed "growing anger among American conservative political elites toward our country. These very powerful (mostly) men in Congress, the Republican hierarchy and the media have concluded that Canada has gone off the rails ... The 'moron' incident [in which a senior prime ministerial aide was overheard referring to President Bush as a "moron" at an international meeting in November 2002] appears to have crystallized their growing conviction that Canada is not as trustworthy or as well-disposed toward the United States as it once was."[50]

The effect of the "moron" incident was reinforced by Liberal MP Carolyn Parrish's remark, "Damn Americans, I hate those bastards" (in a media scrum in February 2003), and later by federal cabinet minister Herb Dhaliwal's negative remarks about President Bush's leadership in the context of the invasion of Iraq. These were all statements, even if unguarded, by members or very senior staff of a supposedly friendly country's government, and while one such episode might have passed without significant damage, a handful of them had a cumulative effect on Canada's reputation as a friendly neighbour, as well as on the strength of Canada's constituency in the United States.

Canada as a nation still had a vaguely positive image among the broader American public. But the notion that Canada was too soft on security (along with the myth that some of the 9/11 aircraft hijackers had entered

the United States from Canada) persisted in some corners of the US public and thus in the US political system, and there was an onus on Canada
to show that its security capabilities were adequate. It did not receive the
benefit of doubt.[51] A major Canadian business lobby noted correctly that,
for Canada, demonstrating good security should be more than just a show
to placate Americans. "All the things Canada gets accused of (being a
haven for terror financing, etc) are no less true of the USA. The border pre-
sents problems in both directions (e.g. handgun imports into Canada).
Canadians should realize they need a better border, not just to serve U.S.
security interests, but to serve their own security interests too."[52]

Corrosively, both sides in the relationship came to see the other as a
security problem. This distrust was exacerbated for Americans by the relative lack of strong visible signs of security collaboration, and the abun-
dance of signs that the two countries were not aligned (notably the comments by Dhaliwal and others, Canada's waffling and eventual refusal of
participation in BMD, its absence from the Iraq coalition, and its constant
preoccupation with keeping border traffic moving). For their part, Canadians remained concerned about importing US patterns of gun use, homi-
cide, and other crime. As Bush's Global War on Terror progressed, Canadian institutions became concerned about allowing data on Canadian
residents (student grades, health records) into the hands of US-based organizations for any purpose, since the data's privacy might then no longer
be assured. It was feared that legislation such as the Patriot Act – a sweeping package of law-enforcement and security measures passed in October
2001, parts of which were later found to be unconstitutional – might
allow US security agencies access to Canadian data, or that those agencies
might not be constrained by considerations of legality.[53] This anxiety
about Canadians' data getting into US government hands, at a time when
the CIA was apparently practising torture and extra-legal "rendition" – the
transfer of suspected terrorists to countries with poor human-rights
records – lingered in the media for years and was an understandable
source of Canadian political reluctance to collaborate too readily with the
United States on security matters.

STRIKING A BETTER NOTE

John Manley, who left cabinet with the advent of Paul Martin's leadership
at the end of 2003, had worked effectively with the American side on
Canada's behalf through those very challenging two years after the 9/11
attacks. One of the testaments to his (and others') success in this period is

how well the US Department of Homeland Security (DHS) continued to work with its new Canadian counterpart, Public Safety and Emergency Preparedness Canada (PSEPC), after he left government. [54]

A new Canadian national-security policy announced in late April 2004 fortunately sent the right kinds of messages to the United States. As our Embassy reported to the administration:

> The policy focuses primarily on "Homeland Security" issues, including maritime security and disaster preparation. It also includes plans for better intelligence coordination and links to Canada's broader foreign policy goals ... The document and the presentations of the strategy by Government of Canada officials have emphasized both that 1) this is Canada's strategy that responds to threats Canada faces, and that 2) Canada is working closely with the United States to combat terrorism and other threats to the security of both countries. [Prime Minister Paul Martin's foreign-policy adviser] stressed to the Ambassador that the Government of Canada is making it clear that Canada itself is threatened, that it is in Canada's interest to address the threat, and that cooperation with the United States is part of Canada's strategy to protect itself. [55]

This was exactly the right note to strike.

In a briefing message to Homeland Security Secretary Tom Ridge for the secretary's October 2004 meeting with Deputy Prime Minister Anne McLellan, Ambassador Paul Cellucci outlined the bilateral security issues while continuing, as he always did, to press the case for sustaining cross-border movement and trade:

> We understand that announcements [by Canada] will include rollout of NEXUS AIR pre-clearance at Vancouver International Airport, succeeding the current CANPASS system, and the opening of additional FAST lanes at key land crossings. Both of these developments will be welcome evidence that we are trying to keep goods and people moving and to decrease "border risk" for low-risk passengers and goods ...
>
> Looking past this round of meetings, in the longer term I believe we need to look at all available options for dealing with border congestion caused by outdated infrastructure, limited space, and traffic that has doubled since the signing of the U.S.-Canada FTA. Continuing the long-term growth trend of cross-border trade is in the interests of both our economies, but our options at the busiest land crossings are

clearly limited and expensive ... Infrastructure development may take
up to ten years before it is operational ... Waiting that long will hurt
our economy.[56]

A record of staff preparations for the same ministerial meeting suggests
how much more balanced the security conversation had become between
the two neighbours over the preceding three years.

[A senior Canadian official] described the 5,000-mile Canada-U.S. border as "a series of gates without a fence" which needs better intelligence sharing for its protection ... Department of Homeland Security
(DHS) and Public Safety and Emergency Preparedness Canada (PSEPC)
discussed sending liaison officers on assignment to one another's
operations centers as a means of furthering communications and
understanding, and to help direct action when a response to a crisis is
required. It was agreed that job descriptions would be prepared for
such detail assignments ...
      As the meetings were taking place, a team of DHS and State Depart-
ment attorneys were meeting with their Canadian counterparts in
Ottawa to examine procedures that would allow U.S. officers adequate
authority [at a proposed Peace Bridge land pre-clearance facility] without violating Canada's Charter of Rights or diminishing U.S. law
enforcement capability ...
      The visit demonstrated that there is a great deal of enthusiasm,
cooperation, and goodwill from both Canada and the U.S. for finding
ways to facilitate trade and the movement of people while at the same
time protecting our common border. Both sides are eager to produce
tangible deliverables.[57]

DIPLOMACY AND THE GLOBAL WAR ON TERROR

US diplomatic relations with Canada were mostly conducted in a practical
and businesslike atmosphere, far different from the press stereotypes about
diplomats in pinstripe suits coddling foreigners with endless dinners and
parties. The anti-diplomatic mentality of the top levels in the Bush administration – "you're either with us or you're against us" – was not so harmful
to relations with Canada as it was to the US Department of State as a
whole. The department was under enormous pressure in 2002–03 to con-
form to the mentality of Global War on Terror, including the notion of a
mission to democratize the Arab world, by force if necessary.

By January 2003, the department's list of strategic goals had been "changed to reflect the order in the National Security Strategy," and read in the following order:

Counterterrorism
Homeland Security
Regional Stability (averting, resolving, or containing local and
    regional conflicts)
Weapons of Mass Destruction
International Crime and Drugs
American Citizens
Democracy & Human Rights
Economic Prosperity and Security
Humanitarian & Other Transnational Issues
Public Diplomacy
Management and Institutional Reform

In this ranking, what might be called national-security objectives held three of the top four places. The economic goal ranked *eighth* on a list of eleven.[58] Two years earlier, it had been *second* on a list of eight. A dozen years later, in 2015, the department had five goals, the *first* of which was to "strengthen America's economic reach and positive economic impact."

Former House speaker Newt Gingrich, who was a prominent Republican on Capitol Hill and elsewhere, was one of the most audible critics of the Department of State and of diplomacy generally. In a speech in late April 2003 he called the department a "broken instrument of diplomacy" and said "the last seven months had involved six months of diplomatic failure and one month of military success [invading Iraq]." Gingrich followed up with a written article proposing a wholesale reconstruction of the Department of State.

> In Washington today, two worldviews on U.S. foreign policy are colliding. One view emphasizes facts, values, and consequences. The other believes in process, politeness, and accommodation ... The State Department needs to experience culture shock, a top-to-bottom transformation ...
>
> [President] Bush made the following statement to a group of Iraqi Americans in Dearborn, Michigan: "I have confidence in the future of a free Iraq. The Iraqi people are fully capable of self-government." He also told them that "You are living proof the Iraqi people love freedom

and living proof the Iraqi people can flourish in democracy. People who live in Iraq deserve the same freedom that you and I enjoy here in America."

Contrast that vision with a recent classified report by the State Department's Bureau of Intelligence and Research titled "Iraq, the Middle East and Change: No Dominoes," which was leaked in March 2003 to the Los Angeles Times. As reported by that newspaper, the document stated that "liberal democracy would be difficult to achieve [in Iraq] ... Electoral democracy, were it to emerge, could well be subject to exploitation by anti-American elements." And according to an anonymous intelligence source interviewed by the newspaper, the thrust of the report argued that "this idea that you're going to transform the Middle East and fundamentally alter its trajectory is not credible."

The Los Angeles Times has also reported that U.S. diplomats (insisting upon anonymity) "said they are profoundly worried about what they describe as the [Bush] administration's arrogance or indifference to world public opinion, which they fear has wiped out, in less than two years, decades of effort to build goodwill toward the United States." Meanwhile, as reported recently by National Review Online contributor Joel Mowbray, a Bush administration official believes the outgoing director of policy planning at the State Department, Richard Haass, has "made it his mission to loosen sanctions on Iran," despite Bush's designation of Iran as part of the "axis of evil."

Can anyone imagine a State Department more out of sync with Bush's views and objectives? The president should demand a complete overhaul of the State Department.[59]

THE BUSH ADMINISTRATION, THE STATE DEPARTMENT, AND COLIN POWELL

Secretary of State Colin Powell, a soldier who had risen from the ranks to top command to be America's top diplomat, said to senators a month later:

Ever since Thomas Jefferson was sworn in as the first Secretary of State, an uninterrupted line of Secretaries of State, from number one to number 65, have been criticized at one time or another of being – what? – diplomats, for trying to find peaceful solutions, to building friendships around the world, to building alliances. That's what we do. We do it damn well. And I'm not going to apologize to anybody.

I'm on the offense for the people who work in my Department doing a great job, and if you come after them, come after them with legitimate criticism. We'll respond to that. We're not above criticism. But if you come after us just to come after us, you're in for a fight, and I'm going to fight back and I'm going to protect my Department and my people.

And I'm also going to defend the policies of the President, which were attacked even more vigorously than any sideways attack on the contributions and the loyalty and the dedication and the courage and the willingness to serve of the men and women of the State Department.

So, hopefully, we can pursue the issue of how the State Department is functioning in a reasonable manner, with constructive comments welcomed and an open debate taking place.

With respect to what's going on within the administration, it's not the first time I have seen discussions with the administration between one department and another. I have been in four straight administrations at a senior level; and thus it has been, and thus it has always been, and thus it should be. There should be tension within the national security team, and, from that tension, arguments are surfaced for the President ... And the President is the one who decides.

Complicated issues come along. How do you go into a place like Iraq[?][60]

Powell was a courageous and deeply credible defender of the State Department and of diplomacy, and his warning to the president on Iraq – "you break it, you buy it" – was very prescient. But his department would remain on the defensive to the end of the Bush years.

A small sign of this showed in the fall of 2004, three years after the September 2001 attacks, when the Canada Desk reshuffled the responsibilities of its five officers and sent the Embassy the new set of informal job descriptions. This job-description list allocated a small handful of officers' jobs – five of them – to covering America's relationship with its largest trade and investment partner in the world, and its largest foreign supplier of energy. When I read the list, I could hardly believe my eyes. Economic issues were hardly mentioned! Though Canada had not had a significant terrorist incident, nor produced a material threat to the United States, in many decades, the job summaries made Canada sound like it might be Iran or Pakistan. I wrote to my colleagues in the Economic Section: "This

is a remarkable document. Of the five portfolios listed, the top three contain both the word 'security' and the word 'terrorism.' 'Energy' makes a
halfhearted appearance in the fourth slot. 'Trade' does not show up until
the third-to-last word. How times have changed."

What I wanted to say, but didn't, was: "When we want to show our great-
grandchildren how much we lost our perspective after September 11, this
is all the evidence we'll need."

THE INVASION OF IRAQ

Differences between US and Canadian government policy priorities and
attitudes to the problem of Iraq became increasingly plain in the later
months of 2002. Iraq was still led by Saddam Hussein, the dictator
behind the invasion of Kuwait in 1990 that had led to the First Gulf War.
Changing the regime in Iraq had been official US policy since 1998, partly because Hussein was allegedly trying to develop chemical, biological,
and nuclear weapons. The top leaders of the Bush administration had a
vision of what they could do to democratize Iraq and other parts of the
Middle East, North Africa, and elsewhere, and they had limited patience
with dissenters.[61]

Unfortunately, Prime Minister Chrétien sent the US administration mixed
signals through the first quarter of 2003 about Canada's willingness to support the coalition to invade Iraq. Ambassador Cellucci believed – and he
assured Washington – that Canada would come on board with the invasion
in the end. The Canadian military had three thousand personnel in the operational theatre on 18 March when Chrétien announced to Parliament that
Canada would not participate.

A small but badly timed and inexcusable incident made matters significantly worse. Chrétien's minister of natural resources, Herb Dhaliwal,
was quoted on 19 March saying outside a cabinet meeting, "I think it's
regrettable and unfortunate that [Bush] made this decision [to invade
Iraq]. People expect the president of a superpower to be a statesman. He's
let down not only Americans, but the world by not being a statesman."[62]
Whatever one may have thought of the president, this was an inappropriate thing for a minister to say and a bad time to say it. Our Embassy had
believed we had agreement with the Prime Minister's Office (PMO) that,
while it would not participate in the invasion, Canada would avoid criticism of what we were calling the "liberation" of Iraq and would merely
use words such as "regret" or "disappointment." The comments by Dhali-

wal not only violated that understanding but also transgressed acceptable boundaries by criticizing the president personally – something that diplomats could not allow to pass without a reaction. As a result, Ambassador Cellucci cancelled a lunch meeting with Dhaliwal that had been scheduled for 21 March.

For our Embassy, and presumably for our friends and contacts on the Canadian side, especially in the energy field, this was an unnecessary and very frustrating setback. A scheduled ambassador-minister lunch meeting takes time to arrange and prepare, and is an important diplomatic and political business opportunity. This was particularly true in Canada-US energy matters at the time. As one of my colleagues noted, the cancellation was "about the Minister's comments, not our energy relationship. I will note that we continue to want to work as intensely as ever to expand the largest, most diverse and most secure energy relationship on earth. I will note that comments like Dhaliwal's do not serve such agreed mutual objectives ... this is a sad and deeply frustrating day."[63]

BALLISTIC MISSILE DEFENCE

Chrétien's government announced two months later that it would pursue long-delayed talks with the United States on possibly participating in ballistic missile defence, a US research and development project that had begun in the 1990s and was aimed at protecting North American airspace against incoming missiles. The decision to talk about BMD helped soothe the bitterness over the Iraq decision, but not by much because it came so late.

The value of BMD, in particular the value to Canada of participating in it, was debatable (like any research and development project, especially a large one at the frontiers of technical capability). The view of one of my former Embassy colleagues – who, before writing this comment on the missile-defence decision for the Center for Strategic and International Studies, had gone on to spend eight years on the Permanent Joint Board on Defence – was that "this decision has been a long time coming. Delay has cost Canada influence on the design of the system, has limited Canadian access to the associated research and development work, and has progressively weakened Canada's negotiating position."[64] The wound would be reopened in 2005 when Canada announced it would not participate in the BMD program after all.

VITUPERATION

The disappointment in Washington with Canada's decision not to join the Iraq coalition was vented tactlessly in early April 2003 by Richard Perle, an adviser to Defense Secretary Donald Rumsfeld. Perle's words provide an example of the less-than-helpful, with-us-or-against-us rhetoric to which senior Bush administration figures were prone.

> The Prime Minister [Chretién] is a lame duck. So that may help explain the failure to appreciate the disappointment that would be caused not only by the Canadian government policy on Iraq, but by the cacophony of [Liberal politicians'] criticism [of the Bush adminis-tration] – much of it ill-informed and much of it simply name-call-ing. There is simply no other way to describe the positions of some countries – not many, but some countries – which is to lend far more support to Saddam Hussein's regime than they may have intended by the positions they have taken ... There will be many people around the world, including many Canadians, who on reflection, if they have an open mind at all, will question whether their government equated itself with the right expression of Canadian values.

Perle reportedly accused Prime Minister Chrétien and French President Jacques Chirac of "an unwillingness to confront" Iraqi leader Saddam Hussein, and also accused Canada of following France in the matter: "If Canada wishes to subordinate its moral and political values to President Chirac – so be it. Chirac and Chretien deserve each other. I would like to believe that the people of Canada will say to Chretien on his way out – 'Why did you put us in this position? This was, in fact, a just war and look at what we now have learned what life was like under Saddam Hussein and there are weapons of mass destruction and how could you have done this to us.'"[65]

Canada could have helped avoid much bitterness of this kind by declin-ing tactfully and quietly (rather than unexpectedly and irritatingly) to participate in the war. As one study later commented, "Canada missed an opportunity to decline participation in the war – as several allies did – *without* registering vocal opposition to an act that the United States con-sidered to be part of its vital national security. What ensued was a climate of mutual suspicion and limited cooperation."[66] President Bush post-poned a state visit to Ottawa that had been planned for 5 May 2003. It was unclear to what extent this actually signaled displeasure about Canada's decision on war participation as opposed to simply reflecting new pressures on the president's schedule.

Ultimately, the longer-run impact on the overall US-Canada bilateral agenda of these differences over, first, continental-security priorities, and then Iraq, should not be overstated. Canada and other nominal non-participants in the war in Iraq ended up making sizable contributions to that country's "reconstruction."[67] Additionally, the US administration remained motivated to liberalize trade and movement within North America, and was very helpful in opening markets for aviation services and energy.[68]

CHRÉTIEN, MANLEY, AND MARTIN

Also, Chrétien shared leadership roles around his cabinet – enough so that strong ministers (such as John Manley) could run their own shows in such a broad and deep bilateral relationship as that between Canada and the United States. As a result, criticism of Chrétien's handling of the Iraq coalition issue had limited impact on slowing progress in other areas. While Chrétien's laissez-faire leadership had counter-productive results in, for example, the case of Canadian heritage minister Sheila Copps and the dispute over magazine advertising and the cultural-diversity treaty, it was a great asset in the case of Manley and sometimes others from 2001 onward.

Paul Martin, waiting in the political wings to succeed Chrétien, had made a statement on 21 March 2003 in response to the decision not to participate in the military action in Iraq.

> First, while we may not agree on this specific – albeit very important – matter, there should be no question of our continued friendship with both Britain and the United States. We share with these nations a common set of values. Our histories are intertwined. Our future will be as well. And let us be clear that there can be no tolerance for heated anti-American rhetoric. We need to remember who our friends are and who they are not.
>
> Second, Canada will continue to work in partnership with the United States to ensure our common security during this time of heightened concern. There is no doubt since September 11th that North America is vulnerable to terrorism and the risk is now very real. We share a continent and a border with the Americans and we must continue to work with them to ensure that our common space remains safe for the benefit of both our peoples.

Third, looking to the future, Canada must be there to assist in the very important reconstruction effort that will surely follow the Iraqi conflict.

Jean Chrétien stepped aside as Liberal Party leader later that year and Paul Martin won the contest to replace him in that role, so Martin became prime minister in December 2003. Martin's preaching about friendship would bear little relation to his words and actions once he became prime minister – driving US administration officials' cynicism about Canada, particularly about the federal Liberals, even lower than it had been at the end of Chrétien's leadership.[69]

4

Casualties

What former House of Representatives speaker Newt Gingrich, when he was criticizing State Department diplomacy in April 2003, called "one month of military success" in Iraq would turn into eight and a half years of effort and vast expense for the United States, its allies, and Iraq – economically, militarily, and diplomatically.[1] In that speech, Gingrich argued that the State Department had failed to persuade Turkey to allow US troops on its soil as a base for the Iraq invasion, had failed to win a second UN resolution authorizing the use of force against Iraq, and had failed to align itself with White House objectives.

While Gingrich's first two points might or might not have had some foundation, demanding that State completely share the White House perspective was neither appropriate nor realistic. Secretary of State Colin Powell noted that government departments should to some degree offer repositories of expertise and dissenting opinion to political leaderships. In retrospect, it is certainly hard to see how what Gingrich described as the Bush administration's "worldview of facts, values and consequences" ended up providing a better framework for advancing US interests abroad than the more traditional State Department world view of accommodation, consultation, and negotiation, despite the latter's undeniable limitations and frustrations.

PLANNING IRAQ'S RECONSTRUCTION

Contrary to some portrayals, the administration did plan for Iraq's post-regime-change reconstruction before the invasion began, though it did not imagine the scale of insurgency that the occupiers would face. One of the leading steps was financial planning. "Government of Iraq funds cur-

rently blocked in the United States ... will be placed in a special account
... to ensure that they will be available to be used to assist the Iraqi people
and to assist in the reconstruction of Iraq ... Posts in the coalition countries and those countries that have previously declared assets to the U.N.
are requested to contact senior finance officials in order to seek cooperation and support for these efforts ... to identify and freeze Iraqi state assets,
as well as the ill-gotten gains of Saddam Hussein and his regime, to assist
in returning funds blocked in the overseas branches of U.S. financial institutions for the benefit of the people of Iraq."[2]

Secretary of State Colin Powell wrote to all Department employees on
31 March 2003, eleven days after the start of the invasion, to lay out the
vision of a liberated Iraq:

> The United States is leading an international coalition of nearly 50
> nations to disarm Iraq and liberate its people from the tyranny of
> Saddam Hussein. Our coalition is broad and deep. It includes part-
> ners from every continent and peoples of every race, religion, and
> ethnic group.
>
> Force was not our first choice. We worked hard to pass United
> Nations Security Council Resolution 1441, which gave the Iraqi
> regime one last chance to disarm peacefully ... The coalition had no
> choice but to use force to disarm that regime ...
>
> Liberation is only the beginning of our commitment to the Iraqi
> people. We are already beginning to supply humanitarian relief to
> help those in need ... Over time, we will work with the Iraqi people to
> help them create a peaceful, democratic, and unified state – one that
> uses its vast wealth to improve the lives of mothers and children, not
> to develop terrible weapons to kill its citizens and its neighbors.

Secretary Powell's message went on to survey other top departmental
priorities: counter-terrorism, North Korea, HIV/AIDS, and the Middle East
peace process.[3]

A more technical message on Iraq reconstruction on 24 April might
have been drafted by a career Foreign Service officer, since it struck a con-
sultative note, saying that the international community was expected join
in a "holistic approach to helping Iraqis rebuild ... [We] are interested in
hearing how other donors think they can best help and how we can work
effectively together to work with and help the Iraqi people." The military
campaign was said to be designed to achieve objectives with minimal loss
of civilian life and minimal damage to Iraq's civilian infrastructure. The

coalition would stay only long enough to ensure that Iraq's weapons of mass destruction were eliminated, terrorist networks destroyed, and the stable foundation of a democratic government established. The president's vision was of a unified, free Iraq, at peace with its neighbours and governed by the rule of law. Presumably, the expectation was that this could be achieved without engaging the United States in a prolonged war.

It is important to note that projections that the campaign in Iraq would be short and affordable were not confined to the US administration. A report by the United Kingdom–based Economist Intelligence Unit in November 2002 said the war "should go well, and quickly, lasting no more than three months, during which the U.S. removes Mr. [Saddam] Hussein and replaces him with a compliant government," and that "the effects of a war should be confined mainly to changes in the price of oil."[4]

LEADERSHIP DOUBTS

As the November 2004 US elections approached, the intervention in Iraq was more than a year and a half old. Weapons of mass destruction had not been found, and US officials would admit after the elections that they were not expected to be found – this search was finished. There was little sign that the invading coalition's goals were on track to being achieved. Targets for handing over power to an interim Iraqi government had been widely missed. If anything, it looked like the allies were being drawn into a longer conflict. This contributed to deepening misgivings in both Canada and the United States about the administration's strategic thinking and, in fact, the White House team's competence.

US journalist and author Seymour Hersh gave voice to some of the criticisms. In 2004 articles Hersh exposed the use of torture at the US-controlled Abu Ghraib prison near Baghdad, which would produce lasting damage to the United States' international credibility on human rights. Hersh also alleged that Vice-President Dick Cheney and Defense Secretary Donald Rumsfeld had bypassed the CIA, the centre of the US government intelligence system, in their eagerness to make the case for invading Iraq. By October, Hersh was warning Americans about the consequences for their country of re-electing President Bush in the following month's election. During a stop in Toronto he told the *Globe and Mail*, "With [John] Kerry [the Democratic nominee for President], at least you know you get a president who can listen. Right now, this guy [President Bush] can't admit a mistake. If he's re-elected, he's got to go ahead. He's incapable psychologically of acknowledging where he is on this war."[5]

Particularly for us in the State Department, the waning of confidence in the administration was deepened by signs that Secretary Powell was no longer part of the inner circle of Bush advisers – apparently because of his dissident views on Iraq. Shortly after the elections, but while Powell was still secretary, we learned that Bush had asked Powell for his view on the progress of the war, and Powell had said, "We're losing," at which point Powell was asked to leave the room. Powell told the media, "A president is not well served when he has people in his cabinet who have points of view but are not prepared to argue those points of view forcefully for fear that it might leak or it looks like members of the cabinet are squabbling."[6] One US observer wrote after the November 2004 election:

The problem in the first Bush administration was not too much dissent; it was too little. Mr. Powell's great failure was not speaking up firmly enough and loudly enough on Iraq and other issues. The Bush foreign policy has been based on a fundamentally flawed world view, a skewed set of global priorities and a self-defeating exercise of American power. These need to be countered and challenged, not reinforced. In that regard, the "get with the team" tone being set for the second Bush term is very disturbing. In addition to [incoming Secretary of State Condoleezza] Rice, two other former White House aides have been named cabinet secretaries, including Alberto Gonzales as successor to Attorney-General John Ashcroft. The new CIA director, former Republican congressman Porter Goss, issued a chilling memo that, in effect, told analysts that their job is to tell the President what he wants to hear. The first Bush team over-politicized policy, relied too much on faith over analysis, and fostered too much "groupthink." The United States doesn't need more of these in any sphere of its national life, and surely not in its foreign policy.[7]

BALLISTIC MISSILE DEFENCE AND CELLUCCI'S DEPARTURE

In March 2005, less than a month after the Paul Martin government's late winter budget announced a five-year program of increased Canadian defence spending, our Embassy team said goodbye to Ambassador Paul Cellucci. The ambassador had delivered results on the main specific instruction he had received from Secretary Powell, which was to encourage Canada to spend more on its own defence.[8] His mantra to Canadians on this had been "Don't do it for us; do it for you," precisely in line with what the wisest Canadian analysts and leaders had been telling their fellow citizens.

In a farewell interview for Canadian television, the ambassador commented on the Martin government's decision, which had been announced by the foreign-affairs minister in February, not to participate in a shared ballistic missile-defence system for North America. Going slightly beyond the press guidance received from the National Security Council, the ambassador framed his comments in sovereignty language that, he had learned, resonated with Canadians:

It is in the vital interest of our country to do ballistic missile defence, and we're going to do it. We felt that our long-term partner at NORAD in defending North America should be at the table participating. So we will deploy, we will defend North America. I think the people who have lost here are the people of Canada, because they will not have a seat at the table. We have this odd situation where the Canadians will participate at NORAD, detecting when the missile is launched, determining where it's heading, and even if they determine it's heading towards Canada, it's at that point they'll have to leave the room because they're not participating. And the United States, we'll decide what to do about the missile. That's why we're more perplexed, we don't understand why a country would give up its sovereignty, which we think Canada has done ...

Part of the surprise here is that, you know, the expectations were quite high here that Canada wanted to participate because it was in Canada's sovereign interest to do so ... We were given that impression in a very direct way for a long time.[9]

Note the ambassador's experience, on BMD as on the Iraq invasion coalition, of being misled by his Canadian interlocutors for an extended period. This would have been enormously harmful to the reputation in Washington of any US ambassador, whose job is to develop contacts that give him an accurate reading on his host country's intentions. The interviewer tried to suggest that Ambassador Cellucci's advocacy of missile defence had produced a hostile reaction that induced the Canadian government to back out of the invasion plan, but if Canadian resistance was triggered by US pressure, it was more likely produced by the unpopular President Bush's unexpected public call on Canada to participate in BMD, which the president made during his late 2004 visit to Ottawa, than by the ambassador.

Cellucci expressed disappointment that neither the Liberals nor the Conservatives had tried to advocate missile defence to the Canadian public. Separately, opposition defence critic Gordon O'Connor said something similar, noting that the Martin government missed a good opportunity to sign on to BMD in the run-up to the president's visit, when the public was more receptive to participating than it would be after Bush personally called for it. "If [Prime Minister Martin] stayed with that and had sought our [the Conservative Party's] support – if the deal was reasonable – ballistic missile defence would have gone through [and] public opinion would have gone with it. Because if the Conservatives and the Liberals together had supported missile defence, I'm sure the public would have agreed."[10]

Canada missed a chance to expand NORAD when the United States formed Northern Command in 2002, and it made matters worse by staying out of missile defence in 2003–04. The result was more than just a reduction of the relative importance of NORAD, and thereby of Canada, in US defence policy; this was also, in retrospect, a perfect opportunity for Canada to position itself once more in Washington as the closest of allies, and that opportunity was squandered.[11] While staying out of the war in Iraq, Canada could still have demonstrated that it was in the inner circle of America's allies.

THE WESTERN HEMISPHERE TRAVEL INITIATIVE

The US Western Hemisphere Travel Initiative of 2005 stemmed from the Intelligence Reform and Terrorism Prevention Act (IRTPA) and also from the recommendations of the National Commission on Terrorist Attacks upon the United States in its 9/11 Report. WHTI was going to require travellers to show a passport when entering the United States from any western hemisphere country, including Canada. Canadians had traditionally been able to enter the United States under very relaxed requirements – for example, US authorities at land crossings generally accepted a person's say-so through the car window as "proof" of citizenship – and many people who regularly crossed the border did not have passports.

Though Canadians were given about two years' notice to get ready for the passport rule, which was scheduled for the end of 2007, anticipation of WHTI requirements produced anxiety in Canada as well as among many Americans with a stake in cross-border traffic. Americans who entered Canada would need to have passports to re-enter their home country, so the requirement affected large numbers of people on both sides. The

British Columbia provincial government, which was busy with plans for hosting the 2010 winter Olympic Games, was afraid that WHTI travel requirements would complicate its hosting of that event because many visitors would not know about the change and would not have passports, creating tie-ups at crossings and airports. Alaska senator Lisa Murkowski shared her concerns with US Ambassador David Wilkins:

> WHTI concerns Alaskans because of its possible negative impact on their ability to cross into Canada easily. For instance, Alaskans living in Skagway often cross the border to shop at the Costco in nearby Whitehorse, Yukon Territory; others, including pregnant women, cross the border to get medical assistance in Whitehorse. Americans on cruise ships traveling in Alaska's Inside Passage make day trips into Canada when ships dock in Skagway ... Many Alaskans in remote parts of the state might have difficulties even applying for a U.S. passport ... native peoples traditionally cross the border with their [caribou] herds without hindrance. Would they have to get special documents? Many of these people, the Senator said, do not even have drivers' licenses or other government-issued documents.[12]

Senior businesspeople also viewed WHTI apprehensively, describing it repeatedly in a major private-sector meeting on NAFTA/SPP as "an impending train wreck."[13] While Ambassador Wilkins urged Canadians to get passports and keep them up to date, he also tried to alleviate the worry by talking up some work the Department of Homeland Security was doing on creating an "equivalent secure document" for Canadians crossing the border (possibly some adaptation of State and provincial driver's licences to contain more security-related data).[14] As a result, unfortunately, some Canadians (including some in the media) then over-focused on this uncertain "solution" of an alternative travel document[15] and constantly pressed the administration about it – overlooking the unavoidable fact that Congress had passed a law regarding passports and that, while there might be an option to develop some other kind of document, as things stood passports were still going to be required at the border. The administration did not have the power to change laws, but rather had to implement them.

Though the implementation of WHTI for air travellers (as opposed to land crossings) in January 2007 had gone well, the government of Canada continued to resist planning to implement it at land and sea crossings. As part of a proposed briefing for the secretary of state, a senior Embassy colleague wrote:

When they say "You (the US) will not be ready (by 2008)" they really mean that Canada will not be ready. Despite bad press about long delays in securing a Canadian passport, the government is still not significantly expanding [passport issuance] capacity, has declined to move from a five-year to ten-year passport, and has not publicly accepted the utility of a Canadian version of the US Passport Card. The Canadian bureaucracy/procurement process adds to the policy problems. It is likely to be between 2009 and 2011 before the Canadians begin producing an e-passport. The Canadians continue to push for acceptance of a modified Driver's Licence and indicate strong support for a pilot program between Washington State and British Columbia, despite leaving unresolved numerous technical and legal (privacy) issues.[16]

In the fall of 2007 the United States accommodated Canada's pressure for further delay. "WHTI amendment has been proposed as part of Homeland Security appropriations bill; one-word change would effectively delay implementation on land to June 1 2009. Appears to have a good chance of passing."

DONE, AT A COST

There was little gratitude expressed on the Canadian side for the delays, entrenching US resentment of Canada's conduct on the WHTI issue. Embassy meeting notes read, "Readout on Rice-Bernier [bilateral foreign ministers'] meeting in Washington on December 19 [2007]. WHTI, passports, ITAR [International Traffic in Arms Regulations]. Little acknowledgement by Government of Canada of the importance of having the implementation of the land border passport requirement put off until June 2009; rather, they moved on to new demands regarding enhanced drivers' licenses."[17]

Asking Canadians to show passports when entering the United States, while it did appear on its face to be a step backward in the openness of the border, and while it produced tremendous complaining from the Canadian side, was a very reasonable measure by a sovereign country. It was certainly on the gentler end of the menu of possible border-thickening measures; worse or, at least, very different things could have happened. For example, the office of a Georgia congressman named Charlie Norwood submitted a staff report to the House Armed Services Committee in September 2006 proposing that the northern border be massively secured against illegal entry. Drawing particular attention to unguarded road crossings from Canada into the United States, the Norwood report said that "the main challenge in securing the border immediately is to deploy sufficient manpower to secure all significant illegal-crossing areas. Total immediate force increases to accomplish this goal for the Northern Border are 10,880 personnel, 400 water patrol craft, and 160 fixed wing aircraft ... All major illegal land entry points on the Northern Border that are currently unguarded – an estimated 1,000 hard-surface roadways – could be secured around the clock with 8,000 National Guard or State Defense Force reserves drawn from all states ... Long term, the number of U.S. Border Patrol field officers on the Northern Border should be doubled."[18]

Along these lines, in August 2008, US Customs and Border Protection (CBP) opened a new Great Lakes Air and Marine Branch, based near Detroit, to strengthen border-security operations. The new branch was planned to consist of over seventy-five agents and support staff and twenty-nine contractor employees, with five helicopters and six fixed-wing aircraft.[19] While this may not have actually thickened the border in practice for Canadians, it would have triggered objections from the Canadian side, made the "undefended" border seem more militarized, and demonstrated that the administration was willing to invest resources in the direction demanded by Norwood and others.

As things turned out, by all indications the implementation of WHTI on land-border crossings on 30 January 2008 went smoothly, and after implementation the whining about WHTI settled down. While a delay of implementation (until January 2008 at land crossings) seems to have been needed for both sides to get ready, in the end no new form of identification was invented; passports were required, many people applied for and received them, and the impact on business was apparently manageable. WHTI genuinely increased the United States' ability to manage people's entry into and exit from its territory, and, unfortunately, Canadians' vocal resistance to it reinforced already strong views in Washington that Canadians were not going to be much help with security issues. By communicating and endorsing, rather than managing, its citizens' concerns about the passport requirement, the government of Canada had solidified its image in Washington as being mostly hindrance and little help on security issues – and on this issue, it had gained little or nothing for the price.[20] This episode, coming on top of Canada's slow, diffident decisions not to participate in the Iraq coalition or the BMD program, undid decades of Canadians' efforts to build their country's image as a reliable and responsive security partner for the United States.

IRRITANTS AND BARRIERS ACCUMULATE

News broke in the press in early September 2006 that the US Animal and Plant Health Inspection Service (APHIS, part of the Department of Agriculture) planned to cease exempting Canadian shipments from the user fees it applied to incoming products from other countries. This meant that people and shipments entering the United States from Canada would need to pay fees that they had not paid in the past, fees that other countries had been paying since the early 1990s. APHIS's position was that "the risk of plant pests or animal diseases being introduced into the United States by way of movements from Canada now appears to be considerably higher than it was in the past because of a general trend toward market globalization coupled with a high demand for new commodities generated by Canada's growing cultural diversity. An ever-increasing variety of agricultural products from all over the world is being imported into Canada. These importations into Canada ... increase the risk to the United States because there is market demand to move these commodities into the United States to meet market demands here that cannot be met through legal importations [directly] into the United States." The Embassy's agriculture counsellor added, "The contention that this is protectionism is the standard Canadian accusation on anything we do. It really has no basis, and in fact the basis for what we are doing is based on over 5 years of research into where the risks are. The Canadian Government has known this is coming for 3 years. We are just imposing what we have on every other country and what Canada imposes on us."[21]

The *Globe and Mail* printed an hysterical editorial piece about the fees (which amounted to $5.25 on a truckload, $70 on an aircraft, and $5.00 on an air passenger):

> What are the Americans doing? Are they trying to bring the Canadian-U.S. border to a complete standstill? ... This is appalling. Whatever happened to the consultations that NAFTA was supposed to foster? There is a NAFTA committee on sanitary measures ... There is a NAFTA committee on agriculture ... Yet International Trade Minister David Emerson said he learned of these measures only two weeks ago. Agriculture Canada found out the details only two days ago ...
>
> There is a larger issue here. The United States is supposed to be our trusted ally and closest trading partner. To hinder agricultural trade, to ask Canadians to pay for U.S. security, to do all this with virtually no notice, is a terrible way to treat a neighbour.[22]

This was overdone. The APHIS fee announcement was a small measure and, like WHTI, not really unreasonable, though the lack of notice was unfortunate. But the announcement felt to some like a tipping point against the Canadian policy establishment's hopes, five years after the September 2001 attacks, that North American economic integration would someday get back on the track it had been on in the 1990s.

Informal notes from a bilateral meeting of top agriculture officials on 13 September 2006 read, "This meeting was requested by the Canadians because they frankly feel that they have been real flexible with USDA [US Department of Agriculture] ... but are not getting the same level of cooperation/consultation in return ... They feel there was little or no consultation beforehand, and no real attempt to meet Canadian concerns or find different ways to do it."[23]

In late November 2006 APHIS announced a delay in imposition of its fee on Canadian border crossings into the United States. However, Canadian Ambassador Michael Wilson continued to cite the APHIS fee and WHTI as examples of "incremental" measures that were taking a toll on the Canada-US border relationship. On 4 December, Prime Minister Stephen Harper wrote to President Bush expressing concern about the fee, in a way that harked back to the perimeter concept – the idea of moving security measures and other protective activity away from the border and instead conducting them (in partnership) closer to the sources of risk.

> The proposed APHIS measures will result in a "thickening" of our shared border ... In particular, we believe that the APHIS rule does not comply with our agreed-upon risk-based approach to interdict high-risk products and goods at the source, rather than at the border. Moreover, it is inconsistent with the principles of our Security and Prosperity Partnership of North America and the Canada-U.S. Smart Border Declaration, which aim to address risks at their point of origin ... Canada proposes putting in place systems and harmonized measures to manage the risks to agricultural products before they reach the U.S.-Canada border, rather than adding on more layers of regulation and control.[24]

Our Embassy team discovered about a month later, on 25 January 2007, that CBP would announce the following day a 10 per cent increase (from US$5.00 to $5.50) in its "single transaction user fee" on trucks entering the United States from Canada. A senior colleague said that "the timing, if true, would be exquisitely bad." It was true. We hurried to warn our con-

tacts on the Canadian side. Our deputy chief of mission stated, "I am wondering whether we could propose a moratorium on this kind of
announcement. Too late for tomorrow's Federal Register [the publication
that would carry the official notice of the CBP fee increase]? We have yet to
catch up with the last one." A National Security Council colleague worried, "Is this going to be another breach of our 'no surprises' rule with the
Canadians?"[25]

It was. Again, while the fee increase was a very small measure in itself,
the timing was unfortunate and the lack of notice or consultation missed
an opportunity to get the Canadian government onside. The border got a
little thicker, but much more importantly, trust in the relationship took
yet another step downward.

FROM MARTIN TO HARPER

Naturally, and particularly given that Paul Martin's 2004–06 Liberal government had deliberately adopted an anti-American stance, Canada's
incoming Conservative Party government pledged to improve the relationship with the United States. But this promise, even if it were genuine,
did not mean that Conservatives knew how to act on it. Prime Minister
Stephen Harper and his government were hardly great relationship-
builders – Harper was seen as having a chilly personality, his team deeply
distrusted most bureaucrats and the whole Ottawa establishment, and
their government was sometimes capable of the same unilateralist impulses the Bush team was accused of. Also, particularly in their early years, the
Harper government was not well connected to big businesses, which are
such essential players in Canada-US relations. While the Harper team's
ways of aggravating relations with Washington may have been less intentional than Martin's or Chretien's, they were still not what was really
needed in the circumstances.

In December 2007 a newspaper reporter asked our Embassy to comment on the following quotes from an interview with International Trade
Minister David Emerson. (Emerson was one of the most experienced and
best ministers in the government, a business Liberal who, by changing
political parties, had moved almost seamlessly from the Martin to Harper
cabinets right after the 2006 election). He was quoted as saying that

the degree to which the protectionist forces in the U.S. and now some
of the rigid mindset of the security establishment is really starting to, I
think, threaten the special relationship that used to be there, where

Canada would get special treatment on various things ... [is] a source of serious concern because Canada cannot afford – frankly neither can the U.S. – to see cross border supply chains start to be weakened ...

I don't think NAFTA is particularly threatened as a legal trade paradigm. I think the threat is that we will just continue this bottom up accumulation of little border-impeding, border thickening initiatives. They really aren't NAFTA issues. They are just ways that protectionism creeps up on you from narrow parochial interests ... inspections or fees or all kinds of immigration related issues ...

You get this absolute supremacy of security trumping everything. And then you get the [US] bureaucrats in the departments and they are all powerful and they don't feel they have to listen to compromise or alternative solutions.

In a way it's a disease of institutional bureaucracy and excessive empowerment. So the broader public interest gets lost in the narrow institutional vision ...

As long as the distributed bureaucracy is out there creating new problems almost monthly, you've got to stop the overall erosion. Somebody at the high level has to say it's time that this stopped, it's time that we really examined every initiative to ensure that we are not undermining the fundamental strength of North America which we all depend on.

While this was better than (say) Minister Herb Dhaliwal's comments about President Bush's statesmanship, it was still fairly open and negative criticism of the administration. Ambassador Wilkins wanted to comment, and I drafted the following as background for him.

There have been independent attempts, by the Conference Board of Canada and others, to see if border security measures have hurt trade. They have found little or no evidence that post-9/11 security measures have hurt bilateral trade volumes, and not much evidence of higher costs at the border.

Bilateral trade is holding up very well considering all the things that are going on in the economy, such as higher costs for energy and transportation, greater competition from emerging markets, and substantial changes in exchange rates. All of these are likely to be just as important, or more so, than security measures.

Yes, there are protectionist pressures in our society. There always will be.

Positive security is something that few people notice. You don't notice the absence of an attack, the non-occurrence of an accident, or the absence of a disease outbreak. Let's keep in mind that maybe our efforts to make our borders and airports more secure may be delivering positive results.[26]

Meanwhile, the post-NAFTA Security and Prosperity Partnership process was crawling forward, so there was still some reason to hope for a broad initiative that would start to set some of these problems straight. The agenda for the second SPP ministerial meeting, held in Ottawa on 23 February 2007, focused on developing a trilateral initiative on energy, working on a coordinated North American response to avian and pandemic influenza, implementing cooperation on emergency management, looking for ways to improve security while facilitating movement across borders, and devising means to improve North American competitiveness in world markets.

At that meeting, Homeland Security Secretary Michael Chertoff refloated the perimeter notion, which had been pecked to death by Canadian media back in 2001. This suggested that the three NAFTA countries should "look at security perimeter objectives[,] noting that the more effective we are along the North American perimeter, the less we have to worry about the barriers between us." (It is not clear why Canadian ministers present did not pick up this theme and seize the opportunity to renew the perimeter discussion.) Reflecting sensitivity to some Americans' attacks on SPP, "Ministers acknowledged that governments need to communicate to our publics what we are doing under SPP – and what we are *not* doing (i.e., no common currency, no intention to re-create the EU in North America)."[27]

Three weeks later, the two countries signed a civil-aviation agreement that facilitated opening of routes to third countries and for cargo flights, allowed more market-based pricing, and instituted liberalized rules for charters. Air Canada, which had transitioned from public to private ownership but still at the time had a virtual monopoly on scheduled international flights to and from Canada, was resisting these changes behind closed doors. But the Canadian government forged ahead, and the agreement led to much greater competition and lower fares for passengers on cross-border and international routes in subsequent years, as upstart airlines such as WestJet, Porter, and others moved into the business.

At the end of January 2008, Ambassador Wilkins was asked by a magazine interviewer whether he foresaw even closer integration between

Canada and the United States. I suggested an answer that I thought was cautious but truthful:

> In the sense that communication and travel keep getting cheaper, making the whole world smaller – then yes, we will likely keep getting more integrated with each other, just as we will keep getting more integrated with the rest of the world.
>
> The question would seem to be, is there something beyond this that we'd choose to do as a matter of policy. A look at our shared history would suggest that we have tended to make those choices positively in the past. Less than 200 years ago we fought a war against each other. Until about 100 years ago, the United States was not Canada's top economic partner; Britain was. Less than 70 years ago, before World War 2, we were not allies in any formal collective security arrangement. It's less than 45 years since we agreed to trade autos and parts back and forth without restrictions.
>
> We no longer argue about whether those past decisions to grow closer together were good or bad. They look wise in hindsight. So we can certainly say, there's no reason not to be open-minded about what else we can do together.[28]

This really just put the best face on a bad situation; I saw no hope of a new integration push for years to come.

CLASHING PERSPECTIVES ON THE BORDER

In February 2008 international-trade expert Michael Hart published an article on the thickening of the Canada-US border. Hart wrote that "the border as presently constituted protects Canadians and Americans from each other, not from global security threats," and that politicians should admit that "much of what is done at the border in the name of security and other objectives serves more as a symbol of their concerns than as a palpable deterrent to terrorism, crime and other risks" – meaning what is sometimes called "security theatre," measures intended more to satisfy or reassure a constituency than to control security risks. In an accompanying piece, columnist Terence Corcoran wrote that "the world's longest undefended border has become a trade war zone through which fewer goods and services are moving."[29]

These two items triggered discussion among my Embassy colleagues. One grumbled, "Canadians tell us all the time that 'our complicated' border is costing 'them billions.' But is there any hard evidence that this is actually the case?" A Department of Homeland Security colleague wrote:

The United States ... should not kow-tow to the idea that the border can go back to the "way it was." Nor do I think we should play into the idea that it is all of the "security" measures that are the problem ... We have not had substantial discussions on these issues with the Government of Canada in several years. The Interagency Border Facilitation Working group led by HSC [Homeland Security Council] is just now beginning to look at the Northern Border and talk to Canada – this is a good start.

Further, while we have made progress on several joint security initiatives, the fact is that we still have significant differences in our security regimes. For example, screening and vetting of incoming passengers from outside North America (e.g. US-VISIT in the U.S., and ?? for Canada? – they don't collect biometrics). These "gaps" are of concern to the United States. Without more synchronization of our security regimes, we must place security measures where we have authority – at our border. Not the ideal, but we are mandated to do so, by Congress and our mission.

Finally, both Canada and the United States must acknowledge that there are persons of concern within North America that we must take every opportunity to identify and whose movements we must track. [Homeland Security] Secretary Chertoff stated as much in quotes in the press this past Sunday. Canada does not wish to speak about this issue, and, in fact, takes offense whenever we state there is an issue, but this is one major reason for increased security at the border. And limitations on sharing of information [since the Maher Arar detainee case] is hindering our ability to cooperate in this area as well.

My personal opinion is that we must be more forceful in pushing the security agenda. Additional cooperation on these issues would have benefits at the border. However, we cannot, and will not, "decrease security" while we face a strong threat, not *from* Canada directly, but, just like in the Cold War, we have to be concerned about what comes *through* Canada. And, for its self-interest, Canada should be just as concerned ...

[There is a] difference of perspective between Canada and the U.S. on the border right now. We no longer look at the border as primarily a regulatory compliance mechanism, but a protective frontier to prevent terrorists, terrorist supporters and terrorist weapons from enter-

ing the country. That is our primary mission at the border. As long as
the difference in perspective on the border remains, we will have difficulty engaging in the type of dialogue necessary, and we will be
accused of inflating or overblowing the threat and our response. I
would also challenge the presumptions in this article that the measures taken are "symbolic" and do nothing to prevent terrorism. This
is a canard that is repeated often, since we cannot publicly tout our
successes, in many cases, the results of these measures are not seen by
the public, so they do not believe they are effective.[30]

The difference between this statement and a reply, written later the
same day, from a Washington-based State Department colleague illustrates
the divergence between the State and Homeland Security perspectives on
these issues:

[It is true that] border infrastructure problems did not begin on Sept.
12, 2001. We had problems with inspection capacity long before. But
it's also true that our new security measures have not helped. There
were strong arguments in favor of implementing tougher screening
without waiting for changes that might have mitigated some of the
adverse effects – we needed to close potential gaps right away. It does
not follow, however, that we should therefore continue ignoring or
delaying those mitigating actions, nor that such actions must in all
cases take a back seat to additional security-related measures. Events in
the world forced the security-facilitation balance to swing heavily
toward security. There is nothing wrong, however, with now, six years
later, assessing whether we can swing it back a bit toward the center ...
     There is no point in thinking we can "bring around" the Canadians
to our point of view. For Canada, the border is their lifeblood ... They
have become far more interdependent than we will ever be. Canadians
simply cannot accept that security trumps trade in all aspects. This difference is going to be an enduring fact in our dialogue. We need to
accept this fact and move forward, rather than let it stifle the discussion.
     Every time we say things like "the northern border is a protective
frontier," Canadians hear "we don't trust you as a security partner."
Even if some quarters might have reservations about Canadian capabilities or will, this approach is not going to get us anywhere in trying to create a partnership. In the Cold War context, NORAD worked
because we made Canada a partner. We made them part of the
defensive "wall" to prevent attacks through Canada on the U.S. We

didn't ask for their cooperation while building a separate "wall" behind them.

We've made great strides in security cooperation with Canada, but I think there's tremendous potential to do more ... The world has dramatically changed in both the security and trade realms. It may be time to dramatically redefine what a border between two partner nations means, and look to greater cooperative efforts.[31]

The Homeland Security viewpoint was naturally defensive and assertive; the State Department perspective was intellectual, couched in historical context, and tried to place itself in the other party's shoes – a vital ingredient to successful negotiation. They were different cultures. While it is important for Canadians to know that a diplomatic culture exists in the United States, including in its foreign-affairs and national-security establishments, they must recognize that it may be a minority voice and one that won't necessarily carry the day in a Washington inter-agency debate.

FOREIGN EMPLOYMENT OPPORTUNITIES

Among the legacies of the Bush era was the effect of the prolonged conflicts in Iraq and, to a lesser extent, Afghanistan on the careers of many Foreign Service personnel. By July 2005, the US establishment in Baghdad was so large that the State Department issued a formal call to its locally engaged staff to volunteer for service there. The details of this invitation give insight into the state of the allied effort in Iraq early in the third year of the war.

To continue the vital work of Iraq reconstruction ... [the Bureau of Near Eastern Affairs] is offering Iraq temporary duty opportunities to locally engaged personnel. Iraq remains the department's top priority and posts are strongly encouraged to approve and assist ... Embassy Baghdad will make all final selection decisions ... Selected volunteers will undergo further security vetting [and] attend the 7.5 day anti-terrorism course ...

All permanent staff is housed in modular units on the heavily guarded and fortified Embassy compound [the so-called Green Zone]. The units are fortified on all sides by sandbags and provide little privacy, as they are placed close together. The compound also houses U.S. military assigned to the Embassy annex ... Most personnel will be required to share a single room with one person or live in barracks-style housing in large rooms or in tents on the compound.

Each modular unit consists of two separate rooms with a shared bathroom/shower ... The average is 80 square feet per room, which means that as long as rooms are shared, each person will have about 40 square feet to call his own ... Use a tape measure to mark out 40 square feet so you know the actual size of your living space ...

The U.S. Embassy, regional offices and embedded sites are located in an active combat zone with frequent attacks on facilities and personnel. Types of attacks experienced are indirect fire from rockets or mortars, vehicle-borne improvised explosive devices, [other] improvised explosive devices, suicide bombers, rocket-propelled grenades, and small arms fire. These attacks are unpredictable and usually occur with little or no warning.

Travel anywhere outside the international zone (IZ) is extremely dangerous ... conducted in heavily armed convoys of armored vehicles ... Even with this visible armed presence, these convoys are attacked. The main route between the IZ and Baghdad International Airport is sometime closed because of attacks ... Travel outside of the IZ for non-official business is prohibited.[32]

While I had been in the same job for fifteen years at this point, and I had considerable appetite for new experiences, it did not take long to decide that this opportunity was not for me.

Three impressions remain from the gossip I picked up from and through my colleagues about life on the compound in Baghdad. First, many people serving there were mainly drawn by the extra pay and low living costs: it was a rare chance for those with financial troubles (such as men with heavy alimony and/or child-support payments) to ease their money problems. However, these were not necessarily highly motivated patriots; on the contrary, many had significant personal baggage. Secondly, very few women volunteered, so those who did said that they received a great deal more male attention than they were used to, whether they liked it or not. Thirdly, there were only really three ways to fill the time (other than work) on the compound: exercise, eat the free food, or drink. Based on which of these three activities one gravitated toward, Baghdad long-timers became, it was said, "hunks, chunks or drunks."

A comment in a well-respected column of the *Washington Post* later in 2005, on the challenge of recruiting Iraqis to the US-led "reconstruction" effort, helps explain the need to recruit from other countries. According to the *Post* writer:

> We received this cable the other day from the U.S. Embassy in Baghdad about exciting new job opportunities there.
>
> "The hiring of [Iraqi] locally engaged staff (LES) has been a slow, cumbersome and sometimes fruitless process at Mission Iraq," the embassy wrote last month to Secretary of State Condoleezza Rice. "Due to the security situation and a lack of a well-established national security structure, performing proper background checks on LES candidates is very difficult and yields uncertain results."
>
> A second problem, Baghdad noted, is that the "insurgents' intimidation campaign has touched our LES corps personally: two of our LES employees have been gunned down in execution-style murders, and two others barely escaped a similar fate in August. Our LES employees live in fear of being identified with the Embassy of the U.S. ...
>
> "For the first half of 2005 ten of 14 [resignations] were due to security concerns. Of 58 job offers, thirteen employees did not show up for work or resigned within 30 days. The reality is that the embassy can offer them little protection outside the International Zone (IZ) and is not in a position to grant their repeated requests to house them and their families within the IZ."
>
> So what to do? Embassy Baghdad says the situation "has led us to consider making greater use of Third Country National (TCN) employees."[33]

Fresh calls for LES, such as myself, to serve in Iraq – either with the Embassy or with Provincial Reconstruction Teams (PRTs) – came in April and again in June 2007. In addition to a 50 per cent pay increase, the department offered an "Iraq benefits package" that included language-incentive pay, administrative leave, and visitation and recuperation travel. Twenty assignments lasting six months to a year were available in visas and consular work, computer management, storekeeping, vehicle management, finance, cultural affairs, information resources, political analysis, and public diplomacy.

For US diplomats who served in Iraq, too, pay was increased significantly in 2007. A senior colleague with US Army experience passed on the announcement with the comment, "Not surprised to see this. The much higher pay limits, especially for senior officers, make Iraq service much more attractive ... Of course, if one should be killed, there are additional benefits for survivors, but obviously that 'recognition' would not be mentioned in this solicitation."[34]

A management-focused Foreign Affairs Council report in June 2007 said the State Department's budget request for 2008 was $5.86 billion, of which $1.88 billion – 32 per cent! – was for Iraq. The report said hundreds of State Department jobs, particularly the junior and training slots, were unfilled or their creation had been stalled because available people were being soaked up in Iraq, Afghanistan, and other hot spots. The result was that the strengthening of the Foreign Service achieved under Colin Powell had been reversed.[35]

About that time, an internal online survey of US diplomats who had returned from hazardous overseas postings found that over 40 per cent said that their mental health, emotional state, social well-being, or capacity to function was affected by the posting, and more than a third reported symptoms of post-traumatic stress disorder. The number of "unaccompanied" jobs in the State Department – those deemed too difficult or dangerous for employees to bring their families – had tripled since 2001. Still, most of the respondents said they would volunteer for another hardship post. Perhaps this only reflected the importance of the pay increment to so many volunteers.[36]

Of course, the toll taken on US diplomats by the wars in Iraq and Afghanistan was nothing compared to what it did to the armed forces through casualties, trauma, and repeat tours of duty. A chief of staff later said, "When the volunteer force was conceived in the mid-'70s, no one thought it would be asked to do what it's been asked to do recently. It has performed magnificently. But there was a period there when we increased the pace of deployment to 15 months away and a year at home, and we almost broke the force."[37]

EMBASSY BAGHDAD'S GROWTH

Criticism of the State Department's Iraq work focused less on the situations faced by diplomats and employees – which paled in comparison with those endured by soldiers – than on why staffing in Iraq needed to be so large. The 104-acre Embassy compound in Iraq was becoming a heavily fortified town-within-a-city housing more than one thousand State employees plus many private-sector security contractors. Its budget for 2006 – not even counting the PRTs – was said to be twenty times that of the US Embassy in Beijing, China. Rather than an Embassy, Iraq's team was a would-be occupying government, yet one that was unable to govern.

This, not a diplomatic effort, is what I would have been joining, had I let myself be recruited.

Embassy Baghdad employees complained that the shipping-container trailers they slept in, though surrounded with sandbags, had not had their roofs hardened against rocket and mortar fire because of cost. One said that it was "criminally negligent" in these circumstances not to reduce the size of the Embassy staff, but that "they're not going to send us home because it's going to be another admission of failure."[38]

The new US ambassador to Iraq, Ryan Crocker, complained in an unclassified cable to Secretary of State Condoleezza Rice in May 2007 that he was not getting the people he needed. "I need more people, and that's the thing, not that the people who are here shouldn't be here or couldn't do it," he said in an interview. Ambassador Crocker also said the security rules for diplomats hampered their work and should be loosened to the levels required for military personnel. Others noted that too many of those sent to Baghdad either were too young and inexperienced or were less-than-ideal workers trying to salvage flagging careers by taking high-priority assignments.[39]

Lawrence Eagleburger, a former secretary of state and member of the Iraq Study Group (ISG), was quoted saying, "I defy anyone to tell me how you can use that many people. It is nuts ... it's insane and it's counterproductive ... and it won't work."[40] One anonymous government official, recently returned from Baghdad, reportedly said that a well-managed political section of fifty of the right people was what Ambassador Crocker really needed.[41]

In June 2007 the department announced a "Special Iraq Assignment Cycle" which put the staffing of Iraq and its PRTs ahead of any other staffing decisions. The official statement from the secretary hinted that Iraq assignments might even be made mandatory if not enough volunteers stepped forward. "It is my fervent hope that we will continue to see sufficient numbers of Foreign Service and Civil Service employees volunteering for Iraq service, but we must be prepared to meet our requirements in any eventuality."[42]

"Baghdad dwarfs everything else. It is becoming a monster that has to be fed every year with a new crop of volunteers," one diplomat was quoted saying.[43] A former Foreign Service officer said the Baghdad Embassy "will be a symbol of the U.S. occupation and the near-total separation of U.S. embassy staff members from the society with which they are supposed to interact. Indeed, the planned embassy reminds me of the huge, cavernous buildings that housed Soviet missions in eastern Europe during the cold war. They were hated by the local population for all they stood for: secrecy, arrogance and domination."[44]

A former colleague, who had been US consul general in Halifax and in 2007 represented an association of Foreign Service employees, said it more politely: "Diplomats, in order to carry out their mission, need to be able to get out regularly and move about freely to cultivate professional relationships with a broad cross-section of contacts in local government and society. If security conditions prevent them from doing so, it raises questions about the usefulness of a heavily staffed embassy."[45]

This detachment from life at street level compounded a problem the invaders and occupiers of Iraq had faced since the start of their effort in 2003. As one of my senior colleagues who had extensive Mideast experience put it, "the mindset, priorities and cultural norms of the locals are often vastly different than what we would automatically assume from our own background. That's one of the main problems we have faced in Iraq. The Administration made a major mistake when it systematically excluded experienced State Department officials from planning and involvement in the post-war reconstruction of Iraq. Many current problems were predicted four years ago and could have been avoided or at least mitigated if these experts had been heeded."[46] This problem of contrasting mindsets was hardly peculiar to Iraq. It is at the heart of much diplomacy. Overcoming it is precisely what you need diplomats for. But the whole situation that had been created in Iraq and the structure that had been built up there made such outreach and engagement all but impossible.

An obviously related problem for State Department employees in Iraq was poor relations with their Department of Defense counterparts (the atmosphere was described by one source as marked by "venom and hostility"). The two departments had fundamental differences on how to revive the Iraq economy. Presumably the Defense crowd were inclined to assume they had the White House behind them; I am sure the State crowd made no such assumption. As I would have sought an economic "reconstruction" role had I gone there, this was another strong reason not to want an Iraq assignment.[47]

WESTERN ALLIES' DIVERGENCES OVER IRAQ

As the scale of the Bush administration's errors in the Iraq conflict became clearer, and as Americans themselves recognized this, it became much more justifiable (and easier) for Canadians to dissociate themselves morally first from the war and then from the whole US response to the Sep-

tember 2001 attacks. In the process, sympathy with the United States in
the later aftermath of 9/11 began to disappear.

Costs of the war would include much more than the immense bud-
getary outlays (estimated in 2006 at US$750 billion to $1,184 billion).
They would also include economic costs of lost lives, injuries, changes in
earnings, and higher oil prices worldwide. Taking an even wider view,
Financial Times economic columnist Martin Wolf also considered

> costs consequent upon creating a link between Iraq and the jihadi
> movement that did not, on the evidence, previously exist; costs of
> increasing the income of some of the world's least desirable regimes,
> above all, Iran's; costs of throwing away the option to fight ground
> wars elsewhere or to fight in Iraq later on, under better conditions,
> better information and a better state of preparedness; costs of enrag-
> ing many Muslims; costs to the effectiveness of the U.S. military; costs
> of fragmenting the western alliance; the loss of Iraqi lives; the cost to
> U.S. credibility of going to war on a false premise; and the cost to the
> U.S. reputation of the torture scandals.
>
> It is possible to argue that the benefits for Iraq, the Middle East and
> the world will outweigh all these costs. But that depends on the emer-
> gence, in Iraq, of a stable and peaceful democratic order. That has not
> yet been achieved.[48]

A colleague of Wolf's at the *Financial Times*, Gideon Rachman, saw
another major cost: the ending of the neo-conservative political movement
in the United States. That movement, he said, had had a liberal, democratic element that had done much good:

> The central plank of the neo-conservative world view has been splin-
> tered by Iraq. Who now believes that U.S.-led military intervention is
> an appropriate way of spreading democracy around the world? As that
> idea dies a grisly death in Iraq, the struggle is on in Washington to
> define a new basis for U.S. foreign policy.
>
> Looking back on the Iraq misadventure it seems the neo-cons were
> not as free of liberal wishful thinking as they fondly imagined. Their
> big mistake was grossly to overestimate how easy it would be ... Offi-
> cially, the Bush administration is undaunted. Unofficially, it is shelving
> the "freedom agenda" ...
>
> [Henry] Kissinger himself – while scrupulously polite about the
> freedom agenda in public – has been heard to "joke" privately that: "I

supported the invasion of Iraq for geostrategic reasons, but it never occurred to me that they would be stupid enough to try to turn the country into a democracy." The realism espoused by Mr. Kissinger is coming back into fashion in Washington ...

While some correction of the excesses of neo-conservatism is inevitable after Iraq, it is important not to over-correct. The neo-cons were reacting against what they regarded as the amorality of a Kissinger and the weakness of a Carter or a Clinton. They were right to point out that détente was too ready to write off the liberation movements of eastern Europe ... the market in ideas – like the market in shares – has a tendency to over-shoot ... the world may end up regretting the demise of neo-conservatism.[49]

Rachman's warning certainly looks prescient a decade later.

THE WAGES OF ANTI-DIPLOMACY

By the fifth anniversary of the September 2001 terrorist attacks, the war in Iraq had become a worldwide disaster for the United States in diplomatic terms if nothing else. In many European and Arab eyes, no connection was seen between Saddam Hussein's regime and the 2001 attacks, yet the president persisted in trying to uphold the myth that they were somehow connected. Around the world and even in the United States, the Bush administration and the national-security establishment were seen as having exploited the September 2001 events to advance a unilateral agenda. Bush's leadership had lost credibility, and many felt it had made the world less safe. At best, greater security for Americans at home was seen as being purchased at the cost of more danger for Arabs and Muslims almost everywhere.[50]

Late in 2004 the *Ottawa Citizen* had asked selected Canadian protest groups (who were planning to demonstrate against President Bush's visit to Ottawa) to list the specific US policies to which they objected. Among the better-articulated answers were those from an umbrella group of Quebec civil-society organizations called Collectif Échec à la Guerre (Stop the War Collective): "An approach to world affairs that is unilateralist and militaristic, including: failure to uphold the rule of international law (waging illegal war); failure to honour international commitments (NPT [Non-Proliferation Treaty] Article VI obligation to scrap nuclear weapons); refusal to sign international agreements (Kyoto, International Criminal Court, Comprehensive Test Ban Treaty); planning to weaponize outer space; post 9/11 erosion of civil liberties (Patriot Act, homeland security measures)."[51] Such views were not limited to fringe groups. At the start of 2005 American writer Michael Lind, again writing in the *Financial Times*, commented on the effect that the Bush team's anti-diplomacy was having on the international system:

> A new world order is indeed emerging – but its architecture is being drafted in Asia and Europe, at meetings to which Americans have not been invited ... Today the evidence of foreign cooperation to reduce American primacy is everywhere – from the increasing importance of regional trade blocs that exclude the U.S. to international space projects and military exercises in which the US is conspicuous by its absence ... The other great powers, with the exception of the UK, are content to let the U.S. waste blood and treasure on its doomed attempt at hegemony in the Middle East.
>
> That the rest of the world is building institutions and alliances that shut out the U.S. should come as no surprise [and] ... has probably been accelerated by the truculent unilateralism of the Bush administration ... Ironically, the U.S., having won the cold war, is adopting the strategy that led the Soviet Union to lose it: hoping that raw military power will be sufficient to intimidate the other great powers.[52]

In late September 2006 a US National Intelligence Estimate was widely reported to have found that the war in Iraq had made terrorism worse and that the status of the Global War on Terror was very different from its portrayal in the president's speeches. The State Department's media response summary read

> International media don't consider it a revelation that a National Intelligence Estimate reportedly finds that the war in Iraq has made terrorism worse. A Saudi editorial comments: "Any layman in any country could have told the world that the war in Iraq has definitely increased the threat of terrorism." [Broadcast news network] *Al-Jazeera* interviewed a U.S.-based "terrorism expert" who believes [September 2001 attack mastermind Osama] Bin Laden "is very happy" that Bush undertook the war in Iraq because it is exactly what Bin Laden wanted. [Pan-Arab newspaper] *Al-Hayat* claims that the report "contradicts" statements made by President Bush. Headlines in Europe and East Asia highlight that the "Iraq War Has Created a New Generation of Islamic Radicals." A UK daily quotes an official who says the report is "stating the obvious." Newscasts in Europe lead with the story; French TV comments that the war "has in fact created a new generation of terrorists who have nothing to do with Bin Laden."[53]

To those in diplomatic service, and many others, the administration's disdain for diplomacy and its preference for using armed force had borne predictable fruit over the five years since the 2001 attacks, and US diplomats could have been forgiven if they felt vindicated that the administration and the war were failing.

THE NOVEMBER 2006 SHIFT

The US mid-term elections in November 2006 shifted congressional power toward the Democratic Party, leading to the resignation of Defense Secretary Donald Rumsfeld. But, while Iraq may have been the main issue that drove that shift, it remained a war that Democrats had very little ability to affect. Not only were the president and the administration still in charge of the US prosecution of the war, but by 2006 the US military engagement in Iraq had become unpredictable and seemingly uncontrollable.

Congress had commissioned a bipartisan Iraq Study Group in March 2006 to assess the war and make policy recommendations. The ISG reported on 6 December, a month after the elections, and the media characterized its recommendations as calling for a major shift in Iraq policy. The State Department worldwide media summary noted: "Several analysts express resentment that the U.S. seems to be walking away from the chaos that it created by invading Iraq. *Al-Jazeera* focuses on the impression that the report holds Iraqis responsible for worsening security. It shows Iraq's National Security Advisor complaining that the U.S. seems to 'think that four years is enough to build capable institutions.'"[54]

Following the Republicans' electoral losses in 2006, Rumsfeld's resignation from the post of secretary of defense, and the release of the ISG (or "Baker-Hamilton") report, Americans engaged in a national debate about withdrawing troops from Iraq. In late March 2007 the House of Representatives voted to set an August 2008 (seventeen-month) deadline for the withdrawal. This confirmed the power shift in Washington and Bush's loss of the confidence of at least a narrow majority in Congress.

In January 2007, Edward Luttwak of the Center for Strategic and International Studies offered the Senate some historical perspective:

During and after the Second World War, after very detailed preparations, the U.S. Army and Navy governed the American zone of Germany, all of Japan and parts of Italy. Initially U.S. officers were themselves the administrators, with such assistance from local officials as they chose to re-employ. Since then, however, the United States has eschewed the role of the Occupier, preferring in both Vietnam long ago and now in Iraq to leave government to the locals, while assuming the rather awkward role of a disproportionately powerful ally with combat forces in place and provider of military assistance, but not of everyday civil administration.

That reflects another kind of politics, manifest in the ambivalence of a United States government that is willing to fight wars, that is willing to start wars because of future projected threats, that is willing to conquer territory or even entire countries, and yet is unwilling to govern what it conquers, even for a few years.[55]

Nine days later before the same committee, former national security adviser Zbigniew Brzezinski appealed to Congress to assert itself and force a change in direction in Iraq:

The war in Iraq is a historic, strategic, and moral calamity. Undertaken under false assumptions, it is undermining America's global legitimacy ... the final destination on this downhill track is likely to be a head-on conflict with Iran and with much of the world of Islam at large ... Initially justified by false claims about weapons of mass destruction in Iraq, the war is now being redefined as the "decisive ideological struggle" of our time, reminiscent of the earlier collisions with Nazism and Stalinism. In that context, Islamic extremism and al Qaeda are presented as the equivalents of the threat posed by Nazi Germany and then Soviet Russia, and 9/11 as the equivalent of the Pearl Harbor attack ... [a] simplistic and dangerous narrative ...

Vague and inflammatory talk about a "new strategic context" which is based on "clarity" and which prompts "the birth pangs of a new Middle East" is breeding intensifying anti-Americanism and is increasing the danger of a long-term collision between the United States and the Islamic world ... practically no country shares the Manichean delusions that the Administration so passionately articulates. The result is a growing political isolation of, and pervasive popular antagonism toward, the U.S. global posture.[56]

In the same vein, West Point military academy professor and retired General Barry McCaffrey darkened his own previous views of the situation in Iraq. He wrote in March 2007 that the US-backed Iraqi government had little credibility, and as a result the US military was in "strategic peril" in Iraq.[57]

President Bush's response, announced in January 2007, was not a step back but rather a step forward known as the "surge": sending five additional combat brigades and other units to Iraq for a year. This meant about 20,000 more soldiers augmenting 132,000 already deployed. As part of trying to get the "surge" accepted politically, the Bush administration was trying to sound less dismissive of the ISG report and more willing to accept its recommendation to intensify diplomatic efforts.[58] Bush designated the State Department as a national-security agency alongside Defense and Homeland Security.

It was a continuing challenge that a wide range of civilian functions were needed to help rebuild and run Iraq's essential systems (like roads, electric power, agriculture, financial oversight, police, and the judiciary) and people were needed to perform these functions. Yet even local Iraqis, for whom the US Embassy pay must have been very attractive, continued not to want to work there because it was too dangerous. The State Department could not get Americans (particularly experienced diplomats), or third-country nationals like myself, to go there either – much less to the Provincial Reconstruction Teams in more remote and less secure places.

So Secretary of State Condoleezza Rice told Defense Secretary Robert Gates that her department needed six months to staff positions in Iraq, and State asked the US military to fill about 40 per cent of more than 300 recently created State jobs there. The military, already stretched, didn't like this request, feeling that civilian agencies like State weren't stepping up to their share of the job.[59] On the other side, senior State people were still bitter at having been cut out of the planning earlier on by a Pentagon that thought it could do everything itself. "There's some outrage that the collective capacity of American reconstruction capability was ignored prior to the war. And now we are expected to clean up the mess."[60]

TRANSITIONAL COUNTRY

US Embassy Ottawa's strategic plan in the spring of 2007 set as its top priority "to further our common-cause partnership with Canada in transformational defense and security diplomacy worldwide."

> In doing so we will better prevent attacks against North America and our allies and partners around the world. We will work with Canada to stem the collapse of fragile and failing states in order to prevent resulting anarchy and widespread human rights abuses. We will expand our bi-national, bilateral and multilateral defense, security, and diplomatic part-

nerships with Canada. We will increase cooperation to combat terrorist groups and the proliferation of weapons of mass destruction. We will encourage Canada to invest more in its defense, and to deepen collaboration among Canada Command and U.S. NORTHCOM, NORAD and other elements of our armed forces and diplomatic and security services.

The Embassy's senior political officer noted that obviously the defence and security partnership was our top priority on global grounds, and not because there was a problem of any kind in Canada; on the contrary, he opined that the United States had "a great ally in the Harper government." The next highest Mission goals were creating a modern, efficient, and secure border, and closing the perceived US-Canada gap in law enforcement and counter-terrorism cooperation. Integrated markets and environmental protection (the latter including climate change) came fourth and fifth respectively.[61]

Canada was the seventh-largest international donor to the Iraq reconstruction effort, granting over $200 million by the end of 2007 (by which time the United States had spent some $29 billion on reconstruction alone).[62] But the government of Canada did not participate in a series of meetings called the Friends of Iraq conferences, on the grounds that it wanted to focus on its involvement in Afghanistan.

As one of its efforts to seem more accommodating after the chastisements of the 2006 election losses and the ISG report, the Bush administration announced on 14 February 2007 that it would allow about 7,000 Iraqi refugees to come to the United States in 2007, versus 202 allowed the previous year, and that it would contribute US$18 million to a worldwide resettlement and relief program. But an estimated 3.8 million Iraqis had been displaced since the start of the war, which was a direct result of US policy.[63]

In July 2007 State Department employees received yet another message from Secretary Rice urging us all to consider serving in "transitional countries." One of my officer colleagues muttered wryly that Washington, DC, real estate agents used "transitional" euphemistically to describe a rough street that was hard to get decent folks to move onto. At the time US Embassy Baghdad had upcoming vacancies for some thirty-two Foreign Service generalist officers: ten political, six economic, two political-military, four public affairs, nine management, and one consular.

Another colleague wrote:

As most of you know, this is just the latest in a series of similar messages from the Secretary. Repetition doesn't make her plea any more compelling ... While I won't speak for others, I've become skeptical about what we can still achieve in Iraq, whose government remains dysfunctional, whose security forces, even after years of training, are ineffective and unreliable, and whose people largely want us out of there. Ambassador Crocker's cables also illustrate the Baghdad government's continued inability to get its act together, and it appears unlikely that this sorry state of affairs will change soon. Afghanistan service would be a better bet for Foreign Service Officers who want to have "the greatest immediate impact."

It's unfortunate the Secretary is laying down a "guilt trip." In doing so, she's denigrating the hard work of those of us who serve in "non-transitional" countries (which is most of the world).[64]

In a separate note two weeks later, the same colleague, who had experience both in the military and in Arab countries, wrote: "I laughed when I read that we now have 'unique opportunities' to study Arabic. This should have been done many years ago ... 'hard-to-fill' assignments used to be filled last and so turning the process on its head might have salutary effects ... [and] the Department does not have enough resources ... but I see few signs that Condi [Rice] and [John] Negroponte are trooping up to the Hill trying to pry more money out of Congress to hire more staff and repair rundown Embassies. [Secretary of State Colin] Powell and [Deputy Secretary of State Richard] Armitage did make that effort, but to little effect."[65]

TOWARD WITHDRAWAL

With less than two years to run in the Bush presidency, Democrats were looking ahead to problems a Democratic president might inherit in 2009, assuming their candidate won the White House; then they would have to take ownership of the Iraq mess. All sides had an interest in thinking responsibly about exit strategies.

A report in July 2007 noted that the US command in Baghdad had prepared a Joint Campaign Plan that anticipated a decline in American forces in late 2007 or 2008 (the end of the surge), but the plan also assumed continued American military involvement through at least 2009. A senior Embassy colleague grumbled, "If we had unlimited time, this plan might work. For better or worse, however, I am afraid that this is completely unrealistic given the mood of Congress and the American people."[66]

Keith Mines, a Foreign Service officer who had held the post of "Coalition Provisional Authority Governance Coordinator" for Al Anbar province of Iraq in 2003–04, was working in our Political Section during this period. In December 2007 Keith published an opinion item on the website of the Foreign Policy Research Institute called "After the Surge: The Only Iraq Worth Fighting For." He wrote:

> The best way for a big power to fight an insurgency is to avoid fighting it in the first instance ... The second best way is to engage proxies who know the terrain, the culture, and the internal politics driving the insurgents, and who will not feed the nationalistic narrative that fuels insurgencies. The worst way is to fight an insurgency directly ... The U.S. military is still the biggest faction on the block and wields the greatest influence locally and nationally. The U.S. military is also both cause and effect in the insurgency: its very presence is what is causing the majority of attacks and generating recruits for the insurgents ... the U.S. military must begin to remove itself from the mix.[67]

REGRET ON ALL SIDES

Anticipating "directed" (mandatory) State Department assignments to Iraq, American Foreign Service Association President John Naland wrote to his membership on 30 October 2007:

> the well has finally run dry of State Department Foreign Service volunteers to serve in the war zone in Iraq ... if volunteers could not be found for 48 remaining positions by November 12, then directed assignments would begin.
>
> While there are many Foreign Service members who have not (yet) served in Iraq, only a small fraction possesses the regional, language, or other expertise that Ambassador Ryan Crocker says that he needs ...
>
> During the Vietnam War ... Saigon (except during the 1968 Tet offensive) was rarely as dangerous as Baghdad has been ... [yet] the State Department today gives Iraq-bound Foreign Service members only around two weeks of pre-deployment training compared to the four to six month comprehensive training regimen provided to Vietnam-bound diplomats ...
>
> Only 20 percent [of American diplomats surveyed] believe that the Administration is doing a good job of defending the Foreign Service. This lack of support arguably weakens the State Department's moral authority to order unarmed diplomats to serve in the war zone in Iraq.[68]

In the end, Secretary of State Condoleezza Rice called off the need for "directed assignments," ostensibly because "a large additional number of Foreign Service employees have volunteered to serve."[69] In December it was announced that diplomatic posts at the department and at embassies worldwide would be cut by 10 per cent in 2008 to accommodate heavy staffing demands in Iraq and Afghanistan.[70]

An article by writer/journalist William Langewiesche put the Baghdad Green Zone in the historical context of the development – and failures – of US foreign policy, globally and in Iraq, and particularly the Bush administration's insistence on seeing a "new Iraq" rising from the mess in Baghdad:

[In 2004–05 Baghdad] industry had stalled, electricity and water were failing, sewage was flooding the streets, the universities were shuttered, the insurgency was expanding, sectarianism was on the rise, and gunfire and explosions now marked the days as well as the nights. Month by month, Baghdad was crumbling back into the earth ... Inside the Green Zone the talk of progress slowed and then died. The first of the nominal Iraqi governments arrived and joined the Americans in their oasis ... the Green Zone defenses kept growing, surrounding the residents with ever more layers of checkpoints and blast walls ... containing 21 reinforced buildings on a 104-acre site [that will] cost $600 million to build, and is expected to cost another $1.2 billion a year to run – a high price even by the profligate standards of the war in Iraq.

Langeweische generalized his observations to the whole class of US New Embassy Compound (NEC) designs:

These embassies are the artifacts of fear. They are located away from city centers, wrapped in perimeter walls, set back from the streets ... They are politely landscaped, minimally intrusive bunkers, placed as far from view as is practical, and dependent as much on discreet technology as on sheer mass – but they are bunkers nonetheless ... the static diplomatic embassy, a product of the distant past, is no longer of much use. To the government this does not seem to matter ... Faced with the failure of an obsolete idea – the necessity of traditional embassies and all the elaboration they entail – we have not stood back to remember their purpose, but have plunged ahead with closely focused concentration to build them bigger and stronger.[71]

In late March 2008, on at least three occasions, rockets were fired into the Green Zone in Baghdad, and five US government employees were seriously injured, at least one dying of his injuries.[72]

STILL ALLIES

The war in Iraq, much like the war in Vietnam, was a major conflict prosecuted by the United States in which Canada took minimal part and in which the US cause ultimately failed. More so than in Vietnam, the war in Iraq was initiated by the United States and the Bush administration bore responsibility for it. Also, Arabs and Muslims in many countries view Iraq as an ancient heartland of civilization, so their anger at its ravaging has deep historical context and meaning. For these reasons, it seems that the Iraq War did greater damage to US diplomacy and the credibility and capacity of US global leadership than Vietnam did. The Iraq experience did even more to drive the United States and Canada apart. It not only further reinforced anti-Americanism in Canada; with the help of poor management and conduct on the Canadian side, it also greatly strengthened previously negligible anti-Canadianism in the United States.

During his years in Ottawa (2004–08), Ambassador David Wilkins did not appear to focus as much as his predecessors on asking Canadians to devote more resources to the military – perhaps because this had been a major theme of Ambassador Cellucci and plans for increased defence spending had been announced in 2004. Our Embassy's 2005/2006 report on allied contributions to common defence had almost nothing critical to say: "While the [Canadian] government does not participate in stability operations in Iraq, it is a leading contributor to both Operation Enduring Freedom and the NATO-led International Security Assistance Force [ISAF] in Afghanistan." Canada's ISAF contribution at the time included an infantry company, an engineer squadron, a combat support company, and a health- and medical-support unit.

But our report noted that Canada's defence spending as a proportion of GDP remained among the lowest in NATO (at 1.1 per cent) and that "most defense insiders believe Canada will need a defense budget of over US$20 billion by FY2012 to implement [its own February 2005] Defence Policy Statement." It also remarked that "the Canadian Forces has a limited ability to recruit and train new forces. The accession and training of the 5,000 new regular forces will only just fully man existing units and will take five years to fully implement."[73]

While Canadians should associate strengthening their defence capabilities with reinforcing their own independence – rather than with showing support for allies – they tend not to do so. The deep mess in Iraq, the fading of Canadian support for the Global War on Terror, and political disaffection with US leadership generally were more likely to restrain than encourage Canadian public backing of increased defence spending.

For Canada's forces, the promise of the Stephen Harper government that took power after the federal election of 2006 involved as much a change of culture as enhanced resources. As one columnist put it,

[Harper] seeks to promote the role of the federal government within its own areas of exclusive jurisdiction, the three most important areas of which are justice, defence and foreign affairs ... For half a century now, Canadians have seen themselves as a nation of peacekeepers. But the age of peacekeeping is past. Today's geopolitical hot spots are found in lawless lands and dysfunctional states that breed anarchy and harbor terrorists. Canada has a role to play in these places by helping to protect civilian populations while nurturing institutions that can enforce the social contract.

This is dangerous work that can lead to guerrilla warfare with higher casualties than Canadians are used to. Nonetheless, although a Liberal government authorized the Kandahar deployment, Mr. Harper has embraced it. He wants Canadians to be proud of what their troops are doing in Afghanistan, and willing to accept these necessary sacrifices as part of Canada's new and more aggressive role in the war on terror. And he despises critics who say this is not Canada's fight, that we should quit the place.[74]

Certainly, the prevailing US government view at the time was that the Harper government was delivering the kind of things that the relationship needed, if not perhaps on hard-to-fix files like softwood or intellectual property, then at least in defence and security. The mandate of NORAD had been renewed indefinitely and expanded to include maritime security. After Canada's 2008–09 budget was tabled in Parliament in February 2008, a colleague put together a list of measures in it that were considered helpful or at least of interest to the US Embassy. The list included:

C$75 million over two years to help the Canadian Border Services Agency better manage the border
Introducing a high-security 10 year electronic Canadian passport by 2011
C$14 million over two years to expand NEXUS (a border-crossing "fast lane" service)

c\$6 million over two years to support provinces introducing electronic drivers' licenses

c\$26 million over two years to incorporate biometric data in Canadian visas

c\$15 million over two years to establish a permanent facility to enhance security of the Great Lakes/St Lawrence Seaway

c\$29 million over two years to meet SPP priorities

Sufficient funds to deliver on pledge to double Canadian assistance to Africa in fulfillment of a G-8 pledge

c\$450 million to the Global Fund to Fight AIDS, Turberculosis, and Malaria

c\$100 million in additional assistance to Afghanistan

c\$720 million for a new Polar-class icebreaker

c\$20 million over two years to collect data and legal work to support Canada's submission to the UN Commission on Limits of the Continental Shelf.[75]

The following month, in March 2008, the House of Commons passed a bipartisan motion extending the Canadian Forces' mandate in Afghanistan's Kandahar province until the end of 2011. Under the Harper government there was thus the beginning of a greatly needed return to the perception on the US side that, while Canada might not always share US views on foreign policy, it could be counted on as an ally.

DETAINEES AND CITIZENS

The cases of two Canadians who were detained by US authorities during this period, Maher Arar and Omar Khadr, would receive intense media focus and become long-standing bilateral irritants.

Omar Khadr was born in September 1986. He and his family were all Canadian citizens, but they spent considerable time in Afghanistan and Pakistan and lived with Osama bin Laden and his family at times between 1996 and 2000. Around May 2002, when Khadr was fifteen years old, his father arranged for him to receive basic insurgency training, including on how to construct improvised explosive devices. He then operated with an al-Qaeda cell, constructing improvised explosive devices targeting US forces in the area of Khowst, Afghanistan, until he was captured in July 2002 (still aged fifteen) after an engagement with US forces in which Khadr allegedly threw a grenade that killed a US sergeant, Christopher Speer.

Khadr was the only Canadian citizen known to be held at the US prison at Guantánamo Bay, Cuba, where he stayed for several years. Canadian Forces' transfer of detainees (or complicity in transferring them) in Afghanistan between national authorities, and how those detainees might subsequently be treated, became a prominent issue in Canadian media in the spring of 2007, and this led to a focus on Khadr, particularly because he had been a minor when detained. Reports in the major newspapers said that the Department of Foreign Affairs had had no "significant" involvement in the arrangement for the transfer of detainees, that is, that Foreign Affairs was "not consulted" or was "shunted aside" –thus encouraging the impression that US authorities were exclusively responsible. Defence Minister Gordon O'Connor responded with an assortment of comments that did not do much to clarify the issue.

Notes from one of our staff meetings read, "Issue dominates Parliament this week. It is difficult to understand Defence Minister's remarks. Surely U.S. and other NATO countries turn over their detainees to Afghanistan authorities. And if evidence of abuse is detected, it must be reported to Afghan authorities. No other option if Afghanistan is truly on a track to self-governance."[76] And from the meeting a week later: "[Canada's] Chief of Defence Staff, Gen Hillier, is in Afghanistan and has launched a PR counterattack which brings the troops into the issue, and tries to highlight the positive work being done in that country. Evidently the gov't plans to ride out this issue and are trying to link problems in the management of detainees to the previous (Martin) government ... We need to remain out of all this."[77]

Apparently not satisfied with the Canadian government's handling of the issue, the Conference of Defence Associations sent an e-mail on 2 May to key political leaders clarifying some facts. "The negotiation of the agreement on the transfer of detainees was the subject of intensive collaboration between DFAIT and DND [Department of National Defence] over many months, with all the expected responsibility centres in both departments involved. These included at DFAIT the International Security Bureau, the Asia Bureau and the Legal Bureau; and at DND, Director-General International Security Policy and the Judge Advocate General ... it is tragic that the mission in Afghanistan is being obfuscated by false debate."[78]

In mid-2007 many offices in the State Department were asked to search their files for documents relevant to the Khadr case. Much as with Freedom of Information Act (FOIA) requests, the search was thorough and required a response from all offices that were approached, but, of course, while the request came to us we had nothing relevant in the Economic Section.

TORTURE

Much worse even than the effects of the failing campaign in Iraq for Canadian and international attitudes to the United States were allegations,
later found to be true, that the Global War on Terror had caused people
to be abducted from various locations around the world and transferred
to countries where they were held indefinitely and secretly, and mistreat-
ed in various ways, including being tortured. As noted earlier, the practice
became known as "rendition."

Canadian attention to this issue focused disproportionately on the case
of Maher Arar, an innocent Canadian of Syrian birth who was detained
during a stop at a US airport, kept in solitary confinement, sent to Syria
rather than his home country of Canada, and imprisoned and tortured.
The human-rights issues at stake, and the consequences for US influence
and credibility internationally, were enormous. As one US columnist put
it, referring to allegations about torture and secret CIA prisons: "We will
remember this whole misguided administration for deciding to wage the
fight against terrorism in a manner that not only mocks our nation's
values but also draws new recruits to the anti-American cause. We will
remember this White House for unwittingly helping the terrorist cause
perpetuate itself."[79] In effect, in the name of counter-terrorism the United
States had shifted from being a proponent of the international rule of law
to a proponent of American exceptionalism and unilateralism, undermining its alliances and its political support almost everywhere.[80]

Canada's security policies and practices at the time might have been
better than those of the United States but they still had their share of
blemishes from a human-rights perspective. On 23 February 2007 the
Supreme Court struck down provisions relating to secret evidence in the
use of "security certificates" to detain foreign nationals in Canada. While
the Court ruled that the detention of foreign nationals without warrant
did not infringe the Charter of Rights and Freedoms, it found that deny-
ing suspects the right to refute secret evidence against them violated the
right to a fair trial, as well as guarantees of life, liberty, and security of the
person. It suggested less intrusive alternatives, such as the use of special
advocates who could hear the secret evidence on behalf of the accused. To
the government and to law-and-order voters, the court ruling reinforced
the Harper team's narrative that the Canadian judiciary was too easy on
crime and terrorists.

Canada negotiated a so-called Safe Third Country Agreement on
refugees with the United States that was scheduled to take effect during

2008. The agreement's purpose was to reduce both countries' refugee-processing burden by requiring refugee claimants to request refugee protection in the first safe country they arrived in. A Canadian Federal Court judge struck down the agreement in mid-January 2008, two weeks before it was to take effect, saying that Canada had not ensured that the United States respected international rules governing torture and refugee rights. The Canadian government appealed this ruling, and eventually prevailed.

In early 2008 the media obtained a copy of a Canadian government training presentation for diplomats on how to recognize torture cases abroad (this was an apparent failing of Canada's in the 2002–03 Maher Arar case). The presentation listed Guantánamo Bay (along with Afghanistan, China, Egypt, Mexico, Saudi Arabia, and Syria) as a place where torture was likely practised, during a period when a Canadian citizen, Omar Khadr, was known to be imprisoned there.

Through 2006 I was exchanging occasional e-mails with my old mentor David Beatty, who by then had retired from Mount Allison University but was still writing and publishing. David had exhaustively studied the development of Canadian-American defence expectations and obligations in the 1938–1940 period.[81] On the defence situation and our relations with the United States in 2006, David wrote, "I do not think that the Canadian situation today is terribly different than it was in 1940. We are getting drawn into an awful black hole." I replied that, in a way, 2006 looked worse:

> I wonder every day whether the parallels with the Second World War are being taken too far by some writers. If one needs something big with which to compare the current world situation, WW2 is certainly the biggest thing handy. But I can't help feeling that this is too easy – by relying on the analogy, we relieve ourselves of seeing all the things that are different now. German conduct in 1939–45 broke many of the rules that Chamberlain et al. thought they could count on among European gentlemen. But even so, as Churchill points out, many German officers were horrified, and tried to observe civilized conventions. They were still Europeans. Even in the Pacific, the Japanese had a code of honour that eventually became intelligible to Americans and for which MacArthur developed some respect. Postwar reconstruction at both ends of the world built on these social structures and was amazingly successful. What kind of postwar reconstruction will ever be possible this time round?[82]

A decade later these doubts seem to have been borne out. I see no way the United States can recover in less than a generation or two from the reputational damage caused by the Bush administration, at least not in the Muslim world, and probably not elsewhere either.

CANADIAN MUSLIMS

A report on Canada's big-city Muslim populations was produced in the fall of 2004 by our Embassy, with help from three of our consulates:

> The possibility of international terrorist networks using Canada as a staging ground for attacks on the U.S. is very real and has led to an extraordinary level of law enforcement and intelligence cooperation between our two governments. Real and potential terrorist networks notwithstanding, our operating assumptions are that the vast majority of Canada's Muslims are peaceful, law abiding citizens who are shocked and revolted by terrorist acts carried out in the name of their religion. That does not mean that Canada's Muslim communities support U.S. policy in Iraq [or] the war on terror ... the experiences and reactions of Canada's Muslims to U.S. policies and American society exert a strong influence on broader Canadian public opinion ... In absolute numbers, Canada's Muslim communities are not huge. But the "mosaic" of ethnic communities looms large in contemporary Canadian society, magnifying the importance of ethnic communities beyond their absolute size ... this argues powerfully for a more systematic public outreach effort.[83]

On 2 June 2006 a wave of counter-terrorism raids in Ontario, which resulted in the arrest of the so-called "Toronto 18" suspects, briefly brought international-security issues closer to home for Canadians. But, as with so many North America-grown "terrorists," a calm look at the details could make the threat far less frightening – if one had the patience to wade through media exaggeration in both directions (the Canadian media played its usual game of initially distorting the story one way and then creating the opportunity to debunk this with an opposing distortion in the next news cycle). As one of my Political Section colleagues commented a few days later: "In the course of a week these 'terrorists' have gone from being junior Zarqawis [Abu Musab al-Zarqawi, an alleged founder of the Islamic State of Iraq and Syria] to the Keystone Cops. It now appears that everything they did, from paintballing, to buying fertilizer, to smuggling weapons, was tracked. From being a material threat on Monday, on Friday they are seen as just knuckleheaded kids with a juvenile grudge." My colleague noted the different conditions between Canada and Europe, or even the United States, for fostering home-grown terrorism. "I know Paris, and there are large sections of it that are more Algerian than French. I don't see that here. It seems the low income housing policy (every neighborhood must have a share of low income housing so it isn't all in one place ...), immigrant integration policy, good economy, welcoming attitude to newcomers (no MP could ever win office with a nativist policy here as in London and Paris, to the contrary they would win office by playing to immigrant concerns), etc. really has produced a nation without the seething ethnic communities of Europe or the invisible ethnic communities of the U.S."[84]

As an economist, I had long readily seen the case for immigration to low-birth-rate Canada and especially for the productive integration of immigrants into Canada's society and labour market. Generally, societies that can and do attract immigrants, and give them room to live productive lives, benefit from it through innovation, creativity, entrepreneurship, and international linkages. I had done community work among immigrants since around 2001. I felt a deep personal stake in Canada's modest progress in this area – and correspondingly deep dismay that it was not paralleled in other places, nor its benefits so well understood.

ESTRANGEMENT AND ISOLATIONISM

US Defense Secretary Robert Gates was quoted in January 2008 saying that some or most of the NATO members' forces in Afghanistan were "not properly trained" in counter-insurgency. It was not clear at first whether this remark included US forces or was aimed only at other NATO members. Gates later the same week called the defence minister of the Netherlands, which had sixteen hundred troops in Afghanistan at the time, to express regret for any consternation his remarks had caused. A Dutch security commentator wondered, "Why did he not criticize those NATO members which stay well away from the fighting?"[85]

Analyzing a poll that indicated very low levels of popular support among Canadians for sending troops to Afghanistan, military historian J.L. Granatstein echoed this view:

> 2300 of our soldiers will almost certainly face roadside bombs, rocket and grenade attacks, and suicide bombers ... Peacekeeping has largely

disappeared, replaced in the new world disorder by much more robust operations run by the UN or other organizations ... Afghanistan is not the first such operation nor will it be the last ... The war on terror is a reality and Canadians are targets, no matter how we try to convince ourselves that the world loves us. It doesn't. Our superpower neighbor, the nation to which 87 percent of our exports go and on which our security depends, has been attacked and is still under threat, but somehow Canadians have not grasped that they are involved. We are.

Canadians see Afghanistan as an American war, a direct response to the al-Qaeda terror attacks of 9/11. That may have been correct in 2002, when the aim was to drive the Taliban government that sheltered al-Qaeda from power. Today, the goal is to assist an elected government in establishing itself in the face of attacks from Taliban remnants. Unfortunately, that difference doesn't appear to matter to Canadians. Afghanistan is still the Americans' war, George W. Bush's war, and automatically, large majorities of Canadians still believe it must be wrong. Canadian anti-Americanism is at a record peak in 2006, and this strong feeling colours every question.[86]

Blaming America for the world's troubles is Canada's brand of isolationism. It is an easy, simplistic way for Canadians to explain why the world is such a difficult place, and from there it is a short step to absolving ourselves of our own responsibility to deal with the world. We may still feel obliged to go out and do nice things for other countries (like "peacekeeping"), but while we do them we can feel even more superior – because we can believe not just that we are wise and good toward the less fortunate, but also that we are wiser and better than others who create all these problems.

Blaming America is so appealing because it seems to make dealing with the world much easier, and doing it at all optional, since one can always put the problems at America's doorstep.[87] Unfortunately, a deepened comfort with blaming America has been one of the lasting costs of the US reaction to the 2001 attacks.

5

Non-Americanism:
Be Careful What You Wish For

I had conversations with family, friends, and acquaintances during 1990 and 1991 about my unusual new job at the US Embassy in Ottawa. These conversations prompted some thinking on my part about citizenship and national identity.

Many people are surprised to learn that embassies employ staff who are not citizens of their home countries. But many non-diplomatic roles – accountants, clerical and maintenance workers, drivers, gardeners, and cooks – are usually needed to support an ambassador and even just a handful of Foreign Service personnel. And there are many non-salary costs (such as long-distance travel, housing allowances, home leave, and private schooling) that add to the burden of employing official, accredited Foreign Service staff. There are consequently great savings available from using local employees wherever possible, even in a high-wage country like Canada.[1]

Businesses often hire foreign-country sales representatives or consultants who understand the local market better than an employee from head office ever could. For governments, similarly, international legal or commercial problems may be best untangled by a lawyer or former official who is resident in another country. In my case, prior knowledge of the Canadian parliamentary system and also of the organization of Canada's government, federal bureaucracy, and federal-provincial relationships were essential to our work. In analysis and advocacy, such knowledge gives one a big head start over a rotational Foreign Service officer who is only in the country for two or three years.

If a government is reluctant to employ another country's citizens, it can likely find expatriates of its own nationality living in the host city, and hire them on local terms, rather than using individuals expensively posted from the home capital. In our case, the US Mission to Canada had some staff who were locally engaged Americans who had been living in Canada before they were hired.[2] They might know little more about Canada than a new arrival would, but at least they did not have to be paid the costly allowances due Foreign Service personnel.

NATIONALITY, PRINCIPLES, AND LOYALTIES

A less frequent but still common reaction among people who learned about my job at the Embassy was surprise that the highly security-conscious US government would trust a non-US citizen to work inside Embassy walls (where there would presumably be sensitive documents and perhaps covert activities being concealed). And finally, there was surprise that a Canadian could, in good conscience, agree to work (some even said spy) for another country's government, particularly that of the United States.

I would say that, between allied countries, much of the work of an Embassy is developing and maintaining a smooth working relationship in which both countries' capitals and citizens can pursue their interests – and interests are better pursued when they are mutually informed and coordinated. Even at low points in their relationship, Canada and the United States have substantially similar values and interests, and our governments are trying to accomplish mostly similar goals. The US Embassy in Ottawa and the Canadian Embassy in Washington work to build a constructive relationship and to pursue those shared goals.

I was surprised by how novel this explanation appeared to be to some of my friends and acquaintances around 1990. They really hadn't thought of diplomacy with the United States as a friendly, mutually constructive activity. This shows how much the media focused on differences and conflicts in the relationship, and on how Canadians were culturally and educationally conditioned to view the United States with suspicion.[3]

In any event, I wondered, why should we assume that each of us will, automatically and for life, be loyal to the national interests of the country of which he/she was born a citizen? Will everyone who is born into a family of a certain religion (or political party, or sports team) adopt that loyalty for life? Why should an official limit his career in government to working for his country of birth, any more than he should only ever cheer the hockey team his grandparents supported? At least one's family presumably made a free choice sometime in the past about which hockey team to support, but they probably had no choice about what country they came from.[4]

Over the years, the same questions would return to my mind around issues of security clearance and formal authority. As a non-citizen of the United States, it was clear from the start of my employment that I would be permanently limited in my career advancement within the US government, and while this seemed logical at first, over time it led to more reflection.

I accept the reasonableness of the assumption that US citizens are more likely to be loyal to US national objectives than those who are citizens of other countries. Still, as a result of the way this assumption was applied in the security-clearance system, I could work loyally for the Embassy for decades, developing a reputation throughout the government for reliability, forming solid employer-employee trust, becoming more knowledgeable about US government policies and practices than many of my American colleagues, and yet still not be officially considered as trustworthy as a security-cleared American of whom little of this might be true. This came to seem questionable, as did the fact that, when I took a temporary assignment in Canada's public service after sixteen years at the Embassy, the Canadian government saw no problem with giving me "Secret" security clearance, even though I remained a long-term US Department of State employee during the period when I sat each day within the Canadian government.[5] On the other hand, a person who became a Canadian only in mid-life can be granted Top Secret clearance in the Canadian government while being a dual citizen of both Canada and her country of origin.

CANADIANS' GREAT, BLIND BIGOTRY

Our Embassy's Public Affairs Section had the job of monitoring, and making efforts to improve, Canadians' views of the United States and its concerns. In addition to disseminating information about the United States, writing speeches and other public materials, and maintaining relations with academics and the media, my colleagues in this office tracked polls of Canadian public opinion on matters of potential interest to the US government.

Newly arrived Public Affairs officers with little or no experience of Canadian affairs, but entering Canada typically with open minds and friendly attitudes, were usually surprised to find how prevalent, and how intense, anti-American sentiment could be among people who the official rhetoric said were their "best friends and closest allies." Having likely heard truisms about Canadians' reserve and civility, they were also surprised at how rude Canadians could be, even in normally polite situations. The rudeness was the more striking because it would appear only after my colleagues revealed their American nationality, at which point some Canadian might suddenly vent years of pent-up national hatred. Hostility breeds hostility even in the best people, and after three years or so of these experiences, some of my colleagues left Ottawa feeling much less friendly toward Canadians than when they had arrived.

As I went about my own ordinary personal life as a Canadian, I began to notice casual expressions of anti-American bigotry that I would not have thought about before I joined the Embassy. Paradoxically, these sentiments were strongest among those who considered themselves progressive and preached tolerance and diversity.[6]

One of my Public Affairs officer colleagues – a person with a reputation for sophistication and scholarship – was adventurous enough to attend the 1993 annual conference of the Canadian Association of American Studies. He later wrote:

> Within the association free, objective and articulate intellectual enquiry is having a hard time holding its own against rampant trendiness, ideological biases, vociferous political correctness and – if this conference is any indication – the most egregiously obfuscating babble of which deconstructionist cultural, social and literary criticism is capable ... Many well-intending academicians are as uneasy as we are with the domination of American studies in Canada by the radical left, but have yet to translate their concern into action. William Butler Yeats best described the situation here: "The best lack all conviction, while the worst are full of passionate intensity."
>
> We cannot escape or gloss over the fundamental fact that the United States is regularly demonized by large segments of the Canadian intelligentsia. This is most glaringly the case in the universities, where courses in American literature, history, politics and society are often controlled by radical American immigrant professors who, to paraphrase Shakespeare, would rather bury the U.S. than praise it. To make matters worse, the expatriates' unregenerate 1960s version of anti-Americanism has now found common cause with a new generation of ideological zealots and scolds.

The reference to a "new generation of zealots and scolds" was not just hyperbole. Anyone who experienced the prevalent atmosphere on North American university campuses in 1990–92 might recall the interest among campus activists of the day in dictating the parameters of acceptable behaviour to everyone they could find a way to bully. They wanted to tell the rest of us which words we could and could not use, even in private conversation. We are very fortunate that such petty tyranny did not spread much beyond the campuses, though it did seep into the media and local government. For all the intellectual left's disdain of business, an industry audience is now likely to be one of the most intellectually open and least judgmental.

My Public Affairs colleague continued: "Despite strong economic ties, a long history of political and military cooperation and close personal associations between both countries, Canadian knowledge of the United States is derived mostly from such ephemera as popular entertainment, major-league sports, cross-border shopping and winter vacations in Florida ... In the post–cold war era, bilateral relations no longer have the cement of anti-communist defense or foreign policy. We mislead ourselves to think that Canadian geographical proximity translates into understanding of American values and institutions, which ... is pathetically lacking."[7]

When people are confident that they know all they want or need to know about a subject, they sometimes cease learning, close their minds, and eventually can become quite ignorant of that topic as a consequence. This is the situation of many Canadians who feel no need to learn anything about the United States. Perhaps they have told themselves from childhood that "we know so much more about them than they know about us." Or they have decided that the United States is somehow bad and therefore not morally deserving of our attention. Either way, minds become closed.

Moreover, Canadian public-school curricula seem to avoid informing students about the United States; certainly it did when I went to school in the 1960s and 1970s. Given the United States' importance in the world and to Canada's interests, this is much harder to understand than Americans' tendency to overlook their northern neighbours.

The Embassy's Public Affairs Section tried to analyze and explain these national attitudes for Washington readers. After commissioning and sifting through a national public-opinion survey, it concluded in early 1993:

[There is] a distinctive Canadian mindset which resists conventional wisdom or easy categorization ... [and] poses a unique, often under-appreciated challenge to U.S. public diplomacy ... Canadians react on different levels to the United States in seemingly contradictory ways ... Because the U.S. is in fact a powerful economic force here, Canadians always are acutely sensitive to any perceived slight or offense. The U.S. is a convenient, plausible scapegoat.

The ambivalence also surfaces in the survey question about US ability to handle world affairs. A majority (58%) has a great deal or fair amount of confidence in the U.S. But a substantial number (39%) has little or no confidence. That minority, in our view, is a fairly high response for America's closest neighbor and longstanding ally, especially taking into account the string of foreign policy successes during the last few years. A large, often outspoken majority in Canada is viscerally suspicious of U.S. foreign policy behavior.

Canadian negativism toward the U.S. is particularly strong in judging U.S. influence on Canada and its culture. Three-fourths of all Canadians assert that the U.S. has too much influence over their country. A smaller majority (52%) believes that American culture is a threat to Canadian culture. Canada has more exposure to U.S. media and culture than does any other country in the world. Canadians are avid consumers of U.S. cultural exports, but they are equivocal and remain apprehensive about the impact on their own cultural institutions.[8]

MORAL SUPERIORITY

I was even more irritated than my American colleagues were by Canadian wilful ignorance of the United States, "non-Americanism," and anti-Americanism (even though the latter two sentiments were thrust more directly in their faces than in mine). Perhaps I just let my irritation show because it was more acceptable for me to show it than for them to do so, and diplomatic discipline kept them quiet. I vented my views in an internal discussion paper in October 2003:

While Canadians consider themselves tolerant, respectful and well-informed, these qualities all too often vanish when they discuss America and Americans. Prejudice, stereotyping and dismissive treatment of the United States and its people sometimes seem to be acceptable among Canadians to a degree that would not be countenanced toward other nations or groups ... Far too prevalent among Canadians are stereotypes of the United States based on popular myth and mass entertainment. To far too many Canadian minds, American society appears as a frightening collage of polarized incomes, illiteracy, inaccessible health care, electoral chaos, gated communities, urban poverty, environmental degradation, organized crime, gangs, gun violence, black-white racial conflict, religious hypocrisy, jingoistic patriotism, government secrecy, and an arrogant, ignorant foreign policy.

These delusions thrive among the relatively well-educated and travelled, who ought to know better. They prevail most strongly among those who have never, or seldom, visited the United States – and who, all too often, take pride in this insularity. Canadians need to learn that they do not know nearly as much as they ought to know, nor than they believe they know, about America and Americans, to absorb positive impressions about U.S. society's past and present leadership in key areas (1) which Canadians claim to value and (2) which challenge Canadians' habitual assumptions about America, to be reminded that prejudice, intolerance, verbal abuse and stereotyping of America and Americans runs contrary to Canadian values.[9]

The US ambassador to New Zealand pursued similar themes in a 2004 speech:

If you have forced us to avoid complacency, you will have contributed to making the United States a better nation and Americans a better people. We are a nation that has been as open to constructive criticism and new ways of doing things as any in history. Our political institutions are designed to encourage a diversity of views and competition among ideas ...

In order for collective security to work, it must aim for the security of all the members of the collective. Ignoring the real concerns of any member, including the United States, undermines collective security. Using U.N. institutions as a means to limit U.S. economic and military power is not only doomed to failure, it undermines the very concept of collective security. Those who try to use the United Nations ... [for example] to restrict America's highly successful trade in cultural goods and services ... are not just anti-American – they are anti-United Nations ...

Who is hurt by anti-Americanism? I close with a quote from John Parker of the New York Times: "the costs of anti-Americanism will be borne not by Americans, but by others ... Cubans, North Koreans, Zimbabweans, and countless other suffer and starve under their respective tyrannies because the democratic world's chattering classes, obsessed with denouncing the United States, can't be bothered with holding their criminal regimes to account ... the global anti-American elite has massively failed to fulfill the most fundamental responsibility of the intellectual class: to provide dispassionate, truthful analysis that can guide society to make proper decisions."[10]

One American who had been living in Canada for a few years offered other Americans this view:

I've learned it's not all beer and doughnuts. If you're thinking about coming to Canada, let me give you some advice: Don't ... As attractive as living here may be in theory, the reality's something else. For me, it's been one of almost daily confrontation with a powerful anti-Americanism ... There's nothing subtle about it ... Canadians bring up "the States" or "Americans" to make comparisons or evaluations that mix a kind of smug contempt with a wariness that alternates between the paranoid and the absurd ...

Part of what's irksome about Canadian anti-Americanism and the obsession with the United States is that it seems so corrosive to Canada. Any country that defines itself through a negative ("Canada: We're not the United States") is doomed to an endless and repetitive cycle of hand-wringing and angst ... As a Canadian social advocate once told me, when her compatriots look at their own societal problems, they are often satisfied once they can convince themselves that they're better off than the United States. As long as there's still more homelessness, racism and income inequality to the south, Canadians can continue to rest easy in their moral superiority ...

In "officially multicultural Canada," hostility toward Americans is the last socially acceptable expression of bigotry and xenophobia. It would be impossible to say the things about any other nationality that Canadians routinely say – both publicly and privately – about the United States. On a human level, it can be rude and hurtful. (As it was on the afternoon of Sept. 11, 2001, when an acquaintance angrily told me that she would now have to curtail her travel plans because she was afraid she might be mistaken for an American.) And there's no way to argue against it. An American who attempts to correct a misconception or express even the mildest approval for the policies of U.S. institutions is likely to be dismissed as thin-skinned or offensive, and as demonstrating those scary nationalistic tendencies that threaten the world.[11]

THE ROOTS OF NON-AMERICANISM

English-speaking Canada's roots among refugees from the American Revolutionary War ingrained views that the new United States of America was violent, disrespectful of authority, politically flawed, and socially inferior. Canada not only *was* better than the United States because it retained British institutions; the Loyalists *needed it to become* better in order to justify their sacrifices and sufferings during the war and afterward, as they surrendered their property and migrated northward to start new lives in harder territory. As well as creating an attitude of moral superiority – a thin-skinned snobbishness – in Canadians, these circumstances drove Canada's early leaders toward building a very *deliberately non-American* culture.

Following the Second World War, US commercial influence seemed overwhelming to many Canadians, and so Canadian governments established a range of government measures to restrain or roll back US corporate and media hegemony. These measures included requiring proportions of Canadian content on radio and television, expanding the state-owned broadcast system (Canadian Broadcasting Corporation, CBC) and domestic film production (National Film Board, NFB), creating various other publicly owned companies, and extending assorted incentives to Canadian-owned activities and organizations in the arts and media. By the 1980s, the so-called "cultural industries" had accrued a large number of vested interests and supporters in the arts, entertainment, and media fields, and had become a major lobbying force that could perpetuate these protections.

In 1984, just before Brian Mulroney's Progressive Conservative government – the most US-friendly in my lifetime – was sworn into office, Canada's then ambassador to Washington, Allan Gotlieb, confided to his diary that he didn't think even Mulroney's team would be able to repair the damage that had been done to Canadian-American relations by Pierre Trudeau's governments. This was because he thought the Mulroney cabinet team would have too many "red Conservatives" such as Joe Clark and Flora MacDonald, and also because "in the Department of External Affairs, anti-Americanism runs deep and will not, cannot change." Eight days later he added, "Sometimes I fear that the only bedrock policy of the officials of External Affairs is to differentiate ourselves from the Americans."[12]

The pro-market Mulroney government chose to leave existing "cultural policies" largely intact, and the United States acquiesced in the 1989 US-Canada Free Trade Agreement. While the term "cultural industries" was a Canadianism that pre-dated the agreement, the FTA gave the term a sort of official US recognition in the form of a broad exemption clause. This allowed Canada to continue measures to protect and subsidize a wide range of activities that the FTA defined as cultural. These included sound recording, broadcasting, film and video production, publishing, and bookstore ownership. The United States retained the right under the FTA to take measures of "equivalent commercial effect" if its industries were disadvantaged by a Canadian measure that, if not for the cultural exemption, would have been disallowed by the FTA. But the United States has never used or tested this right to retaliate.[13]

   The cultural exemption was carried over into the North American Free
Trade Agreement five years later (and Mexico obtained a similarly broad
exemption for its policies in the energy sector). These industry-wide
exemptions were major concessions by the United States, but they were
worth granting in order to relieve important political sensitivities and
thus cement broader, positive relationships within North America. They
were part and parcel of building a stronger continental economy.

CULTURE CLIMBS THE AGENDA

In my first years at the Embassy in the early 1990s, we had only one cul-
tural-sector issue among our active files, and it was not very active. This
was in feature-film distribution, where Canada exempted several of the
major US film studios from existing restrictions on foreign ownership
because these studios had already been invested in the Canadian market
decades before the restrictions had been introduced.

   In 1993–94 the culture question suddenly climbed much higher on the
bilateral agenda. First, a US-based magazine, *Sports Illustrated* (*SI*), decided to sell a Canadian edition which seemed to use new technology to get
around Canadian protections. Canada took action to shut down the
Canadian version of *Sports Illustrated*, beginning what would become a
bitter and highly politicized struggle.

   Just as this magazine issue was gaining momentum during 1994, Canada (through its broadcast regulator, the Canadian Radio-television and
Communications Commission, CRTC) de-licensed a US-based country-
music cable TV service that was being distributed in Canada, Country
Music Television (CMT), to replace it with a Canadian start-up. Because
CMT had invested in developing the country-music audience and winning
TV viewers, this arguably amounted to expropriating that investment and
handing it to a Canadian competitor. The CMT issue was tentatively
resolved in about a year, though not very satisfactorily for the US side: CMT
was compensated by being allowed to own 20 per cent of the channel that
replaced it – a commercial settlement that only partly redressed the harm
to CMT and required no adjustment by Canada to the policy that had
caused that harm.

   So Canada took two separate, apparently discriminatory actions against
US firms in two media industries – magazines and television – in one
year, both rationalized as "cultural policy" measures. In reaction, the
Office of the US Trade Representative saw a pattern that connected with
certain issues it had with Europe, and it consequently became more alert

and active on the cultural-policy front than it might have been if only one of these issues had arisen in isolation. By the first half of 1996 – even before the Canadian Heritage ministry was established and Sheila Copps became its first minister – the USTR had developed a "Strategy on Cultural Issues with Canada" that viewed Canada's actions in this area as a problem area not just to US interests in one country but for the international trading system.[14]

THE MAGAZINE DISPUTE'S COMMERCIAL AND LEGAL CONTEXT

The magazine dispute of the 1990s began over a particular kind of magazine known as a "split run." This was the industry's term for a magazine edition that used editorial content developed in one country (in this case the United States) but included ads aimed at readers in another country (Canada). Canadian policy from the 1960s onward forbade split runs (though two long-established split runs, *Time* and *Readers' Digest*, were grandfathered). In other words, a US-based magazine such as *Sports Illustrated* was not allowed to modify its US edition slightly by adding a few items of Canadian content, sell the advertising space all over again (this time to Canadian advertisers), and market this Canadianized version in Canada. Prohibiting split runs of US magazines left a little more Canadian advertising revenue available for Canadian magazines than would otherwise have been available to them.

There were three measures that kept most split runs out of Canada until the mid-1990s. First, there was a ban on importing physical printed copies of a split-run magazine into Canada. Secondly, advertisers benefited from an income-tax deduction against the cost of ads they bought in "Canadian" magazines but not for ads they bought in "non-Canadian" ones (including split runs). Thirdly, there was a postal subsidy: Canada Post delivered "Canadian" magazines at cheap rates. (I place "Canadian" and "non-Canadian" in quotes here because the policy judged Canadianness by ownership and control, rather than by content.)

The information-technology revolution provided a route around the ban on physical imports, and this was the immediate trigger for the magazine dispute. By 1993, a Canadian split run which was edited in (say) New York no longer had to be printed in the United States and physically trucked across the border. Instead, once edited and composed in New York, it could be transmitted digitally to a Canadian printing plant and then printed and distributed within Canada – thus avoiding one of the three measures Canada had in place against split runs.

Sports Illustrated, a US general-interest sports magazine, produced six trial issues of an *SI* split run in this way during 1993. This was viewed as a key test of Canada's magazine policy. Canada responded by deciding that *Sports Illustrated Canada* would be limited in future to six issues annually. But the magazine had planned a dozen *SI Canada* issues for 1994 and wanted to increase it to a weekly. Canadian magazine publishers, on the other hand, wanted *SI Canada* cut off completely. So publishers on both sides were quite unhappy with Canada's decision.[15]

My colleagues in the US government recognized and accepted that Canada had negotiated an exemption for its cultural industries in the FTA and NAFTA to which the United States had agreed. Their thinking about the US position in the dispute was legal and quite specific, focused on trade rules that had been determined multilaterally under the World Trade Organization, to which both of our countries had signed and committed. To my colleagues in the USTR, the question was not what Canada's cultural objectives were or should be, but only: Given its commitments in this system of international rules, what means could Canada legitimately use to pursue those objectives?[16]

POLITICAL REVERBERATION

The Canadian government's view was that anything that favoured the growth and profitability of Canadian media and entertainment *companies* should be encouraged. This was an extension of a nation-building, institution-creating, industry-protecting drive that Canadians had been pursuing since Confederation and earlier. But to my American colleagues, particularly those accustomed to thinking in legal or trade-policy terms, protectionist impulses of this kind were always to be expected and countries signed trade agreements precisely in order to restrain them. Surely that had been the spirit in which the FTA was negotiated. If Canadians wanted to promote their culture, they should focus on nurturing *creative products* – films, books, and so on – rather than focusing on the less direct route of nurturing *companies and industries,* which might or might not produce something called culture.

Behind this trade-policy viewpoint, there were also philosophical views on the US side about fundamental freedoms. When governments own news organizations, when laws and regulations tinker with broadcasting content and ownership, and when government policies attempt systematically to shape media content, these factors can be perceived to pose certain risks to democracy. Each was and is present in Canada, though for some reason few Canadians ever seem to see this as risky. On the contrary, my US colleagues were taken aback by the intensity and touchiness of Canadian cultural nationalism, and wondered if it was really healthy for Canadian society.[17] But they wisely kept such views mostly to themselves, and while they shared them privately with me, they did not venture publicly into such broad questions about democracy, politics, and media throughout the prolonged and bitter magazine dispute.

The perception of a clash between culture and trade had reverberations beyond Canada, particularly in France and other countries in the European Union, where questions of cultural integrity and preservation were also sensitive. The magazine problem had various European angles for trade-policy makers. First, the United States had been frustrated for years in its efforts to get the European Union to comply with a certain multilateral trade-panel ruling (on trade in bananas). This meant that how the United States might enforce WTO dispute settlement was a particularly keen question for US trade officials and political leaders at the time. Few in Washington could afford to be seen to be letting any trading partner off easily when the partner had run afoul of the WTO. That would not only undermine years of effort in the bananas dispute but also degrade the WTO, which was less than four years old and was the result of years of multilateral trade-policy effort.

Moreover, trade in what were sometimes called "audio-visual" products – music and film – was also an important area of US-European friction at the time, so the outcome of the comparatively small US-Canada magazine dispute might well hold major implications for trade with Europe. These considerations drove USTR officials to take a firm line with Canada.

The trade-law motives driving the United States were no secret, but they were amazingly little understood by the Canadian side during the magazine dispute. Part of this was insecure Canadian narcissism: a presumption that Canada was, or deserved to be, important for its own sake in the American universe. Part of it was deliberate avoidance of the trade-law details. The Canadian media wanted to portray the United States as trying to "own" or "get control of" Canada's culture, since this would politicize the issue and force the Canadian government to take a hard line protecting its industry. They wanted to make the US position look bullying, greedy, and unreasonable. Drawing any attention to specific and calculated arguments, mostly put together by Washington lawyers who had no apparent interest in conquering the northern half of the continent, would have contradicted this self-serving media narrative.

ESCALATION AND RESOLUTION

The magazine dispute grew nasty in 1998–99, owing in large part to dramatization and distortion in Canadian media, which were not impartial: as Canadian periodical publishing and cultural industry interests, they were really a party to the dispute. When the minister of Canadian heritage, Sheila Copps, took a hard and very political line on magazine policy, USTR officials made plans to retaliate, which the United States had a legal right to do. While US Ambassador Gordon Giffin did all he could to moderate the argument, players in the Canadian media establishment repeatedly misrepresented US motives and Ambassador Giffin's words and actions.[18]

At least the bad-cop side of the US approach – our threat of retaliation against Canadian industries such as steel, plastics, and textiles – was having some political effect. Government caucus members began to state openly their intention to abstain from voting on the bill. The Liberal MP for Sarnia-Lambton, Roger Gallaway, told reporters: "All that nonsense that we have to be able to tell our stories to other Canadians just doesn't resonate in a border community. If our cultural industries are that weak ... maybe that should tell us something about what Canadians really want ... Sarnia is home to 40 percent of the plastics and petrochemical industry in Canada. We estimate that Sarnia exports about $2.4 billion worth of these products to the U.S. every year. Can you make that up on [magazines]? Clearly not."[19] Two weeks later, from the other side of the House of Commons, Reform Party MP Charlie Penson echoed Gallaway's sentiment (along with the distaste for Minister Copps's overheated rhetoric): "Where does 'culture under siege' rank among my constituents' concerns? Or those of steelworkers in Hamilton?"

While all this was happening, cool heads on the US side wanted to think the issues through in a global way. In a November 1998 issue of *Business Week*, Jeffrey Garten, who had been under-secretary of commerce a few years earlier in the Clinton administration, advocated a sympathetic approach. "Countries need cohesive national communities grounded in history and tradition. Washington's crusade for free trade is often seen abroad as a Trojan horse for companies, such as Walt Disney Co. and Cable News Network, that would dominate foreign lifestyles and values. Most Americans react to these fears with a shrug. That's a big mistake," Garten argued.

In May 1999, after several rounds of very discreet talks, the two countries reached a settlement that allowed split-run magazines into the Canadian market on limited terms. Minister Copps's main accomplishment from all the effort invested in this issue (apart from embittering the management of the whole bilateral relationship for a couple of years) was that Canada would transfer responsibility for reviewing prospective foreign investments in "cultural industries" from Industry Canada – where nearly all foreign-investment review functions then resided – to the Canadian Heritage ministry that she led. In fact, some in the Industry ministry preferred surrendering this authority over continually having their use of it second-guessed by their Heritage counterparts.

THE SKY FELL AND LIFE WENT ON

Following the settlement in June 1999, the Canadian magazine industry survived better than its advocates foretold. While the terms of the agreement were quite different from what the Canadian magazine industry had wanted or what the government had originally proposed, there was no "onslaught" of split runs and the Canadian industry was not "crushed," as Copps had predicted (just weeks prior to the settlement) would happen if there was any retreat.

One Canadian magazine industry leader had predicted in 1999 that "few or no Canadian magazines will remain even thirty-six months from now" and that the government's retreat would "devastate a generation of young writers." The magazine industry's website said there would be "potentially enormous migration of ad revenue from Canadian magazines to U.S. magazines," and that "Canadian magazines will be hurt and Canadian content will suffer without a program to mitigate the damage." But nine years later the same website announced that "the Canadian magazine industry continues to expand advertising revenues, having grown faster than other major media ... combined, between 1999 and 2006."

NO SECOND SHOE

At the time of the June 1999 settlement, many (if not most) Canadian observers thought that the magazine dispute had represented the first round in a probable ongoing series of Canada-US conflicts over the media and cultural industries. A friend in the television industry asked me in 1999, "So when are you going to come after us?" It was also widely expected that the magazine settlement would not last, because the fundamental underlying issues were more durable than the solution. Yet it lasted, and other culture disputes have not occurred. Remarkably, since 1999 cultural issues have been less a feature of the bilateral US-Canada agenda than at any time in the previous four decades.

Explanations for this are, in fact, not hard to find: the magazine issue was driven less by fundamental policy differences than imagined, and more by the manipulations of specific players. Canadian observers in the 1990s widely believed that the United States had an overarching agenda to break down Canada's cultural protections systematically. Yet, as I worked day after day on the US side, I never saw or heard any evidence that the United States had such a strategy. Bill Merkin, a former senior USTR official who had negotiated with Canada during the FTA talks, noted this when he lamented the way the dispute had deteriorated.

> I don't think anybody down here [in Washington] is sitting around and taking a look at the different sectors in Canada and saying, "Oh, gee, we only have 30% of this one, Let's target them, Let's go after them" ... This all began with *Sports Illustrated* ... I can candidly tell you that in all my years at USTR and throughout the free trade negotiations we never once had any interest expressed to us in going after the [Canadian magazine policies] which had been in place, what, since '65 or some lengthy period like that. And it's unfortunate that ... change in technology and efforts to find a niche and an inability of the two sides to compromise on the *Sports Illustrated* issue ... [have] led to this. I mean I don't think we need to be here. We didn't need to be here but we are.[20]

The US side respected the cultural exemption in the FTA and NAFTA, and repeatedly said so. It focused on upholding international legal rights that had been confirmed by the WTO. If the United States had a broader agenda, it was to uphold the integrity of the young WTO dispute-settlement system more generally. During the course of the dispute, the United States clarified and strengthened its public position that countries had a right to pursue measures to develop their national identities and cultures – a position that had been established by its allowing the cultural exemptions in the FTA and NAFTA.[21]

MEDIA CONFLICT OF INTEREST

The mistaken expectation of ongoing conflict stemmed from dramatic misunderstandings which had grown in the heated atmosphere of the magazine dispute. Drawing on ingrained anxieties about territorial expansion (from the eighteenth and nineteenth centuries) and corporate control (from the mid-twentieth century), too many Canadians were ready to believe in a systematic US government campaign to subjugate Canada, and some of their leaders were ready to encourage this belief.[22]

The Canadian media outlets that reported on the dispute were in a conflict of interest. The companies that owned them were mostly parties to the case, in that they either owned magazines directly, or were affiliated with firms that owned magazines, or had some other commercial interest in maintaining the policy measures involved. Even had this not been so, the reporters and columnists writing about this dispute were mostly members of a professional group that was deeply committed to the cultural-policy apparatus. Minister Copps and magazine-industry leaders provided a phony narrative of bullying and conquest, enhanced by colourful rhetoric, which the writers then amplified.[23]

The magazine dispute was an aberration, one that was produced by relatively unusual circumstances: a small and unsophisticated (but highly vocal) industry captured the loyalty of a mid-ranked cabinet minister and her staff, who, importantly, were allowed to proceed by the prime minister, while complicit media uncritically and fiercely endorsed the government's position.

MINISTERIAL LICENCE AND LEASH

Why did Prime Minister Chrétien sanction Minister Copps's approach to the dispute for so long? Chrétien had to strike difficult compromises among factions in a very broadly based party. Since he had taken office in 1993, "business Liberals" – pragmatists with good economic and commercial sense like John Manley, Paul Martin, Roy MacLaren, Pierre Pettigrew, and others – had been more or less in the driver's seat. The left-nationalists who had resisted trade liberalization and other Mulroney-era policies were feeling alienated from the Liberal Party by 1997 and were at some risk of slipping away. Chrétien must have felt a need to keep them on board. Not unlike his predecessor, Brian Mulroney, he apparently thought that indulging the cultural lobby was a necessary price of carrying on broader liberalization in other areas.

The dispute seriously hurt Canada's stature and image in US political and foreign-policy circles. Canada and Canadians are normally more or less faceless in Washington. A short list of post–Second World War issues and experiences – such as NORAD, health-care models, the Quebec referenda on separation in 1980 and 1995, disputes on acid rain, magazines, and lumber, Canada's engagement in the Afghanistan conflict – have accounted for most of the impressions of Canada that have stuck in the minds of important members of the US policy-making establishment over the past several decades. US trade officials or diplomats who are newly assigned to the Canada file tend to arrive in their offices with no more than two or three of these impressions – if that many – framing their view. The magazine dispute did not contribute anything good to these impressions. Rather, it represents one of the nadirs of a period when Canadians were seen as being hypersensitive screamers who, once they got worked up about an issue, were almost impossible to bring around to a reasonable, grown-up discussion. Their handling of the WHTI issue seven to eight years later reinforced this image.[24]

Generally speaking, Canadian cultural policy has two problems. First, it is almost entirely directed against one country. Americans realize this and find it offensive. If Canadians are going to sustain this policy, they could at least mitigate the irritation by applying the policy in a reasonable fashion.

WHO BENEFITS?

Secondly, and as with many restrictive arrangements, Canadian "cultural policy" has tended to be captured by those who benefit from it, and its benefits have been at least partially diverted over time toward serving these vested stakeholders rather than to developing "Canadian culture."

The 1994–99 magazine dispute was an extreme example of this: a situation in which a few companies manipulated the Canadian government's defence of minor cultural-policy measures to benefit their small industry at the expense of the real public interests of both Canada and its main ally.

Seen in historical perspective, the policy could be said to have held the industry back (by favouring a small number of incumbents, thus reducing creativity and innovation), instead of helping it thrive creatively in the long run. Foreigners are easily able to see the faults of this policy apparatus – risk of political control, risk of suppressing real creativity in favour of official doctrine of what "good Canadian culture" is, risk of corporate capture, and misallocation of resources. These faults in our cultural policy have been almost invisible to nearly all Canadians during my lifetime, but they should not be.

Few or no other countries shared Canada's intense concern with US cultural influence, and few or no other ministers apparently were as willing as Copps to damage their country's relations with the United States

over an issue that Canada was largely defining. In the wake of the magazine dispute, testing international opinion helped Canadian officials to
accept that they had to soften their message and methods, both with third
countries and with American stakeholders. This is suggested by notes
from a meeting I had with a contact in Copps's department. "The Canadian side has figured out that Americans respond well to language of
'under-represented' or 'under-served' groups, and not to 'cultural diversity.'
They are working on polling and analysis that will help them further
develop language which helps their cause in the U.S. and avoids 'inadver-
tently alienating' Americans on this issue. They are shifting Heritage's
'international activities' from 'dancers and cocktail parties' toward proactive public diplomacy, possibly including advertising and educational
materials, to explain the Canadian perspective in a non-threatening way."[25]

REASSESSMENT AND FENCE MENDING

Our sense during the winter of 1999–2000 was that the magazine dispute
had diminished the status of both Copps and her department within the
government. Budget decisions were not going Copps's way, perhaps
owing to this decline in status. Notably, Copps failed to sell cabinet on an
important pet project, establishing a fund to finance the production of
Canadian feature films – a failure that some of my contacts attributed
specifically to her having expended all her political capital on the magazines issue, weakening her support at the table.[26]

All this was putting Canadian Heritage officials in a more conciliatory
mood. For example, we heard that the department was thoroughly reviewing its relationships with partner agencies (such as the CBC and the CRTC)
with a view to relaxing efforts to control them and instead being more col-
legial. We also learned that Canadian Heritage was working to build up its
expertise on international trade and investment rules. To us, this was a
clear sign of the department's dissatisfaction with the narrow-minded way
the magazine battle had been waged, both vis-à-vis the US side and vis-à-
vis the Department of Foreign Affairs and International Trade, which had
to contain and clean up much of the resulting damage.

An academic paper presented in 2000 by Carleton University's Keith
Acheson and Chris Maule provides a well-written, critical view of Canada's management of the culture dispute. It debunks the two major ratio-
nales for Canada's actions in the magazine battle: that the viability of
Canadian magazines was threatened by US-controlled split-run editions,
and that competition from split runs was unfair by some economic or

legal definition. Acheson and Maule point out that Canada had not enforced its pre-dispute tax and tariff measures to protect magazines; that no split runs other than *Sports Illustrated* ever entered the Canadian market, despite having the option of doing so; and that Canada had never brought any anti-dumping or anti-competition charges against American magazine companies.[27]

In July 2003, pronouncing the magazine industry to be "on a solid footing and enjoying healthy growth," Canada cut the funding programs it had put in place for magazines in 1999. This was a striking shift from predictions made in 1998–99 to the effect that any significant concession to the United States meant disaster for the Canadian industry. It effectively admitted that the threat from market liberalization had been exaggerated. We noted that this admission weakened Canada's case for a multilateral culture treaty that would supposedly strengthen cultural-policy options versus trade rules.[28] Canada also adjusted its programs in order to reach more and smaller publishing firms – an implicit admission that past policy had tended to benefit the largest organizations. While Minister Copps had cast herself as a defender of the vulnerable, it was the largest and most financially sound publishing firms that had benefited the most from both protection and subsidies.

BOOMING INDUSTRIES

A further trend contributed to the reassessment at Canadian Heritage and elsewhere. After decades of struggle, Canadian cultural products were enjoying a wave of international artistic and commercial success. Singers such as Celine Dion, Shania Twain, and Alanis Morissette were huge stage and recording stars, while Canadian writers like Carol Shields and Michael Ondaatje were winning major international literary awards. Most remarkably, in film and television production – the media most completely dominated by Americans – Canadians were not just exporting product across the world but succeeding in the US market.[29]

It is true that some of these successful movies and TV shows were made by US studios operating in Canada, that they were not very "recognizably" Canadian, and that production in Canada was strongly assisted by certain fiscal incentives, wage differences, and the low value of the Canadian dollar at the time. But, still, Canada had clearly become a cultural-product exporter. This made some observers ask whether Canadian creators might be outgrowing the need for government nurturing, especially when those incentives might be helping to fund material such as a biopic about

Chicago Bulls basketball star Dennis Rodman ("Bad as I Wanna Be") – an example of the contradictions of policy measures that necessarily defined Canadianness by ownership or location rather than by content.

As it turned out, the migration of US feature-film production to Canada in the late 1990s in search of lower costs did even more than the magazine dispute to bring Canadian "cultural" policy into bad repute in the United States. Congress became aware of the Dennis Rodman biopic (filmed in Toronto), as well as of Canadian police investigations of Montreal-based entertainment firms for alleged fraudulent abuse of tax-credit arrangements (placing Canadian names on work done by US talent in order to claim Canadian tax breaks).

Our Embassy's talking points with Canadian officials began to include lines like these: "These trends are not likely to help Canada's ability to pursue its cultural policies ... nor will they assist Canada's efforts to advance a dialogue on 'cultural diversity' in international fora. Canada would greatly help its own cause in these areas if it could improve the focus of its cultural policy measures on culture, rather than on industry-building."

VISIBLE DIVERGENCE

As Chris Sands (of the Washington-based Center for Strategic and International Studies) pointed out in a paper in the first half of 2000,[30] there was a growing disparity between the incomes of artists who marketed their products globally and those who aimed at the Canadian market and Canadian themes alone (what Minister Copps called "telling each other our own stories"). This caused considerable tension among artists and advocates, and put pressure on the Canadian government to reorient its support toward creators who chose to abstain from "global culture" in favour of working in the home market.

Canadian film, television, and music producers, and Canadian artists, were making it very big. This was thanks partly to their seamless access to American markets and market expertise. These creators were now stakeholders in the existing policies, and they did not necessarily share Copps's desire to focus on the Canadian market and restrain globalization. In fact, the average, increasingly plugged-in Canadian did not necessarily share that desire either. We told Washington in October 2003:

These changes are not likely to derail the push for the new [international cultural diversity] treaty [but] the Government of Canada's support for the treaty could be somewhat less determined in the future, and/or the Government stance on "cultural policy" could be increasingly out of line with popular attitudes ... Since [the settlement of the magazine war with the United States in] 1999, in order to build international support for protecting "cultural policies," the government has developed a new rationale for these policies – "cultural diversity." Vested interests have adopted this buzzphrase and signed on to Copps' push for a new international treaty, and the new rationale appears to have helped the Government to recruit other governments' support.

At the same time, existing policy measures are inevitably being measured against this new yardstick, leading to awkward questions. For example, do "Canadian content" quotas for radio music encourage diversity – or do they result in a handful of internationally successful artists (e.g. Shania Twain) getting inordinate airplay? Do tax breaks for film and television production help to generate diverse Canadian content, or do they foster large Toronto-based firms (e.g. Alliance Atlantis) [a major film and TV producer and distributor] whose productions are American (e.g. CSI) [a very popular TV crime-drama series] or very similar? ... Some "made-in-Canada solutions" are resented by consumers because of their monopoly positions (such as Air Canada); others are thought to have damaged the industries they were supposed to help (e.g. the Chapters bookstore chain, formed to block an incursion by U.S.-owned stores, has been accused of driving Canadian-owned publishers into bankruptcy). Canadians are less and less willing to believe that Canadian owners or managers can be counted on to promote Canadian culture (or other national policy goals) – something that was taken on faith in the nationalist creed that prevailed in the 1970's.[31]

The resulting crisis of confidence among Canada's cultural-policy establishment led, as might have been expected, to infighting. After a meeting of the House of Commons Standing Committee on Canadian Heritage in March 2004, I reported:

The room was packed [and] the atmosphere was almost hysterical – certainly as charged as any I've experienced in a Parliamentary committee ...
On the question of whether Canada's private copying levy [on blank-recording media, revenue from which went only to Canadian artists] is consistent with the World Intellectual Property Organization treaties ... officials said they could not share such opinions with the

committee, on grounds of Cabinet privilege; [one member] called this "totally unacceptable," saying "if you won't share information with us then you won't have a cooperative relationship with us."

On foreign ownership, [Sarmite Bulte, the committee's chair] goes right over the top with the rhetoric. There is a slippery slope, she says, from telecommunications to cable TV to over-the-air broadcasting to the CBC. "If we budge even a little on foreign ownership, it puts all our cultural objectives at risk." She virtually declares that Americans will end up owning the CBC.[32]

Canada's rhetoric on cultural diversity, driven by nationalist personalities such as Copps and Bulte, was simply out of line by 2004, well into the Internet era. It was an official ideology that had already been out of touch with reality when it was forged in the bilateral magazine dispute of the late 1990s. The result had been a clumsy and tortured effort to fit Copps's protectionist efforts into the world of international-trade law and policy – an effort that was not finished.

TRYING TO GLOBALIZE
CANADA'S CULTURAL-POLICY CRUSADE

Through late 1999 and into 2000, Sheila Copps remained the minister of Canadian heritage and her ministry focused on promoting an "International Network on Cultural Policy" (INCP) – a culture ministers' group that Copps had established in the middle of the magazine dispute and that deliberately excluded the United States until that country pressed to be allowed to send an observer.[33] The Network had its second ministerial-level meeting in Oaxaca, Mexico, in September 1999. As our Embassy described it to Washington:

The Network is "a forum for the exchange of ideas and experiences in the field of culture at the international level." The Ministers "reaffirmed their willingness to defend and promote cultural diversity." The Ministers believe that cultural goods and services ... deserve special treatment. They recognize the right of nations and governments to establish their cultural policies freely, and to adopt the means and instruments necessary for their application. The Ministers thank Canada for its offer to set up a liaison office to support the follow-up work of the Network.

Embassy understands ... that Copps was unhappy about the U.S. presence as a "participating non-member" [represented by the chair-

man of the U.S. National Endowment for the Arts, whose] active participation, directly challenged by Copps, left members with strengthened reservations about U.S. participation in the Network. Some
members of the network, including some on the Canadian delegation,
reportedly believe Canada is dominating it to an undesirable extent –
a belief which was reinforced when Copps dominated the closing
press conference in Oaxaca, upstaging [the Mexican host].34

The International Network on Cultural Policy evolved into a Canada-
sponsored push for a multilateral treaty, later a United Nations Educational, Scientific and Cultural Organization (UNESCO) convention, on protecting "cultural diversity." From 2002 onward, this was an irritating
complication to Canadian and US diplomacy at the United Nations and
with various third countries. Bilateral meetings in Washington in January
2005 discussed the draft UNESCO convention on cultural diversity:

Canada strongly supports a convention that affirms the right of States
to impose quotas on a subset of goods and services that are defined as
cultural. Canada claims to accept that this should be done consistent
with existing international obligations. [A US official] said that we
opposed any cultural policy that would limit or deny an individual
access to information or expression of ideas, which by its nature is
what quotas are intended to do. He underscored emphatically the U.S.
Government position that any convention on cultural diversity should
promote the free flow of information and ideas and should not be
used to create barriers to trade. He stated that the U.S. could not support a convention that could be used to create trade barriers, including
quotas. Beyond this fundamental issue (which may prove to be a deal-
breaker), [the Canadian and US officials] agreed that this convention
should be consistent with human rights agreements and should promote the rights of individuals to express their own cultural identity ...
   [In a larger meeting the same day] the Canadian delegation insisted
that Canada was not interested in violating any trade agreements, but
that for a certain set of goods and services, trade agreements had been
reached without taking cultural policy into account. They stated their
desire that the UNESCO convention be a mechanism to develop cultural policy that would complement the trade policy. Finally, the Canadians explained that a system of quotas should only be used to complement other systems of promotion such as subsidies or state grants. We
explained that for the United States Government, the trade policy

already does complement our culture policy. Further, we stated that policies that inhibit creative expression or free flow of ideas could not complement those that are meant to promote them; on the contrary, the very existence of such policies would work in contradiction to promotion policies.[35]

US REACTION

The UNESCO Convention on the Protection and Promotion of the Diversity of Cultural Expressions was approved in a vote in Paris in October 2005 and entered into force in 2006. The US government's final view of the issue at a global level was summarized in an intervention prepared in late 2006 for an Inter-American Meeting of Ministers of Culture, where Canada was trying to promote the UNESCO convention.

> As one of this hemisphere's most enduring multicultural societies, the United States fully supports the diversity of cultural expressions at home. At the same time, we actively promote the cultural diversity aspirations of other countries. However, we do this not through high-minded words or advocacy to subscribe to legal instruments. Rather, we find pragmatic ways to promote domestic cultural institutions and industries with minimal government involvement, both at home and abroad ...
>
> What we, as governments, can do as partners in that process is to create enabling environments by reaffirming our commitment to and respect for the principles of free trade, the free flow of information and the free exchange of cultural ideas and experiences. Experience has shown before, and will show again here, that no single legal instrument – no matter how well intentioned and no matter how well, or poorly, drafted it may be – can serve as a substitute for allowing cultural diversity to express itself through natural, organic processes, rather than through governmentally controlled, and contrived, programs.
>
> For these reasons, we regret that some at this forum seek to tout the UNESCO Convention as a kind of cultural panacea and to ignore how that Convention's misapplication could endanger vital protections of free trade, the free flow of information and freedom of choice in cultural expression that the global community has striven to achieve over many years.[36]

In a more candid communication for internal use, the State Department told its posts abroad:

The United States opposes this convention, in part because it contains very broad definitions about what can be considered cultural expressions and especially because of ambiguous language about the Convention's relationship to other international agreements, including WTO agreements. These serious substantial flaws raise the possibility that some countries might try to misuse the Convention to try to stifle the free flow of information, or attempt to justify WTO-inconsistent trade protections on items or activities they deem to be "cultural expressions" ...

The United States prefers that as few countries as possible ratify the Convention ... [and] to further limit the potential harm of the Convention, the United States would like countries that ratify the Convention to submit a written "understanding" with their instrument of ratification. The understanding should provide that nothing in the Convention should be interpreted as affecting States' rights or obligations under other international agreements ...

The U.S. proposed amendments to clarify language in Article 20 of the Convention [on the convention's relationships to other international treaties, such as NAFTA and WTO agreements] ... [Eight countries] echoed the U.S. view that Article 20 of the Convention cannot properly – and must not – be read to allow provisions of the Convention to prevail over or modify rights and obligations under other international agreements, including WTO agreements ... By filing an understanding ... they would be adding support to the argument that Article 20 is ambiguous and therefore subject to potential abuse.[37]

In the end, the convention did little apparent harm, but little apparent good either, and its executive (the INCP) faded away.[38] It cost Canada substantial diplomatic effort and capital, was achieved at the cost of considerable acrimony with Canada's closest international partner, and the driving logic behind it – that trade liberalization was unacceptably bad for culture – was never borne out.

As the years passed, my American colleagues were increasingly cynical and derisive about Canada's "cultural policies," of which they had been respectful in the FTA-NAFTA negotiating period. A newspaper article in 2005 outlined the Department of Canadian Heritage's review of a plan by coffee-shop chain Starbucks to sell music (both discs and downloads) from its Canadian stores. Canadian Heritage officials wanted to know Starbucks' projections for levels of Canadian content and employment.[39] One of my senior colleagues circulated this around the US government with a note saying, "Just to remind us all again about the depth and fervor of the Canadian commitment to free trade."[40]

HOW IT FELT

Let me draw on allegory to summarize the experience of American officials involved in the cultural-policy dispute with Canada through the magazines saga and the pursuit of the Convention on Cultural Diversity, and why it made them so cynical.

Imagine that you and I own neighbouring houses on a quiet street. We have had several fairly constructive dealings over the years. A bit unusually, we don't have any fence or hedge between our properties. Because I have a busy life, I don't pay much attention to you, but you seem to watch my activities closely.

I understand that you don't want my dog in your yard, and I nearly always manage to keep it at home, until one day it strays into your yard. You immediately beat my dog with a stick. I complain, particularly since I am a dog lover and I am active in a city-wide campaign against animal abuse. The city agrees with me and tickets you for animal abuse. You delay paying the fine, with the weird excuse that my dog was smoking in your yard (but you present no evidence, and anyhow, under the by-laws, this would have been an offence only for humans, not for dogs). You also threaten to electrocute my dog if it enters your yard again, and you claim that this would be all right, because the law does not ban electrocuting animals (only beating them).

I then overhear you telling your family and friends that I have always wanted to make your yard part of my dog's territory. You also call a meeting of selected neighbours – to which you don't invite me. At this meeting you argue that our town's by-laws aren't strong enough to control my dog, and you attempt to start a neighbourhood vigilante group to solve the problem of roaming dogs.

After months of very difficult negotiations, we agree to a settlement whereby you install an electric fence with a voltage that keeps my dog out of your yard, but is not strong enough to kill it (the latter is the solution you would have preferred, but you realize that it wouldn't look good in light of your recent citation for animal abuse). The neighbourhood dog-control meetings continue, I am grudgingly allowed to attend, and they eventually result in a weak declaration that people have a right to take anti-dog measures.

The outcome is tolerable for both of us, and if pressed, you would argue that the whole dispute was worthwhile in order to gain this settlement.

Surely, though, there were easier ways to reach such an outcome – and, if one really and truly wants to keep one's yard to oneself, surely there must be better ways to do it.

MORAL SUPERIORITY IN THE POST-2001 ERA

Over lunch in early October 2003 I discussed Canadians' anti-Americanism with a Canadian politician who was

a leading booster of the United States in Parliament, a job he says he has found increasingly difficult in recent months. He held a pro-U.S. rally in his constituency during March, but says he and his colleagues currently see no political benefit in making pro-U.S. gestures, due primarily to the border restrictions on beef but also to other trade issues (wheat, lumber). He has proposed some pro-U.S. planks to be added to his party's electoral platform, but he is currently pessimistic that they will be used.

I noted that much for which Canadian voters currently blame "the United States" should really be laid at the door of narrower industries/ constituencies, and that within the U.S. Government there had been sustained efforts at high levels (President Bush, Homeland Security Secretary Tom Ridge, Commerce Undersecretary Grant Aldonas) to resolve problems and make the relationship work. While he agreed, he did not indicate that he had tried to make this point with his constituents. He indicated frustration in his efforts to combat Canadians' negative stereotypes of the United States, given the persistence of these views.[41]

After the parting of ways over the invasion of Iraq in 2003, Canadians drifted increasingly toward the view that America's security challenges, whether they were real or imagined (or partly real and exaggerated by the US security establishment), were more or less America's own problem, and that Canadians – who were, according to their own mythology, loved and respected worldwide – had best keep clear of them. An internal Embassy conversation the following week was revealing. One of my officer colleagues noted, "I'm not the expert on counterterrorism, but it seems there is a disconnect between how Government of Canada intelligence and law enforcement officials view the situation in Canada, and how politicians portray it ... Between the 'it can't happen here' and the 'poor innocent Canadians [are] owed protection no matter what' rhetoric they do seem to be working themselves into an awkward corner if some-thing [a terrorist attack] does happen here."

That "awkward corner" would be Canadian leaders' inability to respond to a real or perceived security situation, a perception among both Cana-dians and Americans in some future crisis that those leaders needed out-side help to deal with such events; and possibly also a view among some that, since US policies were somehow responsible for the security prob-lem, the United States should be the one to respond to it and/or owed Canada protection.

Another, more senior colleague commented, "I believe the Canadian view of counterterrorism is all wound up with its general view on crime – which is basically that when it happens in Canada – murder, rape, etc. – these are only aberrations of Canadian society ... by misguided folks who will respond to gentler, kinder treatment. To repeat a story two criminol-ogist friends told me – the political leadership of Corrections Canada can-not believe that when they put the Internet in prisons, prisoners actually defraud the public via the Internet. I see counterterrorism as the same thing – 'we are nice, not like the Americans – no one in Canada would ever be a terrorist.'"

GAUGING PUBLIC ATTITUDES

The US embassies in Ottawa and Mexico City helped to fund a three-coun-try public-opinion poll in October 2003, which was about two years after the September 2001 attacks and about six months after the invasion of Iraq. The results confirmed "growing negative feelings expressed by Cana-dians and Mexicans about the United States" (31 per cent and 29 per cent respectively held negative opinions) and that "Canadians continue to feel far less threatened by the risk of terrorist attack than Americans." While it is true that negative feelings grew after 2001, the relative weight of these changes must be kept in context and the specific causes deserve analysis. In the 2003 poll for the embassies, Canadians (as well as Mexicans) who held favourable opinions of the United States outnumbered those who did not. Majorities in Canada and Mexico agreed that the three countries should have an "economic union," and 73 per cent of Canadians approved of North American free trade. Even on security issues, the numbers were encouraging for the US side: majorities of Canadians and Americans (55 per cent and 69 per cent) (and 43 per cent of Mexicans) supported "estab-lishing a common security perimeter," and 37 per cent of Canadians said they believed that "stronger counter-terrorist measures are appropriate."

By March 2004, a year after the invasion of Iraq, public opinion had shifted against President Bush on both sides of the border. By then, two-thirds of Canadian respondents said they thought the president had "knowingly lied to the world to justify his war with Iraq." The percentage who thought the United States had made a mistake in going to war had climbed from 47 per cent in December 2003 to 63 per cent in March. (Indeed, according to reports of a US poll, American respondents' approval of the way the president was handling Iraq – admittedly a different question – had plummeted from 75 per cent in April 2003 to 46 per cent in early March 2004. And 55 per cent of Americans thought the administration had "intentionally exaggerated its evidence that Iraq had weapons of mass destruction.")

According to the Ipsos-Reid polling firm, 74 per cent of respondents thought that Canada had made the right decision by not supporting the coalition. Ipsos-Reid senior VP John Wright reportedly said the results showed that Canadians, while pleased with the regime change in Baghdad, believed the end of ousting dictator Saddam Hussein had not been justified by the means. Wright also reportedly said that this was most likely because of what had since been learned about faulty pre-war intelligence concerning Iraq's presumed arsenal of weapons of mass destruction.[42]

In 2005 the Pew Global Attitudes Project found that the number of Canadians expressing a favourable attitude toward the United States had fallen substantially during the Bush administration, from 71 per cent in 1999 to 63 per cent in 2002 and 59 per cent in 2005. Those who expressed an unfavourable attitude were then asked if this were mostly because of President Bush, or because of America in general; a majority (54 per cent to 32 per cent) said it was mostly because of Bush.[43] This blaming of Bush was generally in line with attitudes in the United Kingdom and Europe, though not Russia or China, where "America in general" got relatively more disapproval.

MARTIN DISAPPOINTS

Jean Chrétien's long-time rival for the Liberal Party leadership was Paul Martin, who had served as Chrétien's finance minister in the mid-1990s and led that government's effort to reduce the federal budget deficit. As Martin had been an effective minister of finance and he was seen as a leader of the business-friendly side of the Liberal Party, US government observers hoped his expected eventual succession to the prime minister-ship would be likely to improve bilateral relations.

But by November 2003 some of our contacts were pouring cold water on that optimism. One of my senior colleagues reported, "A pollster and a media guru told me together that we should not expect a big change in the way the new Martin Government will attack issues ... in the wider context of whether Martin will be less nationalistic than Chretien, the consensus was 'no.' The only major difference they saw was that Martin may be less inclined to satisfy the far left of the Liberal Party – and the issues they are most attracted to revolve around culture."

After Martin assumed the leadership and swore in his new cabinet, he seemed to be shifting his posture closer to the left-nationalists in preparation for the coming election. A small chorus of criticism began from close observers of the Canada-US relationship, specifically over Martin's not having visited Washington soon after his arrival in the PMO. John Manley publicly advised Martin: "Go and pay a visit to Washington, D.C., and meet with the President as soon as he will see you. No more dilly-dallying." Roger Gibbins, president of the Canada West Foundation, said: "Despite what we may think of America or George W. Bush, we need to repair our relationship with the U.S. We can't afford cheap shots. We have too much at stake." And journalist and author Andrew Cohen wrote, "You may not want to go to [Bush's] ranch, but you do want to go to the White House and you want to go now. Presidents and Prime Ministers always meet and you're overdue for that ... Improve the tone. End the chatter from the cheap seats. Idle criticism does us no good in Washington. Discipline your caucus and cabinet and ensure you're singing the same tune."[44]

When Hurricane Katrina struck New Orleans at the end of August 2005, the resultant disaster – with the ensuing offers of emergency assistance from many quarters – came as a relief from the persistent bitter Canada-US atmosphere, like having a death in the family during a long, nasty divorce. One senior Embassy colleague noted informally, "A week ago, we were hunkered down in an atmosphere poisoned by the softwood dispute. Little of that had to do with the technicalities of the dispute but it fed a long-standing Canadian view that we play unfair when it comes to them (we're a bully). This disaster reminded them that in times of crisis we are neighbors and friends, we do help them and they help us. There is at once a genuine, spontaneous outpouring of offers; at the same time the minority government did pause[,] wondering how their offers would be received in the 'softwood climate.' They started getting criticized for not offering (when they actually had but just hadn't made it public). They responded quickly."[45]

Calls offering help streamed in to the Embassy and consulates. By the opening of business on 2 September, we had heard from the prime minister's chief of staff (three times), the chief of defence staff, the public-safety minister, four premiers, the CEO of Air Canada, and the mayor of Ottawa.[46] This wave of sympathy did not, however, wash away the problems in the relationship. After a few days we briefed the USTR:

> The [uncooperative] U.S. response to the ECC [Extraordinary Challenge Committee] decision [on lumber] unleashed a firestorm of indignation both among officials and in the media. In the wake of the BSE crisis, and concerns over "border risk" and growing security requirements, the perception that the U.S. was declining to comply with NAFTA seemed to crystallize fears among free-trade supporters as well as those traditionally ambivalent about economic dependence on the U.S. that NAFTA is no longer enough to secure market access.
>
> These concerns persist in the public debate despite the genuine Canadian outpouring of concern over [the damage caused by Hurricane] Katrina, which has pushed the softwood issue partly into the background. Even Conservative leader Stephen Harper, whose political base is in the usually pro-American West, just called for a special envoy and prompt retaliation on softwood, as well as diversification of trade away from the United States.
>
> Ambassador Wilkins has traveled extensively across Canada in recent weeks and borne much of the brunt of media indignation.[47]

The desire to change the mood in the relationship also encouraged Ambassador Wilkins to hold a bilateral ceremony on the west side of the Embassy grounds to mark the fourth anniversary of the 9/11 attacks. The mutual-support rhetoric even went slightly overboard, giving the speeches a hypocritical ring.[48]

In subsequent weeks, Martin's handling of the relationship with the United States was increasingly pitched to the coming election (in which Martin's Liberals would be defeated on 23 January 2006). When Martin called President Bush on 14 October, our Embassy understood that a show was being put on – the main purpose was "to underscore to the Canadian public that he continues to press the U.S. Government on softwood lumber, i.e. election campaign motivations," and Canadian political rhetoric on softwood was about to escalate.[49] From this point on through election day, the Martin government's behaviour – particularly around COP 11, the multilateral climate-change meeting it hosted in Montreal – was not just hyper-politicized but set to a dumbed-down Americophobic drumbeat designed to win the election by appealing to the worst in Canadians.

LOSING INFLUENCE

A binational poll in the spring of 2005 was interpreted as showing that
Canadians and Americans viewed each other less and less as their country's closest friend and ally. But the poll also seemed to show some convergence in social values between the two populations. Columnist John
Ibbitson summarized it this way:

> The old political establishment needed to believe that somehow, some
> way, Canadians were different from Americans. No, not different, bet-
> ter. Only by convincing ourselves of the innate superiority of Canadi-
> ans' values – multiculturalism, multilateralism, public health care, pub-
> lic education – could we retain our distinct identity. And what was
> that identity? It was those values, of course. The loop closed in on and
> reinforced itself, endlessly, over drinks and dinner, in the university
> seminar and in the newspaper column.
>
> There were only a few thousand people who ever cared about this
> myth, and they all lived within a few blocks of each other in Toronto,
> Ottawa and Montreal. The rest of the country never really bought into
> it. As today's Ipsos-Reid poll reveals, they're buying into it less and
> less. People aren't listening to the establishment any more.[50]

A report from a think-tank event in New York in February 2005 expressed the situation eloquently:

> After weeks of equivocating, the government of Prime Minister Jean
> Chretien jarred the Bush administration when it publicly revealed its
> decision not to join the U.S.-led "coalition of the willing" in the inva-
> sion of Iraq. The announcement, carried live on CNN, was made in the
> House of Commons among cheering MPs, a setting not compatible
> with either the gravity of the decision or the importance of close U.S.-
> Canadian ties ...
>
> Part of the problem has been the continued reluctance of Canadian
> politicians to make a case to the electorate for increased defense
> spending ... Many Canadian politicians pledge to defend their coun-
> try's independence and distinctiveness from the United States, even
> when there is no real menace to either ...
>
> We are witnessing something new in the relationship: the emer-
> gence on the American right of a troubling anti-Canadianism, albeit
> confined to strident voices in the media ... who regularly contrast

American values with those of a soft and self-indulgent Canada. Nonetheless, this misguided impulse pales beside the disturbing and persistent currents of anti-Americanism in Canada [that] thrives on images of a peaceable northern kingdom living apart from the belligerent giant to the south ...

It is by now evident that Canada is losing influence in Washington. There are many reasons for this. The world has changed and Canada has declined in the international political hierarchy ... Much of the current breach in the Canada-U.S. relationship stems from the fact that the collapse of communism deprived us of common purpose, but did not result in the easier, safer world both countries anticipated ... At a time when Canada and the United States need each other more than ever, each has diminished standing in the other's country.[51]

A fundamental part of the dynamic was that too many Canadians saw continental security as being mainly a US problem – that if Canada did anything about security, it would be as a favour to the United States rather than as necessary self-defence. Behind this attitude lay two views. One view was that the United States was going to do all the work anyway, so Canada always had the option of riding along for free. By this logic, anything Canada did was more than it needed to do – it was optional.

The other view was that the whole problem was really America's doing: nobody would attack Canada if it wasn't allied to the United States; security and defence measures were necessary only because of Americans and their actions. The latter view got stronger as 9/11 receded into the past. Public attention focused on the state of the war in Iraq, then became weary of it, and finally turned to criticism of the Bush White House. During this period, anti-American views in Canada were also reinforced by bitterness over the unresolved disputes on softwood and BSE. A majority of Canadian business leaders even said they believed that the hard-line US positions on softwood lumber were a reaction to anti-Americanism in Canada.[52]

OFF THE RAILS

Work released in late November 2005 by the Canadian Defence and Foreign Affairs Institute was very critical of the Martin government's foreign policy. Kim Nossal, Derek Burney (Prime Minister Mulroney's former ambassador to the United States), and others said that the improvement in bilateral relations that the Martin government claimed to call for in its

International Policy Statement could not happen without better leadership. Nossal accused the government of "spinning fantastical castles in the air" with an ambitious "responsibilities agenda" composed of "ideals [that] are nothing more than feel-good and sound-good rhetoric."[53] Burney tore apart the government's handling of relations with the United States. "The most serious deficiency to date in managing Canada's most important bilateral relationship has been the uncertain, erratic policy stewardship from the top," he wrote.

> Real, effective leadership requires signalling top priority – confidently and clearly – to the manner in which we manage relations with the United States ... Talk of greater integration contradicts the more evident fragmentation of foreign policy delivery instruments, whether through the pointless decision to split the integrated department of Foreign Affairs and International Trade, or the sub-contracting of vestiges of foreign policy to the provinces. Nor will adding more resources to Consulates in the United States achieve much if the substance of our relations is skewed by inexplicable decisions on basic policy in Ottawa.
>
> Canada has every right and good reason to be concerned about what the United States will do, unilaterally or otherwise, with its massive military power. But, if we hope to influence the U.S. on decisions of that kind, we need to establish a more mature platform of trust that will facilitate constructive dialogue. We also need to back our positions with commitments in kind. And when we choose to differ, we should learn to express our difference in a manner that can be understood as serving a distinct Canadian interest.
>
> That is where the decision to stand down on Ballistic Missile Defence was most perplexing to Americans and many Canadians alike. It defied logic in terms of either Canadian national sovereignty or security. Who doubts that we are now further than ever from having the degree of trust and respect in Washington that would be required to make the ... commitment to "revitalize" the relationship a reality?[54]

This wave of attacks, coming from a range of media and political sources, did not faze Prime Minister Martin. He seemed to be doing whatever he could to pander to anti-American sentiment by criticizing and irritating the United States during the election campaign. Soon thereafter, his government made a handgun-ban announcement in Toronto that implicitly blamed the United States for violence in Canada.

COP II

But that was just the warm-up for an appallingly hypocritical public slap at the United States, one that Martin made in the presence of Under-Secretary of State Paula Dobriansky and Ambassador David Wilkins in his speech to the climate-change conference in Montreal known as COP 11. Weeks before COP 11, US officials cautioned that the emerging Canadian position for the conference was "dictated solely by politics. The Canadian position is being driven by an aggressive Environment Canada stance and the U.S. Government may have to push back somewhat."[55]

At the time, Environment Canada had a reputation for being staffed by former activists – and lacking the bureaucratic and diplomatic senses to navigate the complex, multi-stakeholder federal and international policy game. In this case, that problem (if real) was combined with the fact that Canada was hosting a major international environmental meeting in the middle of an election campaign, one that the Martin team had decided to fight in America-bashing colours. It was clear to some on the US side that this was likely to become a mess.

At COP 11 Martin preached to a huge multinational audience, "To the reticent nations, including the United States, I say there is such a thing as a global conscience and now is the time to listen to it." This not only singled out the United States for criticism on the most visible of platforms, but also preached to it about "global conscience" as if America lacked a conscience (or wouldn't listen to it), and did it in a crude grab for domestic political gain. And, of course, because there was a Canadian election campaign on, Martin knew that US representatives would bite their tongues and stay quiet, rather than feed the fire by being accused of interfering in Canadian politics.

In our weekly meeting the next day, the ambassador and Embassy staff brushed this off, since it was too late to undo what had happened. We focused our discussion on the substance of climate policy:

> [The public-affairs officer] remarked on how much is happening in the Canadian media that concerns our Mission. The Ambassador opined that we should appear as little as possible given the election campaign.
>
> There was a brief discussion of the historical response to the Kyoto Accord by the United States. President Clinton initially signed the accord and it was submitted to Congress in the last days of his Administration, but did not go to a vote. A resolution by the U.S.

Senate indicated that an accord which did not include reduction targets for all countries would not receive Senate approval, and so President Bush recalled the Accord from Congress.

This led to a discussion of the fundamental conflict in economic policy objectives (in the short run) between economic growth and emissions reduction. Advocates of the Kyoto approach either deny this conflict, or else claim willingness to sacrifice economic growth. The U.S. approach to climate change simply acknowledges that this conflict exists and attempts to resolve it in the longer run through technological change.

A related discussion took place of the trends in U.S. trade with Asia.[56]

Martin's America-bashing was calculated to help him in the election, in which his party was overdue to be tossed out, and for a while it seemed to be paying off in the polling data, so he kept it up. The prime minister even rearranged his schedule to hold a joint appearance at the climate conference with former Democratic President Bill Clinton, who had also been critical of the Bush administration on climate change. As columnist Jeffrey Simpson wrote, "Imagine, circa 1995, how the Chrétien government would have felt had the White House made a big fuss over Brian Mulroney at some conference in Washington."

Martin was deliberately offending a sitting administration of one party, while at the same time going out of his way to cultivate a past president of the other political stripe. There was not even a nod toward the kind of political even-handedness normally to be expected from a head of government, particularly one who was hosting a major international meeting.

RESPONSE

US Ambassador David Wilkins, always gentlemanly, waited until the delegates had gone home from the climate-change talks before he made his one public protest, in which he did not refer to the prime minister directly.

It may be smart election-year politics to thump your chest and constantly criticize your friend and your No. 1 trading partner. But it is a slippery slope, and all of us should hope that it doesn't have a long-term impact on the relationship ... Canada never has to tear down the United States to build itself up.

What if one of your best friends criticized you directly and indirectly almost relentlessly? What if that friend's agenda was to highlight
your perceived flaws while avoiding mentioning your successes? What
if that friend demanded respect but offered little in return? Wouldn't
that begin to sow the seeds of doubt in your mind about the strength
of your friendship? ...

I get election-year politics. I understand political expediency. But
the last time I looked, the United States was not on the ballot for the
January 23 election.[57]

A newspaper editorial discussed the episode, including Martin's response:

What has happened to Paul Martin, the once dignified Liberal leadership candidate who promised to foster closer relations with the United
States? More than two years after that vow, the suave statesman has been
eclipsed by a posturing politician who delivers nationalistic tirades with
exaggerated indignation. It is a distasteful reminder that it is all too easy
to exploit latent anti-American sentiments in the Canadian soul.

And it is all so unnecessary ... [Reacting to Ambassador Wilkins's
speech] Mr. Martin took the low road. He could have responded
diplomatically as the Prime Minister of Canada, soothingly emphasizing the close and supportive relationship between the two nations,
cordially treating the matter as a disagreement between friends.
Instead, in a theatrical retort staged at a lumber mill, Mr. Martin opted
to behave as the scrabbling Liberal candidate – and upped the stakes.
"I will make sure that Canada speaks with an independent voice now,
tomorrow and always," he declaimed.

It was a short-sighted and ungracious performance. And, while it
has backroom Liberal strategists cackling with glee, it has the potential to boomerang. As Toronto pollster Michael Marzolini has
observed, Mr. Martin's tough-talking act could help the Liberals if the
public believes he is defending national sovereignty. But "it could also
cripple the Liberals if he is seen to be picking a fight with our best
friend just to win political points." That is exactly how it appears.[58]

In a staff meeting later that week we considered the situation:

The Deputy Chief of Mission [DCM] noted that while there was frustration in Washington over Prime Minister Martin's remarks last
week, the Ambassador's decision to speak out, and the manner in

which he did so, were his own. The DCM invited comments from the room ... the Liberal Party's predictable "hidden agenda" attacks on Conservative Leader Stephen Harper have begun ... several media outlets have interpreted the Ambassador's "slippery slope" remark as an implied threat ... the Ambassador meant only that emphasizing the negative would have costs.

Six months into the job, the Ambassador's efforts to focus on positive aspects of this bilateral relationship have not been reciprocated ... When there is a positive development, such as on a trade dispute, some Washington players do not want to acknowledge it lest they irritate U.S. industry or other interests, who do not want the impression conveyed that any concession has been made to Canadian pressure.[59]

CHOOSE YOUR CANADA

The Liberal Party's America-bashing strategy reached a crescendo in the weeks just prior to the 23 January 2006 election with a series of half-minute "Choose Your Canada" television advertisements. These implied in various ways that voting for the Liberals was equivalent to voting for Canada, while voting for the Conservatives was somehow voting to become Americans. Following is the text of three of the TV ads, as reported in the *Washington Times* on 2 December 2005:

"Canada may elect the most pro-American leader in the Western world. Harper is pro-Iraq war, anti-Kyoto and socially conservative. Bush's new best friend is the poster boy for his ideal foreign leader. A Harper victory will put a smile on George W. Bush's face. Well, at least someone will be happy, eh?"

"Stephen Harper spoke to a secret, ultra right-wing American think tank. In a Montreal hotel, off limits to press and public, he said, 'America, and particularly your conservative movement, is a light and an inspiration to people in this country and across the world.' No. We did not make that up. We're not allowed to make stuff up."

"Who paid for Stephen Harper's rise to the head of the party? We don't know. He refuses to reveal his donors. What do you suppose he's hiding? We do know he's very popular with right wingers in the U.S. They have money, maybe they helped him. We just don't know. He just won't say."

An item in the same series, and still more insulting to viewer intelligence, was released by the Liberal Party only on its website – not as a paid advertisement – but it was replayed by various media outlets: "Stephen Harper actually announced he wants to increase military presence in our cities. Canadian cities. Soldiers with guns. In our cities. In Canada."

It was clear that the ads had gone too far when parodies circulated just as quickly: "Stephen Harper has a dog. You know who else had a dog? Hitler. Adolf Hitler. That's who. Did Stephen Harper train his dog to attack racial minorities on command? We don't know. He's not saying." And, "In 1963, in Dallas, democratic president John F. Kennedy was shot and killed. Where was four-year-old Stephen Harper? We don't know. He's not saying. We didn't make this up."

It had already been clear at the time of COP 11 in early December that the Liberal Party of Canada was out of energy and integrity – and that the Martin team was prepared to scorch Canada's foreign-policy earth to survive in office. The attack ads tipped the whole business into the realm of comedy and ridicule. US-bashing faded from the Liberal campaign after mid-December.[60]

THE COSTS OF THE MARTIN GOVERNMENT

Columnist Jeffrey Simpson captured the foreign-policy scene at the start of December 2006:

Canada is a moral superpower in its own mind . . . [this conduct] plays well at home, but badly abroad ... Everyone close to the climate-change file knows the dirty truth, and has known it for years: There is absolutely no chance that Canada will meet its [greenhouse gas] emission-reduction commitments by 2012.

Indeed – and this will come as a thundering slap at Canada's habitual moral superiority vis-à-vis the United States – the Americans, under that arch-demon George W. Bush, have slowed their increase in greenhouse-gas emissions faster than Canada has, and might continue to do so up to 2012 – without having signed the Kyoto agreement. From 1990 to 2003, the U.S. increased its emissions by "only" 13.3 percent, compared to 24.2 percent for Canada. Some U.S. states have implemented bolder carbon-emission reduction programs than anything found in Canada.

This U.S. change has occurred, remember, within a political system that Canada's ambassador to Washington recently called "dysfunctional." It also happened in a country against which, in various ways, the Liberal Party is running its campaign ...

And, all the while, the Chrétien-Martin governments kept insisting that Canada was a good and faithful servant of the Kyoto Protocol, knowing privately that it was a lie or a fib (choose your word).

Now, morally superior and brazen to the end, Canada has invited the world to its door, where only good manners prevent guests from exposing their host as a fraud.[61]

As I look back nearly a decade later, my own analysis of the short-lived Paul Martin government and its anti-US 2006 election campaign is that this campaign marked the final disappearance of any credible pretension by Canada to be the United States' best friend. Canada had already effectively lost its status as the United States' closest ally to Britain. That status had long been weakened in any case by the gradual withering of our defence establishment since the 1950s. If we hadn't lost the "closest ally" moniker with the decision to stay out of the Iraq War, then we certainly lost it with the way we revealed that decision to Washington and London. And if not at that time, then we lost it a few months later by refusing – after much delay – to join in the BMD program.

After all this, Canada's list of reasons why it mattered to the United States had been whittled down to "longest border" and "largest trading partner," and it was not clear how long we might hold the latter (versus Mexico or China). In any event, being the largest trading partner does not necessarily count for all that much in foreign-policy terms, not when a power has the list of worldwide political and security concerns that the United States did in the early 2000s.

PERSISTENT REFLEXES

The US-baiting seen in that 2006 election campaign was a behavioural streak inherited from the Chrétien years. It has much in common with the demonology constructed by the left-nationalist wing of the party under Sheila Copps and others. That culture had previously bloomed during the magazine-advertising dispute of 1995–99. While this culture hurt Canada's foreign relations and did nothing for economic policy, it was tolerated in the Liberal Party and then revived by the 2005–06 campaign team under Paul Martin for electoral purposes. It failed only because they overdid it and made it ridiculous, not because it was not fundamentally effective with the Canadian electorate.

This behavioural streak is still latent in the younger generation of the Liberal Party. Questioned by reporters in April 2016 about the propriety of Liberal Party political fundraising events, Prime Minister Justin Trudeau avoided the question by talking about the superiority of Canada's party-financing rules to those in the United States and the role of money in the US political system. The Liberals' deeply ingrained answer to criticism of their governments remains what it was fifty years ago: it is essentially, "Whatever our flaws, we're better than Americans." This is neither a good way to measure Canadian conduct nor healthy for the relationship.

In the Bush administration's second term, the United States began correcting past policy mistakes. It tried, whether well or badly, to restore diplomatic engagement, to face up to climate change, and to mitigate human-rights abuses around detention and interrogation of alleged terror suspects. However slow, late, and inadequate such turnarounds may have been, had Canada been a true friend to the United States, its government would have taken the opportunity to encourage the improvement and work with it.

Instead, Canada's prime minister and governing party chose to manipulate the president's unpopularity in Canada for the sake of a partisan agenda, maliciously demonizing the United States on climate change at COP 11 and then running an election campaign on a nakedly Americophobic platform. This disgraceful and futile behaviour did not save the government at the polls; it succeeded only in telling Americans they had better friends elsewhere in the world. That attitude took root.

In late 2008 a friend of mine, a young Liberal Party intellectual, told me with pride that although he was not a US citizen, he had travelled to the United States to work as a volunteer on the Obama campaign. I have heard through the media that Liberal Party members also organized themselves to do this to support the 2016 Hillary Clinton presidential bid. I have two objections to this. First, it is unethical to meddle in the election campaigns of a democratic jurisdiction where you are neither a citizen nor a resident nor a voter. My friend's reaction when I made this point in 2008 was that the Obama presidential campaign was just too important for him not to be a part of it (in other words, he dismissed the question entirely). Secondly, the risk of a backlash against Canada and Canadians if and when news of such meddling was publicized could easily offset any imaginable benefit to Canadians from influencing a US election in a few localities. Again, deeply political people dismiss such concerns.

What I've learned is that, to the hard-core politically minded, their activities are not really about outcomes and are even less about principles.

It's only about participating in the game. This helps explain to me why I have never felt really comfortable in political circles. It also explains the conduct of so many parties and governments that will disregard principles and outcomes to keep themselves in play.

While Prime Minister Martin inevitably held responsibility for his team's behaviour in 2005–06, one could take a kinder view of events and maintain that the US-baiting was not entirely Paul Martin speaking. It did seem somewhat out of character. Just as Minister Copps's mostly futile escalation of the magazine dispute in the late 1990s did not truly reflect Prime Minister Chrétien's approach to policy, but rather was tolerated by him because it played well on Canada's political left where he needed to hold his support, similarly in 2005–06 the Liberal election strategy and tactics were controlled by a campaign team, and my own suspicion is that Martin let that team continue unimpeded because he was absolutely desperate for support and the strategy and tactics seemed to be working.

PERMANENT DAMAGE

An important distinction between the Copps and Martin fiascos is that the magazine dispute of 1997–99 occurred against a background of otherwise expanding trade and investment, and general good relations between the White House and the Prime Minister's Office, which could rebound from even a very nasty dispute in a single area. The situation in 2005–06 was very different, with a negative background to the relationship on both the economic (softwood and BSE) and political (Iraq and missile-defence) fronts, and a terrible atmosphere at the leadership level. There was less than usual common ground on which to rebuild relations after the politicking was done and the election was over.

In this context, letting the campaign "war room" have its way with Canada-US relations (if that is indeed what happened) was liable to do much greater damage than the magazine dispute had. And it did. Had the Liberal government survived the January 2006 election, I see no way that it could have undone the damage inflicted on the relationship, at least not any earlier than three years later when the Democrats under Barack Obama succeeded to the presidency.

Allan Gotlieb, the former Canadian ambassador to Washington, added to the well-justified criticism of Martin a few days after the 2006 election. "The defeat of Paul Martin's government marks the third time in the past half-century when a Canadian government has fallen after mismanaging the Canada-US relationship. John Diefenbaker's Conservative government made a mess of the defence relationship, Pierre Trudeau's last Liberal government made a mess of the economic relationship and Paul Martin's Liberal government made a mess of the relationship as a whole ... Common sense suggests that Canadians expect their government to be competent in dealing with our paramount international relationship and the source of much of their wealth and prosperity."

If so, it must be said that common sense is mistaken. Populations from Argentina to Zimbabwe show nearly endless willingness to back leaders who blame outsiders – including the most benevolent ones – for the leaders' own ruinous policies. Voters will generally buy into narratives about foreign enemies if the yarn is half well told. The Martin team just did it badly.

Gotlieb went on to list the mistakes he thought Martin's government had made in managing the relationship: downplaying diplomacy, overestimating the role of Congress and of lobbying, undervaluing defence, and so on. In all this criticism of Martin by Gotlieb, Simpson, and other incisive commentators, the faults in the US side's conduct were not completely forgotten, but they were overshadowed by contempt for how the Martin team had behaved.

Adding to the chorus a few weeks later, on his last day as ambassador to Washington, was Frank McKenna. McKenna said that "being gratuitously offensive" had hurt both Canada's image among Washington officials and the Martin government's electoral prospects.[62]

The more Canadians obsess about their relationship with the United States, the less they understand the wider world and deal with it maturely. Columnist Robert Fulford hinted at this point at the close of 2005. "Radical Islamists have declared war on all secular democracies, including Canada, yet we believe there are more important matters on our agenda. In current politics, our relations with the world beyond the United States barely exist – and we see the United States not as democracy's champion but as a malign force whose oppressive trading practices must be fought by brave Canadian politicians ... Canadians have made indifference to this [Islamo-fascist] menace almost a virtue. We have apparently decided that it's an American struggle, promoted by oil-hungry jingoists."[63]

ARRIVAL OF THE HARPER ERA

In mid-January 2006, as the Conservative campaign seemed to be gaining momentum, one of my senior American colleagues asked what the Conservative Party's campaign had been saying on the topic of US-Canada relations. My summary answer was that we should expect very little change on international-trade policy and that "the critical change would not be in policy directions, but in the degree of sincerity ... in dealing with foreign governments including the United States Government."[64]

On 23 January 2006 Stephen Harper's Conservatives won 124 seats (to 103 for Martin's Liberals), beginning five years of minority government by the Conservative Party of Canada, followed by a four-year majority. Harper's reinvented Conservative Party was assumed by both friends and opponents to be both pro-business and pro-American, but it was really neither. Most of Harper's cabinet had no particular sympathy with corporate or urban Canada. Some ministers did have a sincere desire to improve Canada-US relations, but their team did not necessarily possess the sophistication to do it, particularly not in very difficult circumstances, working as they did under the burden of the Global War on Terror, in addition to the burdens of past (IPR, BSE, lumber) and emerging (Keystone pipeline) disputes.

In the first quarter of 2006 our Mission produced three analyses reflecting on the political and economic situation in Canada in the future. One, which was a survey of the role that economic policy had played in the election campaign, correctly guessed that federal-government fiscal deficits were likely to return – particularly if the Conservatives formed the government, because they would cut taxes.[65] A longer analysis written after the election, on "Canada's Evolving Federalism," set some of the new government's challenges in the context of national unity.

> While Canada is a very successful country as judged by socio-economic measures, its federal political system struggles with chronic problems of national unity ... Without an effective Senate or some other mechanism to represent provincial interests, distributing federal dollars is the Government's primary device for assuaging discontented regions and groups. To the extent that provincial leaders succeed in correcting the "fiscal imbalance" in their favor, they will be weakening Canada's federal glue.
>
> Alternatively, incoming Conservative Prime Minister Stephen Harper may manage to construct a different uniting vision of Canada which is more respectful of the constitutional division of powers. But the unity challenges Harper faces are multi-dimensional, including the sharp socio-economic divide between Canada's industrialized and resource-based regions, and a political divide between urban and rural areas (Harper's caucus has no representatives from any of the three largest cities) ...

During the constitutional turbulence of the early 1990s, the Government shifted somewhat from its usual strategy of warning about the dire consequences should its constitutional project fail, and turned toward emphasizing the economic benefits of Canada's federal system. These benefits are significant, including a large internal market, efficiencies in regulation and other federal government services, shared defense, and greater negotiating strength with international partners. But this argument was (and still is) weakened by decades of low investment in defense, persistent inter-provincial trade and labor barriers, low socio-economic status of native peoples, and mismanagement of ocean fisheries.[66]

DISSECTING THE CONSERVATIVES

In March 2006 a cable from the Consulate in Calgary examined the ideology of the Harper Conservatives' intellectual mentors at the University of Calgary:

> Their group has for more than 20 years now been arguing for fundamental changes that would realign the balance of federal-provincial powers and the relationship of government to the individual ... The group opined that PM Harper has already made a shift to "the left" to gain Canadian electoral support ... The "shift" to the left does not appear to have ruffled many feathers among Albertans.
>
> The group suggested that Albertans are more satisfied with the fact that they now have a voice through a western elected Prime Minister, and are not particularly concerned about what PM Harper might do on a national level. The bottom line ... is one of reducing the federal government's influence on the lives and pocketbooks of Albertans who, according to the group, simply "want to be left alone" ... the group made no apologies for the province's embarrassing riches or how they would be spent, and there was general consensus that the provinces need more autonomy with respect to how transfer monies are spent ...
>
> If the comments we heard are any indication, the PM can expect to have a wide latitude to build a national consensus for his party – even tilting a little to the left – without eroding his base support in Alberta.[67]

On the morning after the January 2006 election, an official in our Consulate in Quebec City commented on the extent to which Quebecers had voted Conservative, particularly in the Quebec City region.

They voted Conservative because they desperately wanted the Liberals out of power in Ottawa, and they believed this could only be done if some of the Quebec ridings went to the Conservatives. It was a purely strategic vote. They were not particularly voting against the Bloc Quebecois (although we see by yesterday's vote that there is no strong brand loyalty to the Bloc). "We've still got enough Bloc deputies to look out for Quebec interests in case the Conservatives don't deliver," one person told me. Quebec voters are now waiting to see if the Conservatives will deliver what they promised to Quebec – lower taxes and fixing the fiscal imbalance, for starters ... Quebec voters showed us once again that "leaving Canada" is not what drives them ... They want Canada to work for them, and they are willing to give Harper a chance.[68]

HOPES FOR HARPER

There were great hopes on both sides that the change in Canadian leadership would improve Canada-US relations. One US writer glowed, "Mr. Harper, unlike Mr. Martin, respects the United States ... That's why Americans should rejoice in the crowning of Canada's new, dynamic prime minister."[69]

We at the Embassy spent much of February 2007 analyzing the state of Canada at this turning point, watching the new government take shape and speculating about its directions. An example is my record of a lunch in mid-month with an energy/environment consultant who said:

The challenge is to better integrate and reconcile what business wants with what the rest of the body politic wants. Harper's nature is not to compartmentalize [issues] (what Martin tended to do) but to integrate, so that actions in various areas will be compatible with each other and will achieve common goals.

Arrival of Jim Prentice, the new Minister of Indian Affairs and Northern Development, is excellent news. He understands native affairs, northern development, and the oil and gas scene. He will integrate these different considerations, which is necessary in order for big projects (notably the Mackenzie Gas Project) to truly succeed. Big projects are not just about business objectives; they have many other dimensions. The pipeline is not just a corporate timeline past a string of regulatory points; it is about native self-government and the whole course of northern development ...

On climate change, the Department of Finance has been made a full partner, to be engaged on all decisions on this file. This will help

end the NRCan-Environment battle, and integrate climate change policy better with economic policy generally.[70]

By the beginning of May 2006, our Public Affairs Section said that the
bilateral situation showed great improvement over a year earlier, and that
the outlines of an agreement on softwood lumber, which had been negotiated in the rough in April, felt like a turning point.

> Many contacts in Ottawa are telling us that this is a major break-
> through in the relationship. Media play, albeit grudgingly in some
> cases, has also embraced the softwood agreement as a major advance
> in the relationship. The Embassy will embark this week on a major
> initiative to highlight the positive tone we have heard in the relation-
> ship since the President and the Prime Minister met in Cancun at the
> end of March, with particular emphasis on the softwood lumber reso-
> lution. We expect to maintain this initiative through the lead up to
> the next official visit ...
>   Talking point for emphasis: Think back a year ago. The big issues
> on the bilateral agenda were BSE and softwood lumber. Those were
> two huge irritants in the bilateral relationship. Our governments
> worked together and got BSE settled and off the bilateral agenda. Now,
> our governments have worked together and hammered out a deal that
> will resolve the divisive softwood lumber issue and end the costly liti-
> gation for at least seven years.
>   But think back further for just a moment. Remember Pacific
> salmon? And PEI potatoes? We solved those issues also. Because that's
> what friends and neighbors do.[71]

At long last it was again possible to tout the positives in the relationship
– as Ambassador David Wilkins had struggled to do in his early months
in the job, against the unhelpful backdrop of the Martin government.

HARPER'S ECONOMIC AGENDA

I accompanied Ambassador Wilkins on several of his courtesy calls to
meet members of the new cabinet. Two of the senior ministers we saw
were Treasury Board President John Baird and Finance Minister Jim
Flaherty, both veterans of the Progressive Conservative governments in
Ontario a few years earlier. Baird made little impression at the time;
our main talking point with him was to applaud signs of military-

procurement initiatives by Canada. Flaherty had more to discuss and he struck me as a more thoughtful type, with a broad perspective on the country's situation.

Flaherty, an experienced and successful provincial politician, was frank about plans to address the complex of issues surrounding federal-provincial tax and fiscal arrangements. "The equalization system had a sound basis originally, but the Liberals did one-off, asymmetric deals with individual provinces. It can't work that way." The new government is already having discussions about this and PM Harper is "thinking about who does what and who pays for it."

In Flaherty's personal view, "the government that wants to spend the money should raise it. I'm not a fan of transfers as a routine matter." Such transfers, he said, create "insidious intrusion" which the provinces are right to dislike and which is especially irritating to Quebec. "We need to get away from this intrusive federalism. We have enough responsibilities of our own in defence, foreign affairs, banking, monetary policy" and other areas.

Our report commented, "The Conservatives came into power promising to 'fix' the 'vertical fiscal imbalance' between the federal and provincial governments. Flaherty's comments sound surprisingly similar to the view among Finance officials that there is no such imbalance: sub-federal governments have the authority to raise needed revenues through taxation if they choose to do so."[72]

A conversation I had a few weeks later with a senior Alberta government official echoed Flaherty's remarks about fiscal federalism:

[On health care] Former PM Martin "gave away the store" to provinces two years ago. So funding from the Government of Canada is okay right now. Still, this doesn't solve the basic economic trend in health care costs: inevitably provinces will have to look at major change.

[On fiscal imbalance] Alberta is not complaining about being a "have" province and putting money into the system, but there has to be a system – not a bunch of one-off deals like former PM Martin started cutting. Martin "gave away the federation for seven seats in Newfoundland." You can't run a country that way.

[On international representation] Alberta's office in Canadian Embassy Washington is up and running. A top concern is managing the Government of Canada's tendency to talk about the oilsands internationally. "The Government of Canada does not control the oilsands and has no expertise on them." On cultural diversity at UNESCO, the federal government allowed Quebec equal time as long as its message was the same as the federal one. Alberta could have stopped this by demanding equal time to deliver an opposite message [on UNESCO]. Alberta doesn't mind Quebec having an international platform, but Alberta expects to receive the same treatment.[73]

THE CONSERVATIVES' FIRST BUDGET

With hindsight, the 2 May 2006 budget had the mark of the Harper government's style – even though it had to be crafted to obtain support from other parties in a minority Parliament. Our report read:

This budget was designed for popular appeal rather than economic principle ... there is little room for error if the economy turns downward. Economists, while generally positive, judged that the budget will mildly boost an economy which is already running at full capacity. This means that tight restraint on other spending commitments will be needed in order to contain inflationary pressure and limit the need for interest rate hikes. Even so, the appreciating Canadian dollar seems set to continue its climb above 90 U.S. cents. This will deepen the rift between sectors which are prospering (energy, commodities) and those suffering (manufacturing, tourism) ...

While it put the government's tax-cut and "frugality" messages foremost, Flaherty's budget speech also outlined a range of major spending promises [for infrastructure, child-care allowance, defence, farm support, housing], with little mention of the offsetting cuts which these imply ... Cuts are expected in public sector labor agreements, programs for native communities and the environment ...

The current mix of high energy costs, tight labor markets, rising interest rates and currency appreciation (not to mention global competition) has been especially painful for central Canada's manufacturing base, and for them, no relief is in sight.[74]

I appended my personal views in an accompanying e-mail to contacts at Treasury and State:

The sub-text here is that the Harper government is beginning a long-term rearrangement of the distribution of federal and provincial government roles in Canada – an effort that they will continue more openly if they remain in power. The see it as an effort to restore the balance of powers contemplated in the Constitution, focusing the federal government more on defense, foreign affairs, natives and oceans, and less on nationwide socioeconomic policies and programs ...

I am more concerned than most observers about the downside risks to the economy and to the fiscal balance. A macroeconomic downturn is a significant possibility, particularly now that the stage is set for more monetary tightening and a near end to the housing boom. The Conservatives have announced a swathe of tax cuts and spending plans with virtually no details on offsetting cuts to spending. Their party has a poor track record of maintaining fiscal balance – neither the federal Conservatives in the Mulroney years, nor the [Conservative Ontario Premier] Mike Harris team on which Flaherty served as Ontario's finance minister. The net result is that all the risks to the economic and fiscal picture are on the downside now, and their likelihood has moved upward a big notch over the past week.[75]

Regardless of the Harper government's later rhetoric about Canada being an island of economic stability during the financial crisis, and its endless self-branding as the party Canadians could trust with the economy, the stability through the 2007–09 crisis had much more to do with Canada's having an old-fashioned conservative banking system – one that had not overextended credit – than with the government's management.

For Prime Minister Harper, what mattered most in 2006–07 was how to move up from minority to majority government. The Harper team rolled out an election budget and a "green plan" in the spring of 2007 with plans to go to the polls, but, as one of my colleagues put it, "the numbers never quite got there and Quebec went squishy every time something bad happened in Afghanistan."

Preston Manning, the prime minister's political mentor, told a US official that the environment and climate change would not be important priorities for Harper with a majority, since he was not convinced either that climate change mattered or that the public would continue to care about it. On the other hand, the prime minister was a believer in the effort in Afghanistan. Politically, Manning noted, Harper's team faced difficult challenges: selling themselves in the Toronto area to win seats; addressing the loss of industry in southern Ontario; repairing relations with the (nominally but not very Conservative) Maritime premiers and also those in the west who were irritated by the party's lip service to the climate issue; fixing a rift between two wings of the party (coast versus interior) in British Columbia; and addressing relations with Bay Street.

THE HARPER GOVERNMENT AND THE ECONOMY

In May 2007 I sent Washington a twenty-one-paragraph message titled "Main Street vs. Bay Street: The Harper Government and Canadian Business" that blurred the line between economic and political work. It was designed to protect US government officials from having a too-simplistic view of the Harper team as being merely a reincarnation of Brian Mulroney's business-friendly (and America-friendly) government.

The report explained the Harper Conservatives' background as populist Reformers, showing how Harper's party was the result of the takeover of a remnant of Mulroney's party by a populist protest movement (a point many Americans working on Canadian files might not realize). We pointed out that the January 2006 election that brought Harper to power produced a striking rural-urban split. Voters elected no Conservatives from any of the country's three largest cities, where most of Canada's corporate and financial interests were based.

In its minority phase the government had already taken a series of measures that were perceived as being anti-business: a somewhat more confrontational stance toward China on human rights, attacking banking fees, ending the tax break for income trusts, and promising to change the tax-deductibility of interest paid on loans to finance business operations abroad. These were not so much deliberate decisions to challenge big business as reflections of the lack of corporate and urban representation in the new government. This was compounded by the fact that the Harper team – which entered office preoccupied with ethics and "accountability" – had made itself inaccessible to business associations and lobbyists who represented integrated North American business interests in Ottawa and who did so much to inform and guide economic policy.

This lack of accessibility to business, combined with the government's related lack of sophistication about foreign relations, could potentially make US-Canada economic-policy coordination more difficult:

A string of Harper government moves ... have highlighted just how little this western-based, minority government has in common with big businesses. This gap has been reinforced by the tightness of Harper's control within the government and his team's emphasis on "accountability." Business representatives say this rigid, closed operating atmosphere leaves them unable to communicate with and influence the government through their accustomed lobbying channels.

Conservative Party apologists say that Harper's operating style serves his top priority, which is to win a majority of seats in Parliament in the next election (likely in 2008), after which (they suggest) better balance with the business community can be restored and broader economic goals can be pursued. We are skeptical of this view because we see the government's various discords with business as stemming from the Conservative caucus' essential political character, rather than from strategic choice.[76]

Reform Party founder Preston Manning told American contacts that, once a secure majority was gained, Harper would like to focus on competitiveness vis-à-vis the United States (leaner regulation, lower taxes, better education), relations with the United States, the war in Afghanistan, and the law-and-order agenda (even though crime was declining and the subject did not resonate with most Canadians).

BACK TO THE STATE, AND AWAY FROM CONTINENTALISM

A prescient conservative friend – who vividly remembered the 1970s, and had just attended some economic-policy discussions inside the Canadian federal government – warned me in 2005 of an intellectual trend back toward government activism and protectionism, a trend that was centred in the Ontario establishment. I made some notes on the conversation for my colleagues:

Canada's free trade era is truly over. A participant in these discussions says that their parameters have come full circle: monopoly is acceptable again, protectionism is warranted, and it is government's job to shape the economy ... the productivity gap has disappeared from public policy debate.

Partly, the governing Liberal Party has simply reverted to its traditional mission statement – that only the Liberal Party can save Canadians from (1) becoming Americans and (2) being broken up by separatists. This fear-mongering intensifies when the Liberal Party is under stress and/or an election approaches ... Voter fatigue threatens this approach. Eventually you just get so weary of being threatened with something that you may decide to throw caution to the wind and take the consequences ...

North America's economic centre of gravity has moved southward and westward. The southern Ontario establishment ("Bay Street"), which controls the Party and thus the country, senses that over the past generation it has lost economic and social influence on the continent. Open markets – as tested since 1989 by the FTA and NAFTA – have not extended this elite's power. So it is reaching instead for the levers of government. And it has lost interest in federalism ... there is no Canadian elite, only an Ontario elite which holds a controlling interest in the federal system.[77]

While that Ontario elite was pushed further out of power at the federal level in Canada from 2006 to 2015 by the western-based, Conservative government of Stephen Harper, the arrival of the Kathleen Wynne government in Ontario in 2013 and the Justin Trudeau government in Ottawa in 2015 appeared to bring this predicted trend – the old elite reaching for the levers of power – to fruition. Under these governments, advocates and lobbyists almost completely stopped talking the language of economic concepts such as competitiveness, market mechanisms, value-added, or productivity in their conversations, because these words, which had been mainstream in the 1990s in Canada as in the United States, were now completely out of intellectual favour. There was no longer much interest in conversations about the sources of wealth generation or economic growth. These were governments with, at least for the most part, social and environmental agendas, mixed with a misplaced trust that economic problems could be resolved by new technologies.

THE HARPER GOVERNMENT AND THE WORLD

Back in the second half of 2007, on greenhouse gases (GHG) and climate change, the United States was beginning to look considerably more progressive than Canada. Former Prime Minister Paul Martin's gratuitous attack on the United States at COP 11 in Montreal had embarrassed most Canadians who knew anything about foreign relations or about Canada's actual GHG-emissions profile. Canada was a huge per-capita fossil-fuel consumer and GHG emitter, no better than the United States. At least American officials were trying to lead a "Major Economies Process," pulling together the world's big economic powers to work on GHG reduction, while Martin had only wanted to preach and Prime Minister Harper made it clear that he wanted to ignore the climate issue altogether.

While the bilateral atmosphere was inevitably somewhat cleared by the Martin-Harper transition, there was not much greater basis for renewed collaboration under Canada's new government. With the Bush administration still in office, there was no turnaround in Canadians' desire for such collaboration, either. An analyst from the State Department's Intelligence and Research Bureau wrote an informal comment on Canadian public opinion in December 2007:

Of long standing [are] the preference for multilateral solutions to ones led by U.S., [a] view of world as one much more benign where Canada can be do-gooder via development aid, environmental protection, peacekeeping troop contributions, and international law. The facts may be greatly at variance with that in the sense that in per capita terms Canada is like 30th in peacekeeping, behind likes of Uruguay, Chile, or Argentina. The inclination to want to pull down the shades and make threats of weapons of mass destruction, terrorism, energy shortages, an aggressive China or North Korea, Iran, go away are strong, just as for European publics ... there is an equally great inclination toward isolationism and non-engagement in world affairs on tough problems that may require a security response, troops in harm's way or killed, and that are tough sell in domestic political terms ... Canadians, like Spaniards and others[,] would love to believe that we live in a world of nice herbivores and not one with threatening carnivores.

For instance, in the Pew 2007 poll, 70% disagreed with [Bush's] management of world affairs, 92% were concerned about Iranian nukes, yet majorities wanted to "let the UN do it," which as we saw in Balkans, Rwanda and elsewhere looks better on paper than in reality. Note in Pew and EKOS polling re: Canadian troops in Afghanistan, 49% said pull troops out now. Originally, there was about 75% support for that mission but over time, that has fallen by 25–30 points and views are closely divided. On [counter-terrorism], you get a similar erosion: in 2002 68% supported our counterterrorism policies, but that was down to just 38% this Spring. Six-in-ten in recent years have thought the world was more dangerous but fewer than 20% perceived threat for Canada from terrorism (that dropped each successive year after 9/11 ...

Intrinsic anti-Americanism ... is much more a reflection of animus toward POTUS, USG [President Bush and the US government] post-Iraq.

U.S. image in 2002 was 72% favorable, much as it was throughout the
Bush 41 and Clinton years. That dipped steadily to 63% in 2005 and
55% now ... And some polls suggest that concern over "Americaniza-
tion" ... was greater in the 1990s than in the last 5 years.

On some polling indicators Canadians do indeed look more like
West Europeans than Americans – for instance in their median political ideology (more centre-left), on balance more secular, views on welfare state and taxes, death penalty, gay marriage, abortion, immigration, decriminalization of drugs ... environment and social
development being greater world threats than WMD and terrorism ...

Then lastly there is that "cannot be seen as too pro-U.S." factor in
Canada ... When Americans are asked which country is key foreign
relationship, UK wins hands down. When Canadians are asked, it is
U.S. by 3 or 4:1, then UK, Australia. So when one is seen too much as
"U.S. agent," [you] have to invent a non-issue like the Arctic or some-
thing else to prove that you are not really pushing for inclusion of
Canada as 51st State.[78]

Few were surprised that a survey released in September 2007 by the
International Institute of Strategic Studies found that the United States
was losing power and prestige around the world, largely because of its failure in Iraq. "It was evident that the exercise of military power – in which,
on paper, America dominated the world – had not secured its goal ... The
restoration of American strategic authority seemed bound to take much
longer than the mere installation of a new President."[79] A senior colleague
commented: "Some European and Canadian intellectuals think this development is long overdue and that more power and influence by Russia,
Iran, India, and the like, is a good replacement for U.S. power."[80]

Diplomats who had direct experience with the governments and power
structures of such countries could more readily grasp the human cost of
such a global shift of control. Canadians who think that a world with a
weaker United States will somehow be empowering for Canada perhaps
do not understand that Canada's success and security for the past hundred
years has depended on the United States. Its influence with other countries still depends on influencing the United States, and its ability to do
this has been falling for decades. It is hard to see how a weaker United
States could possibly benefit Canada.

6

Smaller in the World

United States-Canada relations began centuries ago with a lengthy period of conflict and competition. European powers battled for colonial territory in North America, and their colonies and successors skirmished along frontiers. This started before the Seven Years' War of 1756–63, and it gradually wound down in the late nineteenth century with the closing of the western interior wilderness and resolution of the territorial boundaries between the two countries.

A great period of alliance, collaboration, and institution building followed. This phase was foreshadowed by the 1854 Reciprocity Treaty (which was abrogated a few years later) and truly got underway with the 1909 Boundary Waters Treaty and the creation of the International Joint Commission a decade afterwards; galvanized by external threats, it reached its height in the mid-twentieth century. The period of collaboration weakened in more secure times under prime ministers John Diefenbaker, Lester Pearson, and Pierre Trudeau. It had a revival under Brian Mulroney and an extension under Jean Chrétien.

We are now apparently in a third phase, in which the two countries (at least for the time being) are neither in serious conflict with each other nor united by external threats that we perceive similarly. We are still formally allied and continue to work together in routine ways, but the era of ambitious collaboration and of building up our shared institutions may be largely over.

For a few years until 2001, at least some North American economic officials foresaw the eventual fading away of the Canada-US border. As in Europe, the removal of border posts and controls was seen as being possible with no great compromise of territorial sovereignty. While this vision was tenuously realized in Europe, it is now in real peril there. In North America it seems to have been lost since 2001.

NUMBER ONE

The United States is, and will likely remain for a long time, the world's leading power, or one of two such powers. Americans built a great and durable system of alliances and partnerships that includes some sixty countries collectively accounting for two-thirds of global economic output and military capacity. Americans also possess immense military and diplomatic assets of their own, neither of which any other country is close to matching. Some Canadians appear to believe that their own country is universally admired, much more so than the United States, and that this somehow offsets the difference in hard power, but that is wishful thinking.

The truth is that most of the rest of the world is barely aware of Canada at all (except possibly through a few symbols and celebrities), while the United States of America is universally recognized – whether positively or negatively – and continues to have iconic appeal to the rest of the world as an ally, an economic partner, and a place in which to invest, to visit, to study and live in, and to emulate. This appeal is not a mistake or delusion and it is not an accident. It has been earned by America's offering people opportunity and freedom, whether the country's detractors like to admit this or not. True, Canada has some of this appeal as well, but it not so widely noticed, and not enough to give us any practical advantage over any other country in conducting our international affairs, certainly not compared with the United States.[1]

Canada's relevance to its big neighbour declined during the sixteen years of the Bill Clinton and George W. Bush administrations, from 1993 to 2009, and that decline accelerated after 2001. The military and security side of this decline may have been impractical for Canadian leaders to avoid, since the shrinkage of military capacity has been a bipartisan trend for decades and thus presumably hard for any one leader to reverse.

AVOIDABLE

But the political and psychological side of the decline in Canada's relevance and stature in the United States was plainly avoidable on the part of Canada's governments. They did not need to spend years deliberately portraying America's rich, free, and creative media world as an imperializing monoculture that deserved to be resisted around the world through government controls. They did not need to dawdle over the Iraq and BMD decisions – Americans, like most of us, prefer honest, forthright differences over waffling or false acquiescence. They did not need to disparage the United States and its president gratuitously and misrepresent its policies in front of international audiences. They did not need to kick and scream about the WHTI passport requirement. The unnecessary, cumulative result of all this was a decline in respect for Canada in Washington and elsewhere.

Whether or not it had to happen, and whatever one thinks of the United States, this decline in relevance and respect matters for Canada. It was not the end of the world, and Canadians can choose to allow and accept it, but they should not delude themselves that it has no costs. The United States is more influential than Canada is in global human, technological, and environmental affairs, by a factor of much greater than ten. Feeling morally superior and imagining that the world loves them will not begin to compensate Canadians on any practical level for losing relevance as a friend and ally to this power. To the extent that the decline in relevance was the result of Canada's own bad management, as it partly was, Canadians should have done their best to prevent or at least avoid accelerating that decline.

Canada had an impressive economic, demographic, and military rise from the 1860s to the 1960s: it went from being an assortment of dispersed, weak colonies to being a G-7 power alongside Britain and the United States. But this was not all Canada's doing. In part, Canada rode along on the economic, demographic, and military coattails of the United States of America, the Anglo-American alliance and its victory in the greatest war in history, and the West that grew from that victory. Canada made the most of this good luck by building a constructive relationship with, and integrating with, the United States (and the international order that it backed) throughout the twentieth century – from the pioneering environmental diplomacy of the 1909 Boundary Waters Treaty to the 1994 North American Free Trade Agreement. Canadians should not forget how wonderfully this combination of strategy and good luck succeeded for them, as well as for their closest neighbour and ally.

MANAGING PHASE THREE

Since the late 1990s, both parts of this combination – the ascendancy of North America, and Canada's integration into it – have struggled. Both remain robust, and will probably endure, but they do not seem likely to strengthen as they did in the past. Canada can play only a small role in determining whether the alliance system and the West continue to succeed. But Canada's integration into North America, the alliance system, and the global institutions in which the United States continues to be influential is something that Canadians can do much about. The less they can steer the first, the more reason to work on the second.

In the game of being integrated with and relevant to the United States after the end of the Cold War, Canada handled some things quite well, such as the FTA, NAFTA, and the 2001 border accords. Some things went badly more or less through the fault of the United States, such as the disputes over softwood lumber, cattle and beef, and aspects of the thickening of the border. Canadians had little choice but to suffer through these and manage them as well as they could, minimizing the collateral damage to the rest of the relationship, and this they usually did.

But Canada also handled too many things poorly. These include the magazine dispute, the response to the WHTI, the decision on BMD, intellectual-property protection, and, most unfortunately, Canadians' unnecessarily insulting displays of anti-Americanism, including by political leaders but of which so many were guilty every day in smaller (though still inexcusable) ways.

BIGOTRY CARRIES COSTS

Some Canadians, at least some of the time, hold negative stereotypes of and prejudices against Americans and are even willing to express these sentiments publicly. This is objectively immoral, it is inconsistent with Canadian values, and it is abusive and offensive to others. Every Canadian has as much moral reason to resist it as they do to resist misogyny, Islamophobia, or white supremacism.

Stereotyping and prejudice hurt human beings, among other ways by preventing us from understanding others. For Canada, failing to understand the United States is no small mistake. It is far costlier than failing to understand other nations, such as Saudi Arabia, Pakistan, Iran, or Israel.

Both Americans and Canadians have cults of themselves. These national cults, a form of egotism, can be serious impediments to relationships. We human beings generally gain by trying to see ourselves as others see us and accepting the legitimacy of those others' viewpoints, even if what they see is not as flattering as we think is warranted. Many US officials, not only in the State Department but also in Commerce, the military, and other arms of government, make efforts to do this with respect to their nation's role in the world, to their great credit. I cannot say whether Canadian officials make similar efforts, rather than pander to the national self-image, but I hope they do.

The impulse to nurse ethnic tribalism and historical resentment, without focusing on making constructive plans to move beyond these things and build something bigger and more inclusive, can be harmful. In Quebec's case, for example, it has been corrosive to the integrity of both anglophone and francophone Canada, and certainly has alienated investors and immigrants, while delivering questionable benefits for Quebecers.

Canadians can identify these resentments as a fault in others, whether in Quebecers, in other groups within Canada, or in the Balkans or in the Middle East. So they should be able to see how nursing their *own* resentments against the United States, resentments that have been reinforced for more than two hundred years, and failing to transcend them and build better, more secure partnerships and institutions will drive opportunities away and produce nothing at all of lasting value.

SECURITY, REAL AND PERCEIVED

The George W. Bush administration's so-called Global War on Terror, which came to be extended far beyond an effort to combat the causes of the September 2001 attacks, and the war in Iraq that the GWOT rationalized, largely reversed Canadians' and Europeans' mood of solidarity with the United States on and immediately after 9/11.

US diplomatic leadership in the international system survived and partially recovered, beginning in the late part of the Bush administration and continuing under Barack Obama's. That recovery reflects not just changes in US political leadership but also the deep strength of America's diplomacy, its system of alliances, its economy, and its enduring cultural appeal, all of which give the United States' paramount position in the world considerable resilience and durability.

One of the pernicious effects of the Global War on Terror and the Iraq War for Canada is that they have strengthened the sentiment of those who said on 9/11 that America had it coming. The episode, combined with Canadians' delusion that they are universally valued and that this confers some kind of practical asset in the world, encourages a conceit that international security problems are essentially America's fault and Canada can disown them – that, with the maple leaf on their backpacks, Canadians should be able to travel, safe and respected, anywhere. As tempting as this idea is to some people, it does not reflect the reality of their security situation, nor does it reflect the true position of the United States and Canada in the world.

On the other hand, taking realistic, hard-headed, clear-sighted responsibility for oneself, and being seen to be doing so, free of myths and delusions and foolish cults of moral superiority, is the foundation of security. It also builds value and credibility with others.

Even a credible show of assuming such responsibility would reduce the risk of Americans thinking that a perceived threat to US security, a threat that involved Canadian territory, would require US intervention in Canada for both countries' sake – because Americans think Canada is not willing or able to handle the situation. Taking vigilant responsibility for Canada's security in the world and particularly in North America, and showing consistent respect for US security concerns even when Canadians do not agree with them, would help protect Canada from such a crisis occurring in the first place and mitigate the likelihood that the United States might intervene if it did occur.

The continental "perimeter" concept that was floated around 2000–01 has value for Canada and should be kept in mind in case an opportunity for its revival arises. Perhaps, just as cross-border trade liberalization had a false start in the 1850s and then enjoyed its heyday more than a century later, so the perimeter concept's failure in the early 2000s could presage a success to come farther down the road.

THE PATH FORWARD

It appears that the main fact of Canadian foreign policy in this new century is that the country matters less than it used to. To other powers, Canada is not relevant territorially or militarily, is slow-growing economically, and is not much of a competitive threat. Generally speaking, unless a country needs some very specific Canadian export product, or needs to marshal one more vote at an international meeting, there are not many strong reasons to have Canada as a friend or strategic partner.

On the other hand, there remain many strong reasons to want the United States as a friend. If America might disengage from your country or your region, for the most part you probably have much to lose. There is very competitive lobbying to keep such engagement, and there are even incentives, particularly for small states, to make trouble to get America's attention, because America matters to nearly everyone.

There will continue to be important things Canada requires from the United States, but Canada will have fewer levers to keep US administrations engaged and Washington now sees reduced value in this relationship. While Canada has many shared arrangements with the United States, these are not levers except if Canada threatens to withdraw from them, which it cannot credibly do because generally that would hurt Canada much more than it would hurt the United States. Tantrums and threats may work for armed rogue states with weapons and weak neighbours, but it should be obvious that they are not credible from Canada and so will not work.

Yes, Canada has big, persistent shared challenges with the United States, on which we have trouble agreeing. But, whatever resentments there may be, preaching to or blaming the big neighbour is futile. More than ever, America has different problems than Canada does, and is unlikely to care what Canadians think.

Epilogue

This book chronicles events in the US-Canada relationship under the Bush 41, Clinton, and Bush 43 administrations and sets those events in the longer context of the post-1945 international order. It was completed in the closing weeks of the Obama administration and then edited early in the Trump era. By the spring of 2017, it seemed likely that, after seventy-five years, US influence and leadership in the international order had seen its peak. In the decade from the mid-term elections of 2006 to Donald Trump's election as president in 2016, this was not so clear.

I visited Washington for a few weeks around the time of Barack Obama's victory in the US presidential election in the fall of 2008. During quiet dark fall evenings I recorded my thoughts, at greater length than usual, in my diary.

> *October* 29: Very pessimistic conversation over dinner this evening with my Ottawa colleague, who is here at Foreign Service Institute ...
>
> My colleague and his classmates, some of whom are from African and/or Muslim countries, are being drilled to defend themselves against hostile questions about U.S. policies and actions and about why they work for the U.S. I ran him through the history of my 18 years with the State Department – from 1990, when we were still living down the U.S.'s support of dictators, Vietnam, Chile, Nicaragua, Ollie North, but when at least the West's economic and political systems were seemingly vindicated by Communism's failure and everyone had an interest in being America's friend; to the upswing brought by the Clintons and their interest in a social agenda and a more outward-looking, friendlier foreign policy; to the moment after 9/11 when the world rallied emotionally and morally behind the USA.

I told him that, for what the present administration did to this leadership, to this advantage, squandered is too gentle a word. They torched it ...

My colleague agreed. The Administration's policies are an utter failure, he said, a waste of trillions, and he doubted whether we are safer ...

If Obama wins, my colleague said, he inherits a dish of poison. Expectations are too high. Africans see an Obama presidency in nearly messianic terms. Millions of others simply think that as soon as Bush is gone, everything will be okay, and we can go back to the way things used to be. But Obama will face insuperable problems and wildly unrealistic expectations. In six months to a year, my colleague fears, this will give way to resentment: "you can't change Americans, it doesn't matter who you put at the top, nothing really changes, they exported their financial mess to us," etc. And Obama will share the blame.

I said that being historically aware, I had always expected an empire to overreach, and that I know all too well that predictions most often go wrong by shortening their time frame; but that nevertheless I expect a period of significant pulling-back of the U.S. from international engagement. He agreed, and moreover thinks it's already begun; the next President will find himself in the middle of it and will be riding it. America's downsizing, he said, could even become a headlong rush for the exits by America's many allies, partners and parasites.

He said he is most worried that with this could come isolationism, a resentment at the world for not accepting U.S. efforts to lead. I told him I'm less worried about this (though I am concerned about economic isolationism and protectionism); that just as Americans seem to have a popular sense of complicity in the mortgage crisis, they also may have a similar sense of complicity in their foreign policy failures, and they may know better than to blame the rest of the world for them.

November 3: After this visit, at the end of eight dreadful years, I believe in America more than ever. I feel as free here as I do at home. I feel like I can belong here. I feel that this society, perhaps even more than my own, is committed to advancing the values I hold.[1]

A few hours later I watched Obama's election win on television in a crowded bar in downtown Washington. The concession speech by his opponent, John McCain, was magnificent: dignified, graceful, and patriotic. Afterwards, I strolled through the small and quiet clumps of people gathered on the street just north of the White House. The mood I remember, in myself and in the city, was one of relief and hope.

While the George W. Bush administration had done lasting damage to America's influence and leadership, recovery seemed possible in November 2008. After all, America has always been dynamic and resilient. The world mostly blamed the Bush team and not the country. The Western-led order still operated. In the end, the Obama team might not have entirely stopped the decline and retraction of American military, financial, political, social, and diplomatic power, but, in the face of incredibly difficult circumstances, they at least made it more orderly and respectable. There was a chance that, with fortuitous events, the next presidency or two could even partly reverse the trend. My analysis in this book therefore implicitly assumed that the ongoing decline in US influence would probably continue, but that the decline was not certain and would be less dramatic than during the George W. Bush years. I was wrong, at least in the short term.

It could be said that the most important deterioration the Obama team failed to slow was that of their opposing political party. The repercussions of 2016's events have undermined not just the United States but democracy itself. One British commentator wrote in April 2017, "The Trump administration's most shocking feature is how rapidly it has turned into a family business ... The Chinese wall separating Mr. Trump from his business interests is invisible ... I have lost count of the number of diplomats from what used to be called the Third World telling me how familiar they find Mr. Trump's Washington. Access to the president's bloodline is the priority. There is no pretence of meritocracy. Patronage and clientelism are in the air."[2] The example this change is setting for the world is terrible, and the responsibility lies no less with the political party that allowed it than with the president himself.

America's powers of self-renewal have always been great, but we seem to be witnessing a decline in US political leadership more sweeping than that of the Bush 43 years. This is again requiring allies of the United States, including Canada, to take defensive, or at least hedged, postures. Worse yet, America's key allies overseas are also entangled in crises that affect foreign policy. Neither the United Kingdom nor Europe seems strongly positioned to resist the Trump administration's effects on economic and diplomatic order. There is seldom a perfect time for anything, but this is not a robust framework for enforcing international law, preventing institutional breakdown, or dissuading destructive actions by rogue states. Our international order depends on, and is intended to defend and advance, healthy democracies. Imperial decline produces various well-known reactions: ideological rigidity and schisms, factional power struggles and distracted government, and a search for scapegoats and the blaming of outsiders.

China has the option of taking up a global leadership role much sooner than might have been anticipated a year ago, and unfortunately at an earlier stage in its diplomatic development than the United States was in the 1940s. This is not ideal, but nor is it hopeless. At least China is reasonably internally stable and has reached a point where it has some vested interest in a rules-based international system.

All this has limited bearing on my book's analysis, which is essentially historical and offers only a couple of prescriptions for Canadians, both of which seem to be only reinforced by recent events. First, anti-American sentiment in Canada waned in the Obama years, but a resurgence can probably be expected given the widening gap in the two countries' directions. This could strengthen the relevance of the book's argument about anti-Americanism. Secondly, the case for Canadians to demonstrate responsibility and competence in national-security matters is now even stronger. The current American administration is plainer than most about wanting its allies to pull their weight. It might have fewer reservations about either intervening on Canadian territory or imposing very disruptive restrictions on border traffic.

Illegal migration is another growing risk for which Canada is poorly prepared. It will require major resources and will create many problems both internally and at the border. It is certainly in Canada's interest to integrate immigrants well and to gain strength from diversity, but that is a completely different question from that of exercising border control – the very essence of a sovereign nation. Canada is now one of the ultimate target destinations for global migrations being driven by the compounded instabilities the world now seems to face. The pressure will be enormous.

And that is just one dimension of what Canada may be in for. Declining international order, if it does continue, is likely to have enormous economic costs for a highly open economy with little capacity to project force abroad or to impose sanctions. Our economy will suffer and Canada will face a need to do far more to back its own citizens and organizations when they operate overseas. This would be a new world for a country that has always enjoyed some form of imperial cover.

By the time of Obama's election in 2008, I had moved from the Economic Section to a management role in the Embassy. Increasingly disturbed by reports on global warming, I strengthened my connections with energy-policy groups. It was, and still is, very clear to the analysts whom I most respected that the successful use of nuclear energy is likely to make or break the Earth's response to our greenhouse-gas problem. When the Canadian Nuclear Association came looking for a policy director, I had found my next job. My colleagues at the US Embassy honoured my twenty years of work by presenting me with a flag that had flown above the Chancery for a day and been ceremonially folded and encased by the Marine guard detachment. I left the Embassy's service in October 2010.

I have spent most of my career advocating for four embattled causes, all of which are often unjustly maligned. One is open international trade and investment, the factual case for which is overwhelmingly positive. The second, closely related to trade, is the reception and productive integration of immigrants into Canada. This is an effort in which I believe intellectually as an economist, and in which I have worked as a volunteer for more than a decade, in the interest of my own city and country as well as to my own great social and cultural benefit.

The third embattled cause is the necessity of investing in clean, reliable, affordable nuclear energy. This already exists on a large scale, and the world needs more of it to close the gap between our current energy systems – including renewable power and storage, unless something changes more than looks likely – and climate change. The fourth cause is the United States' leadership in the world, which, as I have said, must be evaluated against actual alternative power systems, or, even more favourably to the United States, against the consequences of having no leading power at all, rather than against perfection or against anyone's sense of moral or cultural superiority.

As right as these causes continue to look by the evidence, too many of the world's centrist politicians are timid about speaking up for them when they might run against popular sentiment. But things that we know are unfashionable sometime deserve a competent, honest, and vocal defence regardless.

Notes

CHAPTER ONE

1 Churchill also allegedly said that the best argument against democracy is a five-minute conversation with the average voter.

2 Recall the pressure placed on China and Japan in the nineteenth century to allow intrusion by Westerners.

3 The Nicaraguan conflict in the 1980s was a *cause célèbre* of my generation. A left-wing populist government (the "Sandinistas") in a poor Central American country faced resistance from US-supported irregular forces (the "Contras"). The picture that emerged in our eyes was that the Sandinista government drew its support from the majority of ordinary Nicaraguans and, like many nationalist movements, was not initially seeking resources from the Soviet Union. On the other hand, the Contras were encouraged and funded by foreign-based business interests and probably by "covert" (undisclosed or plausibly deniable) operations of the US Central Intelligence Agency. Armed resistance by the Contras hindered constructive government in Nicaragua, and inevitably drove the Sandinistas to seek outside support, making their alleged pro-communist leanings a self-fulfilling prophecy and thus further justifying US intervention. In 1987 allegations surfaced of an illegal, freelance scheme in which Lieutenant-Colonel Oliver North, a US National Security Council staff member, arranged arms sales to the US-hostile Iranian government and used the proceeds to fund the Contras. This became a scandal for the Reagan administration. The overall effect on an idealistic Canadian observer was to make US policy look meddlesome, dishonest, and counter-productive.

4 "Did it not come to mind that for years the same embassy had been violating Vietnam? ... U.S. Embassies are not pristine diplomatic oases, but full-blown governmental hives, heavy with C.I.A. operatives, and representative of a country that however much it is admired is also despised. The point is not that the C.I.A.

should be excluded from hallowed ground, or that U.S. interventions are necessarily counterproductive, but that diplomatic immunity is a flimsy conceit naturally just ignored, especially by guerrillas who expect no special status for themselves and are willing to die in a fight ... During the 10 years following the loss
of Saigon, in 1975, there had been by some estimates nearly 240 attacks or
attempted attacks against U.S. diplomats and their facilities worldwide." William
Langewiesche, "The Mega-Bunker of Baghdad," *Vanity Fair*, 29 October 2007.

5 Stephen Kinzer, a former *New York Times* bureau chief in Nicaragua, wrote: "For
most of the 'regime change' era, the United States did little or nothing to promote democracy in the countries whose governments it deposed ... Each of these
interventions radicalized more people. They ultimately led millions around the
world to support anti-American movements like those that have erupted in
countries from Nicaragua to Iraq." Kinzer's words, though written twenty years
on, sum up how my cohort of twenty-somethings interested in international
affairs already saw America's foreign-policy predicament by the late 1980s.
Stephen Kinzer, *Overthrow: America's Century of Regime Change from Hawaii to
Iraq* (New York: Times Books 2006). In January 2008, the final year of the administration of George W. Bush, I wrote to myself: "If a country at times seems hypocritical, it may be, not that its leaders say one thing and do another, but that
some of its leaders want to do one thing (such as preach a missionary ideal) and
others want to do another (such as pursue what they see as the country's strategic interests). One cannot attribute a single mind to a democratic nation of
300 million."

6 Mohandas K. Gandhi, *An Autobiography*, translated by Mohadev Desai (Boston:
Beacon Press 1993), chapter 38.

7 Irshad Manji, *The Trouble with Islam Today* (New York: St Martin's Griffin 2003),
123. Manji also writes, "We consider it civil to criticize Americans but not Muslims [but] not only will the United States listen to an itemizing of its failures,
the United States will take responsibility for a few of them" (198). "I can choose
not to read a McDonald's menu ... Equating the evils of desert Islam with the
sins of globalization is a mistake committed by the overprivileged, those who've
never known anything worse than the horrors of being marketed to" (202–3).

8 United States Department of State, diplomatic telegrams 1991 Bonn 024905 and
1991 Brussels 12295.

9 United States Department of State, diplomatic telegram 1992 Paris 029720.

10 United States Department of State, diplomatic telegram 1993 London 01710.

11 United States Department of State, diplomatic telegram 1993 Secstate 242351.

12 United States Department of State, diplomatic telegram 1994 Berlin 02994.

13 United States Department of State, diplomatic telegram 1996 Brussels 01325.

14 United States Department of State, diplomatic telegram 1996 Brussels 01667.

15 Daniel Yergin, *Shattered Peace: The Origins of the Cold War and the National Security State* (Boston: Houghton Mifflin 1977), chapter 1.

16 Ibid., 61. Later in the book (84) Yergin describes how the Second World War
    "had transformed the American mind. The American leaders ... felt *responsible*
    for what happened all over the world. They were gripped again by messianic lib-
    eralism, the powerful urge to reform the world that has been called Wilsonian-
    ism. They wanted a world safe for both liberal democracy and liberal capitalism.
    Why else had they joined the war against totalitarianism and tyranny? ... [In their
    own minds] they were liberators, not imperialists" And he describes the roots of
    what he calls the "national security state": "National security ... postulates the
    interrelatedness of so many different political, economic, and military factors
    that developments halfway around the globe are seen to have automatic and
    direct impact on America's core interests. Virtually every development in the
    world is perceived to be potentially crucial ... The doctrine is characterized by
    expansiveness, a tendency to push the subjective boundaries of security outward
    to more and more areas, to encompass more and more geography and more and
    more problems" (96). A noteworthy positive side of the "national security state"
    mentality was a compelling requirement for solidarity among the major non-
    communist powers. At the outset of the Cold War, State Department USSR expert
    George Kennan wrote in his definitive analysis of the Soviet Union: "Their suc-
    cess will really depend on the degree of cohesion, firmness and vigor which the
    Western World can muster ... Every courageous and incisive measure to solve
    internal problems of our own society, to improve self-confidence, discipline,
    morale and community spirit of our own people, is a diplomatic victory over
    Moscow worth a thousand diplomatic notes and joint communiqués." George
    Kennan, in the "Long Telegram" from Moscow to Washington, 22 February 1946,
    Part 5, http://nsarchive.gwu.edu/coldwar/documents/episode-1/kennan.htm.

17 Actually, there were limits. The US Consulate in Bordeaux, France, which had
    been the first US diplomatic station in the world when established in 1778, was
    closed in 1995 for "budgetary reasons." I heard that someone there had written
    a study on the regional wine industry, and that helped Washington make up
    its mind.

18 A cable (or, more archaically, a telegram) is a formal, on-the-record, serially
    numbered message from an overseas post to the home capital or vice versa, or
    more rarely, from post to post. A cable can be routed to anyone in a wide
    range of departments, agencies, and other diplomatic and military posts. For
    well over a hundred years, cables had been the standard route by which posts
    communicated with their home governments. (President Abraham Lincoln
    tracked the Union troops' fortunes in the Civil War from behind the chair of a
    telegraph operator near the White House, where he could read cables the
    minute they arrived.) The older communications system is the "pouch," or
    diplomatic bag, a term for any container carrying physical mail that is protect-
    ed by diplomatic privilege from being opened or searched. Pouched mail
    tends to travel infrequently and slowly. In my career, I used a pouch only once

– to send a final, bound, and sealed copy of a treaty amendment to the treaty vault in Washington.

19 Author's diary.

20 I recall hearing a (perhaps apocryphal) story about Pierre Trudeau seeing the US ambassador's pine-panelled office. If the story is true, it must have happened either before Trudeau became minister of justice or after he left politics, since I can't imagine why a minister would call on the US ambassador in the Chancery. At any rate, Trudeau was said to have looked out the window at the Centre Block and remarked on what a terrific location the room would make for the Prime Minister's Office (PMO). When I arrived in 1990, the search had been on for years to find the Embassy a new home. A green-field site called Mile Circle (in the Rockcliffe Park area) had been considered but was blocked by neigh-bourhood opponents. Our lease on 100 Wellington was due to run out in 1998. We were not aware of any decision about how the old building might be used after we left, but there was speculation it could house the PMO. It was still vacant in 2016.

21 Author's diary.

22 Some say that the name "Asia-Pacific Economic Cooperation" is "four adjectives in search of a noun."

23 United States Embassy Ottawa, memorandum of conversation, September 1997.

24 Author's diary.

25 In Rio it's actually called Carnival. David T. Jones, "U.S. Now Sees Canada as Bush League," *Ottawa Citizen*, 14 July 1998.

26 US ambassadors' frequent urging of Canadians to take responsibility for their own defence contradicted the juvenile accusation by Canadian leftists that the United States "just wanted to take over" Canada, but the left never seemed to notice this.

27 Consulate: "We would prefer to make the call about when the report should go in rather than get WHA excited about something which is a continuation of ongoing provincial activities rather than a noteworthy event." Embassy: "WHA tells us at every opportunity that the way to get the attention of their Front Office is to do reports that relate Canada to the rest of the Bureau." In retrospect, it is hard to either applaud or condemn the bureau shift. It is true that Canada never quite fit into the Latin America bureau. My Embassy colleagues com-plained about WHA's "consistent lack of awareness that Canada has joined them." Still, it's equally true that Canada is no longer connected to Europe as it was in the twentieth century. And, if the Western Hemisphere bureau may not always be near heart of US foreign-policy formation, it is less clear than ever whether the European bureau still is.

28 Incidentally, Lévesque, like myself, although not a US citizen, worked at one time for the US government. Late in the Second World War he was recruited as a

journalist by the US Office of War Information to work for the radio network Voice of America in Europe.

29 John Stewart, "Project, or Faith? Quebec's 1995 Push for Sovereignty and the Realities of International Relations," *Canadian Foreign Policy Journal*, summer 2012. Analysts had argued that a unilateral declaration of independence by Quebec, while legally possible, would be impractical because it would be vigorously contested by Canada and by important groups within Quebec, even at the cost of deepening and prolonging an economic crisis, and also that it was highly unlikely that Canada would agree to joint political institutions with Quebec following secession. There were various narrow but thorny economic problems such as the division between Quebec and the rest of Canada of defence assets and sovereign-debt liabilities. Some noted that, in an effort to secede, Quebec would be susceptible to considerable international interference from international creditors, and that, while able to retain the use of the Canadian dollar, it would lose much authority over monetary policy. Some suggested that the secession movement is economically irrational and driven by a fear of cultural extinction.

30 Anyone who wonders why Stephen Harper had a poor relationship with the media should review the way most reporters and editors treated the early Reform Party.

31 This account of the economic issues around the 1995 Quebec referendum, as viewed from the US Embassy, is recounted in more detail in Stewart, "Project, or Faith?"

32 As William Faulkner wrote, "The past isn't over. In fact, it's not even past." The US Civil War of 1861–65 (also known as the War between the States or the War for Southern Independence) stands as the third-bloodiest war in US history after the two world wars of the twentieth century. Until well into the Vietnam War, more Americans had died in the Civil War than had died in all other US wars combined. The war's fratricidal element and the fact that it ended in total defeat of the vanquished side gave it profound importance not just in American political, historical and military consciousness but also in the shared history of the English-speaking peoples. Kevin Phillips, *The Cousins' Wars* (New York: Basic Books 1999).

33 As Prime Minister Lester Pearson observed after Charles de Gaulle's infamous "Vive le Quebec libre!" appearance, "Canadians do not need to be liberated."

34 In a 1989 interview, former US ambassador Paul Robinson had said of Parti Québécois founder Rene Lévesque: "To me, it is treason. I mean, if the governor of Illinois was saying the things Levesque said, we would hang him."

35 James Blanchard, *Behind the Embassy Door* (Ann Arbor, MI: Sleeping Bear Press 1998), 77–8.

36 Canada, Office of the Prime Minister, "Speech by Prime Minister Jean Chrétien at the Conference on Trade with China," 10 February 1995.

37 United States Department of State, diplomatic telegram 1995 Ottawa 0746.

38 The rule is set out in Article 34 of the 1978 Vienna Convention. Use of this rule had solidified in the 1990s as a practical necessity, since the time and resources were usually lacking to engage in all the renegotiations that would have otherwise been needed with post-Soviet governments. Before that, the United States and others had sometimes chosen to give a "clean slate" to a state emerging from colonial status (deeming it to be free of previous rights and obligations). For more discussion of Quebec-independence scenarios, see Charles N. Brower and Abbey Cohen Smutny, "The Effect of the Independence of Quebec upon Treaties and Agreements with the United States of America," *American Review of Canadian Studies*, spring 1997, 51–61.

39 An analysis by the US Consulate in Quebec City found that the province's expenditure of money and manpower on international affairs was staggering in relation to its size and population. United States Department of State, diplomatic telegram 1998 Quebec 0176. Quebec's Ministry of International Relations had 545 full-time employees, consumed an annual budget of about US$56 million, and maintained delegations, offices, and attachés in more than a dozen locations outside Canada. At the same time, California, with more than four times Quebec's population and more than five times its GDP, had about 150 international trade and development staff on a budget of less than $11 million. California's office in Tokyo, managing the state's immense cultural and trade relationship with Japan, had four full-time employees.

40 The White House, Office of the Press Secretary, "Remarks by the President to Forum of Federation Conference, Chateau Mont-Tremblant, Mont-Tremblant, Canada," 8 October 1999.

41 Kathleen Kenna, "Separation Means Rough Ride on Trade, Quebecers warned," *Toronto Star*, 20 November 1999.

42 Ibid.

43 Occasionally the question arose of why the United States maintained two consulates in Quebec. In 2006 Embassy staff were formally asked for our views on the "rightsizing" of Mission Canada. I commented: "We have two posts in the Province of Quebec, one of which (Quebec City) is a small post engaged primarily in political work. Travel between these two cities is very easy (for example, it is more convenient than travel from Vancouver to Victoria, capital of the next largest province, where we do not maintain a post). This province's economic and demographic weight within Canada is declining. There may be efficiencies to be gained by combining these posts at Montreal. The obstacles are political. By choosing to maintain Quebec City in these circumstances, [the United States government] sends a public message that it is 'holding an option' on Quebec sovereignty. It should be recognized that, while closing this post would be viewed in political terms, keeping it open also sends a political mes-

sage, one which may be less in tune with USG policy positions than it was in past decades."

CHAPTER TWO

1 Conrad Black, *Rise to Greatness: The History of Canada from the Vikings to the Present* (Toronto: McClelland and Stewart 2014), 454.

2 "Uncle Sam" is a nickname for the United States government. He was a lean, top-hatted, white-goateed character who routinely appeared in political cartoons in the nineteenth and twentieth centuries as the incarnation of the USA – or sometimes of a stereotypically sharp-dealing "Yankee trader." I explain this because Uncle Sam's image has been disappearing from popular media.

3 Ronald J. Wonnacott and Paul Wonnacott, *Free Trade Between the United States and Canada: The Potential Economic Effects* (Cambridge, MA: Harvard University Press; Harvard Economic Studies, vol. 129, 1967).

4 Office of the US Trade Representative, Memorandum to the President, "Your July 10 Meeting with Prime Minister Trudeau and Canadian Investment Policies," 8 July 1981.

5 Office of the US Trade Representative, Memorandum to the President, "Status of U.S.-Canada Bilateral Trade and Investment Issues," 30 October 1981.

6 Paul Robinson, US ambassador to Canada during the first term of Ronald Reagan's administration (1981–85), said the FTA was his idea. "My first work day of 1983 ... I announced that we were going to reinitiate the free trade agreement, which you'll remember ... failed in 1911. We knew, of course, that it wouldn't do any good unless it was initiated by the Canadians. It wouldn't fly at all because we would be accused of gobbling up Canada." "U.S. Envoys: Canadians Frightened and Weak." *Ottawa Citizen*, 13 October 1997.

7 Following is a cynical argument for maintaining open trade and investment policies in an imperfect world, an argument that does not necessarily reflect my personal views but that some might find persuasive. While the United States may claim that its interventions in other countries are benevolent (to build democracy and freedom or combat terror), quite often the motives behind them are commercial. For a smaller country, therefore, being commercially open lowers the risk of being hurt by US meddling. This by itself is an argument for having open policies. Fortunately, commercial openness is inherently beneficial anyway, since it raises living standards and is consistent with greater personal freedom. And, while free trade and investment is often accused of leading to foreign domination, cultural homogenization, or various other evils, experience in Canada and elsewhere arguably disproves this. Still, when a country is faced with a much larger partner such as the United States that it is reluctant to embrace, a partner that is a great commercial and economic success but is considered to have an

unsavoury foreign-policy record, the small country might want to add this meddling-avoidance argument to the calculation.

8 Another fascinating senior visitor was Ann Brunsdale, then chair of the US International Trade Commission, who participated in an event at the University of Ottawa law school in 1990 or 1991. As I accompanied her to the airport after the event, she told me about the early days of her career in the 1940s, when she had worked in the Office of Strategic Services (OSS), the wartime predecessor of the Central Intelligence Agency. OSS played an important role in developing American approaches to both global intelligence gathering and covert operations. In 1990–91, at a time when the Cold War was ending, it was remarkable that one could still meet, and work with, people who had witnessed its beginnings more than forty years earlier. Canada's chief negotiator for the FTA, Simon Reisman, was another example. He had worked in international-trade policy during the creation of the General Agreement on Tariffs and Trade in 1947 and was still making speaking appearances at universities as late as 2000.

9 According to the classical economic argument, if local product never needs to compete with foreign product, then the local product costs too much and improves too slowly. Consumers overpay for a limited variety of inferior products – in this case wine and beer. Investment in local industries remains low, and workers remain unproductive and (as a result) poor. Reducing the sorts of market barriers put up by the provincial liquor boards is not easy, because vested interests (local brewers and vintners) benefit from them and work hard to keep them in place, including by contributing to the campaigns of political candidates and then lobbying them once they are elected. Those who would benefit from reducing the barriers (consumers) far outnumber these brewers and vintners, and the total economic gains would outweigh the losses, so that in the long run society would be better off. But, while the brewers and vintners may each have millions to lose, and accordingly put up a big fight, each consumer would benefit by only a few dollars a year, so few of them bother to lobby politicians on this issue, even if they are aware of their potential gains. As a result, politicians tend to favour the few over the many, so industry remains protected and society winds up poorer. Good, constructive trade policy consists of an endless uphill struggle in favour of the many relatively scattered consumers who will benefit from more trade, and against relatively concentrated vested interests who demand to be protected. For economic professionals of a free-trade bent, liberalizing trade and investment is more than a policy choice, it is a moral imperative.

10 Mexico and the United States were contemplating bilateral negotiations, which would have left Canada with its existing FTA and no trade deal with Mexico. If this pattern were adopted, and then followed by the United States with other Latin American partner countries, it would have produced a "hub-and-spoke" arrangement of FTAS with the United States being the hub. In other words, the

United States would be the one partner with preferred access to all the other partners – at least, unless and until the others got around to negotiating FTAS with each other, which would be slow and expensive. Economists such as Richard Lipsey pointed out that a web pattern – one agreement with multiple members – would deliver bigger and wider economic benefits, particularly for the countries that would otherwise have become spokes to the US hub. Canadian officials worked hard to pull the Americans in this trilateral direction, and they eventually succeeded, despite some misgivings in the United States (since obviously the negotiations would be much less manageable with three countries, and moreover, there would be opportunities for the smaller partners' negotiators to collaborate, the better to gain concessions from the United States). As one of my senior American colleagues remarked to me, "Having everyone in the negotiations together like this is great for the Canadians, but as far as the U.S. team is concerned, it's a mess." In the event, however, I would say that the dynamic went as it usually does: while it was complicated having three parties involved rather than two, the United States and Canada probably had more in common with each other than with the Mexicans. Canada ended up providing some help to the US team by helping to articulate and moderate their positions, and perhaps to broker a few compromises.

11 Poor countries were either staying poor – with an ever-widening gap between themselves and the developed world – or, in a few cases, caught up with (converged with) the developed world in just a few decades. These few development miracles (mainly the East Asian "tigers" – South Korea, Taiwan, Singapore, and Hong Kong) could not be attributed to foreign aid, government ownership and control, or natural-resource endowments. The evidence, supported by research in the late 1980s, suggested that they were driven by free markets and strong property rights plus good basic institutions and human capital.

12 As the economist Paul Krugman would later note, the opponents of globalization seemed to think that the developing world was filled with happy peasants in traditional costumes doing their village dances in the rainforest, who would be best served by remaining uncontaminated by development. These opponents would be confounded by the reality of actual people looking for actual jobs in an actual developing economy, who, because they couldn't satisfy their aspirations in Mexico, would risk what little they had in order to get to the United States to work. As a rational argument, the anti-NAFTA anti-corporate rhetoric that purported to be defending Mexicans was illogical.

13 The party's vow to eliminate grants, subsidies, and protectionist measures was qualified in the case of agriculture, a sector in which Reform had its base of support and where multilateral trade negotiations were ongoing at the time. Harper told us that Reform thought Canadian farmers "should offer the rest of the world and the rest of the country a deal leading to a step-by-step reduction in

government agricultural support at home and abroad if other economic sectors and our trading partners will do the same." Such a deal would be accompanied by "transitional support" to farmers, who should also have recourse to counter-vailing duties against subsidized imports, whether or not those imports could be shown to have hurt Canadian producers. Contrasted with Reform's slash-and-burn attitude to most federal spending, this tempered position on agricultural trade indicated an area where the party's ideology was conditioned by reality.

14 United States Department of State, diplomatic telegram 1993 Ottawa 6580.

15 A similar tactic – stimulating fears about sovereignty and constitutional integrity – would be used in the 2000s by American media commentators, who alleged that the three NAFTA countries' Security and Prosperity Partnership (SPP), which in reality was a loose collection of modest regulatory initiatives, was actually a conspiracy to subvert the US constitution and replace it with a continental government.

16 One of the Action Canada Network's few ventures into specific explanation was this: NAFTA was going to "terminate the usefulness of crown corporations" by such measures as committing them to give equal consideration to U.S. and Mexican suppliers when they bought goods and services. One would think crown corporations had been created to provide buyers for uncompetitive Canadian products.

17 Heather Scoffield, "Canada Hollowing Out? It's a World Beater," *Globe and Mail*, 5 December 2006.

18 United States Department of State, diplomatic telegram 1997 Ottawa 2192.

19 The November 2000 elections dropped the party's standing in Parliament from 21 seats to 13 (out of 301).

20 Joseph Heath, *Montreal Gazette*, 20 September 2003.

21 Michael Campbell, *Vancouver Sun*, 20 September 2003.

22 United States Department of State, diplomatic telegram 2002 Ottawa 0851.

23 United States Department of State, diplomatic telegram 2004 Ottawa 066.

24 Canada, Minister of Industry, Speech to the Canadian Chamber of Commerce in Calgary, Alberta, 20 September 2004.

25 United States Embassy Ottawa, informal meeting notes, 12 April 2005.

26 United States Department of State, diplomatic telegram 2004 Ottawa 0894.

27 Canada, Office of the Prime Minister, Speech by Prime Minister Paul Martin at the Sun Valley 2004 Conference, 7 July 2004.

28 United States Embassy Ottawa, "NAFTA Offspring: Barren or Ambitious?" Draft internal briefing memo, 28 October 2004.

29 See chapter 3.

30 United States Embassy Ottawa, internal non-paper, November 2004.

31 United States Department of State, diplomatic telegram 2005 Ottawa 0268. Commended in 2005 Secstate 023479.

32 United States Embassy Ottawa, internal briefing note, September 2004. ·

33 United States Department of State, diplomatic telegram 2004 Ottawa 0625.

34 The event was "Trade Policy in 2005," at the Center for Strategic and International Studies, Washington, DC, 9 February 2005.

35 United States Department of State, diplomatic telegram 2005 Ottawa 1282.

36 United States Embassy Ottawa, internal e-mail, 13 July 2006.

37 United States Department of State, internal e-mail, 16 March 2005.

38 United States Department of State, diplomatic telegram 2005 Ottawa 838.

39 United States Department of State, internal e-mail, 9 May 2005.

40 United States Embassy Ottawa, e-mail, 25 February 2008.

41 One independent analysis that confirms this is by legal and consulting firm Bennett Jones, "Growth in Real Household Income in Canada: 1984–2024," June 2015.

42 SES Research/Policy Options, "Canadians, Americans Agree Both Better off with Free Trade," news release, 30 September 2007.

43 "Maude Barlow Addresses Parliament on the Security and Prosperity Partnership," Council of Canadians media release, 1 May 2007.

44 On this point (climate change as a security threat) May was echoing the UN Security Council decision a few weeks earlier to discuss for the first time the potential threats to international security from climate change.

45 United States Embassy Ottawa, "Summary of Meeting with Elizabeth May, leader of the Green Party, on SPP, 23 April 2007," draft internal notes.

46 House of Commons Subcommittee on International Trade, meeting record, 26 April 2007.

47 United States Department of State, e-mail, 7 December 2007.

48 Campaign websites, cited in Embassy e-mail, 27 February 2008. The Republican contenders, John McCain and Mike Huckabee, avoided direct reference to NAFTA.

49 Thomas d'Aquino, quoted in "Protectionism Is Not the Answer," Canadian Council of Chief Executives (press release), 27 February 2008.

50 United States Embassy Ottawa, e-mail, 27 February 2008.

51 Financial Times, 13 March 2008. I forwarded this to my Embassy colleagues with the comment: "In my own view, this speaks extremely well of McGuinty. Among Canada's provinces, Ontario (both the provincial government and the populace) has traditionally been the least enthusiastic about free trade (and Quebec the most enthusiastic). Despite years of job losses in manufacturing, McGuinty stays positive and does not pander. Bob Rae, as Ontario's New Democratic Party Premier in the early 1990s, denounced NAFTA at the World Economic Forum while in the same breath urging foreigners to invest in Ontario. Somehow, Rae seemed not to grasp the absurdity."

52 Jagdish Bhagwati, "Obama's Free-Trade Credentials Top Clinton's," Financial Times, 3 March 2008.

53 Canadian Consulate General Chicago, "Report on U.S. Elections – CHCGO Meeting with Obama Advisor Austan Goolsbee," diplomatic telegram published on Slate (www.slate.com/id/2185753/entry/2185754/), February 2008. This cable caused a minor political and media stir for appearing to suggest that Obama's position on NAFTA was "nothing more than political posturing." Mike Blanchfield, "Wilkins Forgives Tory Party Leak in 'NAFTA-gate,'" *Ottawa Citizen*, 7 March 2008. Canadian government officials said they regretted any perception of interference in the US political process.

54 United States Embassy Ottawa, diplomatic telegram 2008 Ottawa 378.

55 United States Department of State, e-mail, 28 January 2008.

CHAPTER THREE

1 In the middle stages of the Iraq war fifteen years later, journalists rediscovered the value of questioning what they were told by military officials, because they had been so misled about the reasons for invading Iraq (i.e., its alleged weapons of mass destruction) in 2003.

2 Barbara Ehrenreich, *Blood Rites* (New York: Metropolitan Books/Henry Holt and Company 1997).

3 Canada's role as a security ally to the United States reached a post–Pierre Trudeau and pre–Iraq War low while Lloyd Axworthy was Canada's minister of foreign affairs. Axworthy's international campaign for a treaty restricting the use of anti-personnel land mines (and possibly another on trade in small firearms) caused a split with the United States on arms-trade policy. While the United States said that land mines should be eliminated eventually and while it invested in humanitarian mine-removal efforts, it also took the view that it needed to continue to be able to use land mines in the Korean Peninsula. In October 1997 I heard the Embassy's political minister-counsellor mutter about Axworthy: "I can't believe he buys into this stuff." Our Embassy was also irritated by the fawning reception given in Ottawa to Jody Williams, the American anti-land-mine crusader who would share a Nobel Peace Prize less than two weeks later. Williams addressed a breakfast at the National Press Club, held meetings at the Department of Foreign Affairs, and then delivered another speech at Carleton University, all "with little courtesy to the Embassy" (my colleagues complained) by her Canadian hosts. Whether or not it was justified, there was a strong sense in the Embassy that Axworthy wanted to make his mark in government by irritating or alienating the United States.

4 "Perspectives on Free Trade," set of six research papers, Industry Canada, 2000.

5 "Country mandate" describes a company's Canadian operation being mandated to sell that company's products in the Canadian market, while "product mandate" describes the same Canadian operation being responsible for producing

the global supply of some set of the company's products. During this period Bay Street (Toronto's financial district) had fewer and fewer country analysts whose job was to follow the Canadian market – and more who, while still based in Toronto, followed a global product or sector.

6 Former *New York Times* Canada correspondent Steven Pearlstein, "The Eternal Question: Will Canada Survive? – Canada, U.S. Economies Merging at Mach Speed," *Toronto Star*, 9 September 2000.

7 United States Embassy Ottawa, "Your First Hundred Days – Setting Priority Themes," Memorandum to the Ambassador, 9 May 2001.

8 Stephen Fidler, "Economics Drives U.S. Policy," *Financial Times*, 12 April 2001. Among other things, the Bush team created an international economics unit within the National Security Council (NSC), and put the secretary of the treasury on the NSC.

9 Under a typical free-trade agreement, countries agree to reduce or eliminate tariffs on each other's products, but each country continues to determine its own barriers to goods from third countries. Therefore, officials at the shared border must still control the movement of third-country goods. In a customs union, countries agree to zero tariffs between themselves, and they also agree to joint rules on third-country goods. Therefore, once third-country goods (say from Britain or China) have entered one country in the customs union (say Canada), those goods are free to flow into other members of the custom union (say the United States), and officials at the shared border do not need to check or control them. The shared border normally then is focused on controlling non-goods traffic – mainly people, at least until the countries agree to integrate their labour markets. The European Community went through this stage of integration.

10 Mulroney reportedly said that Canada's national income per capita had fallen to 35 per cent below the US level (perhaps an overstatement), and that if trends continued, it would be 50 per cent of the US level in ten years. This glossed over the role and sustainability of Canadian dollar depreciation. "Mulroney Calls for Canada-U.S. Customs Union," *Ottawa Citizen*, 19 June 2001.

11 "Canada, U.S. Eye Scrapping Border," *Toronto Star*, 28 July 2001.

12 "The Case for Erasing an 'Obsolete' Border – Economic Demands Are Forcing Politicians to Consider Converting the Border into a 'Continental Main St.,'" *Ottawa Citizen*, 4 August 2001.

13 United States Department of State, e-mail, 13 February 2003.

14 EKOS polling.

15 Steven Simon and Daniel Benjamin, "Myths of American Misdeeds," *Financial Times*, 2 October 2001. The writers put responsibility for the attacks on Osama bin Laden and violent religious belief, and they take apart "myths" that 9/11 was the result of the Arab-Israeli conflict, regional poverty, or US involvement in the pre-2001 Afghanistan war. "These myths may make some feel better about their

moral equivocation in the face of the suffering in New York ... But by enabling believers to deny the undeniable threat Mr Bin Laden poses, these myths undermine the capacity to defend our societies from devastating attack right now."

16 I was surprised at the time that I did not read or hear of the containment model being discussed. It might have worked better than the Bush administration's thesis that "we have to take the war to the enemy so they don't bring it to us." See Guy Dinmore, "The White House Reverts to Cold War Containment," *Financial Times*, 13 October 2006, and Andrew J. Bacevich, "Ending Endless War: A Pragmatic Military Strategy," *Foreign Affairs*, September/October 2016, 36–44.

17 United States Department of State, "Key Words and Themes to be Used as Guidance, Updated 09/17/2001 – 1600 EDT, regarding Events on September 11, 2001."

18 US Ambassador Paul Cellucci, "Again I Learn the True Meaning of Friendship," *Ottawa Citizen*, 15 September 2001. The ambassador used the same words in his speech to the Canadian Club of Ottawa on 18 September.

19 Peter Beinart, "The War of the Words," *Washington Post*, 1 April 2007.

20 Conrad Black, *Rise to Greatness: The History of Canada from the Vikings to the Present* (Toronto: McClelland and Stewart 2014), 402.

21 Robert Graves, *Good-Bye to All That* (New York: Anchor Books 1998), 228.

22 See, for example, Bacevich, "Ending Endless War." "During the Cold War, the idea was not to fight but to defend, deter and contain ... The Bush Doctrine of 2002 announced that the United States would no longer 'wait for threats to fully materialize' before striking ... specific assumptions about changes in the nature of war had ostensibly endowed the United States with something akin to outright military supremacy. Thoroughly tested in Iraq and Afghanistan, those suppositions have proved utterly false ... The next president should return to [defence and deterrence], explicitly abrogating the Bush Doctrine and permanently renouncing preventive war. The point is not to specify a fixed hierarchy of interests and then to draw a line, everything above which is worth fighting for and everything below which isn't. That's a losing game ... Instead, keep the weapon oiled and loaded but holstered."

23 United States Department of State, diplomatic telegram 01 Ottawa 2937.

24 The US policy establishment paid surprisingly little attention to the economic risks of over-reacting to 9/11. For example, in remarks to a small group in Ottawa on 16 November, Federal Reserve Chairman Alan Greenspan instead focused his remarks on what he saw as rosy prospects for a long-term productivity revolution driven by information technology. United States Department of State, US Embassy Ottawa Memorandum of Conversation, "Greenspan's Remarks at Ambassador Cellucci's Lunch for Treasury Secretary O'Neill," 16 November 2001.

25 A Transport Canada task force worked constantly on this beginning on the morning of the 11th, and by 9 p.m. that night there were reported to be 8,800 displaced passengers at Halifax, 6,585 at Gander, 4,320 at St John's, and 3,000 at

each of Vancouver and Moncton. Eight other Canadian airports were also affected. Transport Canada told our Embassy's transportation officer that Canada wanted "a clear statement of expectations for reactivating U.S. airspace," and they committed to follow the US Federal Aviation Administration's guidelines for "agreed heightened security measures" on flights departing Canada for the United States. This constrained Transport Canada's ability to get those flights into the air and on their way to the United States in coming days. One limiting factor was the lack of certified personnel to screen passengers, particularly at small airports. Another was the lack of US immigration and customs pre-clearance inspectors at most of the affected airports. The latter meant that flights departing those points could not proceed to any open US airport, but only to those that had immigration and customs facilities. Some airlines based in third countries planned to take their aircraft directly back from Canada to home base, so many US-bound passengers on those flights were trying to continue on to their original US destinations by some other means. By the morning of the 14th, three days after the closure, while 27 per cent of the diverted aircraft were still on the ground at airports across Canada, the number of stranded passengers was down to about 400 in Halifax and 600 in Gander. United States Department of State, diplomatic telegrams 2001 Ottawa 2880, 2896 and 2922.

26 "9/11 Cost Transport Industry up to $2.6B," *Ottawa Citizen*, 9 July 2007.

27 Statement of Paul Cellucci, United States ambassador to Canada, before the Immigration Subcommittee of the Committee on the Judiciary, United States Senate, 16 October 2001. While few Canadian politicians or media noticed Ambassador Cellucci's efforts, they were certainly noticing the economic disruption he was trying to help them contain. In Ottawa two days later, both government and opposition members of the House of Commons Industry Committee attacked senior government officials' presentation of the situation on the border. While officials argued that traffic volumes had rebounded to not far below pre-9/11 levels, and waiting times would eventually be restored to "normal," committee members not only doubted the accuracy of their data but also said that border conditions had been unacceptably long prior to September and restoring those conditions was not an adequate goal. Canada, House of Commons Industry Committee, Sub-Committee on International Trade, hearing 18 October 2001.

28 The same applies to how Canadians view their national interests in the Arctic: preoccupation with "sovereignty" greatly distracts from the real issues and interferes with practical collaboration with other Arctic countries, especially the United States.

29 Auditor General of Canada, reports from April 2000 and December 2001.

30 United States Department of State, diplomatic telegram 2001 Ottawa 3455.

31 André Belelieu, "Canada Alert – the Smart Border Process at Two," Washington,

Center for Strategic and International Studies, *Hemisphere Focus*, vol. 11, no. 31, 10 December 2003.

32　US Embassy Ottawa, "U.S. Relations with Canada in 2002–2003: Notes for Remarks at the Kennedy School of Government, Harvard University, by Ambassador Paul Cellucci, 7 February 2002."

33　Canada, Department of Foreign Affairs and International Trade, "Resumption of In-Transit Preclearance at Vancouver Airport," news release no. 13, 14 February 2002.

34　The US commander of USNORTHCOM is concurrently commander of the North American Aerospace Defence command (NORAD), in which Canada does participate. Philippe Lagasse, "Northern Command and the Evolution of Canada-U.S. Defence Relations," *Canadian Military Journal*, spring 2003.

35　John Stewart, "Canada, the United States, and the Air Corridor to Alaska," Department of History thesis, Mount Allison University, 1981.

36　United States Department of State, diplomatic telegram 2002 Ottawa 3248.

37　The White House, Office of the Press Secretary, "Statement by the President," 18 April 2002.

38　Alanna Mitchell, "Canadians Support Closer Ties with U.S.," *Globe and Mail*, 29 April 2002.

39　Peter Calamai, "Canada Growing Strong, Poll Says," *Toronto Star*, 1 July 2002.

40　Stephen Clarkson, "Lockstep in the Continental Ranks," Canadian Centre for Policy Alternatives, Ottawa, 8 February 2002.

41　Lloyd Axworthy, "Watch Your Step, Mr. Chrétien," *Globe and Mail*, 4 February 2002.

42　J.L. Granatstein, "Now as Then, Defence Must Be Continental," *National Post*, 31 January 2002. See also J.L. Granatstein, "Axworthy Paper Full of Holes," *National Post*, 1 May 2002.

43　Lewis MacKenzie, "We're in This Fight Together," *Globe and Mail*, 31 January 2002.

44　Allan Thompson, "Canada Is Able to Stand up to U.S.: Manley," *Toronto Star*, 9 February 2002.

45　Edward Greenspon, "I Am Manley, Hear Me Roar," *Globe and Mail*, 9 February 2002.

46　US Consulate Toronto, "Meeting with Former Ontario Premier Mike Harris," note to file, 18 November 2002.

47　Quoted in Robert Fife, "Ottawa Says Bush 'Texans' Tried to Bully G8 Host," *National Post*, 13 July 2002.

48　Allan Thompson, "Graham Keen to Take on U.S.," *Toronto Star*, 10 June 2002.

49　United States Department of State, "Review of Canadian Non-Paper" (draft information memorandum), n.d.

50　John Ibbitson, "Searching for Conservative Solace," *Globe and Mail*, 12 December 2002.

51　Still, EKOS Research's Frank Graves reported in May 2002 that "contrary to what you see in the American media or on 60 Minutes or espoused from Congress [about Canada being an actual or potential base for terrorism against the United

States], the American public is really quite confident that Canada is to be trusted in taking care of its homeland security issues." Graves also reportedly said that "by a three to one margin Americans say Canadians should be able to move freely in [the United States], whether as workers or as tourists." Kathryn May, "U.S. Trusts Canadian Security: Poll," *Ottawa Citizen*, 5 May 2002.

52 United States Embassy Ottawa, e-mail, March 2004.

53 See, for example, Simon Avery, "Patriot Act Haunts Google Service," *Globe and Mail*, 24 March 2008.

54 While the US Department of Homeland Security (DHS) generally functioned well, its creation out of an assortment of agencies (Customs, Immigration and Naturalization Service, Secret Service, Alcohol Tobacco and Firearms, Animal and Plant Health Inspection Service, etc.) was a complex management problem with many effects that occasioned a twelve-paragraph analysis from the Embassy to Washington late in 2003. "Unresolved issues from the transition have caused problems for the U.S. Mission to Canada ... There are more than 500 DHS employees in Canada, approximately one-third of all DHS employees stationed outside the U.S. ... As the representative of the President responsible for all U.S. Government activities and employees in Canada, the Ambassador needs a clear chain-of-command between him/herself and all U.S. Government personnel in Canada. In the law enforcement context, this is ensured through the designation of an attaché who maintains oversight over the troops in the field, and reports to the Ambassador. Prior to the formation of DHS, the Customs Attaché coordinated all Customs activities and personnel in Canada, an INS attaché oversaw INS personnel, and an APHIS attaché oversaw APHIS activities. Since the formation of DHS and the creation of the Bureaus of Customs and Border Protection and Immigration and Customs Enforcement (ICE), it is no longer clear who oversees whom. This lack of coordination has resulted in a few 'hiccups' and could lead to a serious security or policy error." United States Department of State, diplomatic telegram 2003 Ottawa 3035.

55 United States Department of State, diplomatic telegram 2004 Ottawa 1099.

56 United States Department of State, diplomatic telegram 2004 Ottawa 2729.

57 United States Department of State, diplomatic telegram 2004 Ottawa 2575.

58 United States Department of State, Strategic Planning Framework Overview, 9 January 2003.

59 Newt Gingrich, "Rogue State Department," *Foreign Policy*, July/August 2003.

60 United States Department of State, "Remarks: Opening Remarks by Secretary of State Colin L. Powell before the Senate Appropriations Subcommittee on Foreign Operations," 30 April 2003.

61 For a very good contemporary view of this democratizing vision, and for a critique of it, see James Fallows, "The Fifty-First State?" *Atlantic Monthly*, November 2002.

62 CBC News, "PMO Silent but Liberal Cabinet Minister Says Bush 'Let Down' the

World," 19 March 2003. A few weeks earlier, another Liberal MP, Carolyn Parrish, had been overheard by media saying, "Damn Americans, I hate those bastards." Parrish said the remark was directed at the administration rather than Americans in general, but that did not make it any more appropriate.

63 United States Department of State, e-mail, 20 March 2003.

64 Dwight N. Mason, "Canada Alert: Canada and Missile Defense," Washington, Center for Strategic and International Studies, *Hemispheric Focus*, vol. 11, no. 22, 6 June 2003.

65 Robert Fife, "Bush Advisor: Canadians Will Rue PM's Stand," *National Post*, 3 April 2003.
    Perle's hope would be disappointed. Chrétien's decision not to join the coalition invading Iraq was accepted in the short run and vindicated in the long run, though it would have been helpful if he could have found a way to let Ambassador Cellucci know in advance that his decision might fall in that direction. Not doing so must have hurt the ambassador's credibility in Washington. On Perle's remark about Chrétien and Chirac: while Americans occasionally think they can explain political behaviour by Canada or Canadians as "following France," even French-speaking Canadians have had slight contact with France for more than two and a half centuries, and nothing important in Canadian politics can be explained that way. A case in point is the political crisis over military conscription in the two world wars: French Canadians were the group least interested in engaging in wars to liberate France from an invader.

66 Alexander Moens, Cassandra Florio, and Sean McCarthy, "Canadian-American Relations in 2007," Fraser Institute Digital Publication, May 2007, 4. I only partly agree with these authors' subsequent remark (5) that the resulting undermining of relations with the White House cost Canada support in border issues and in bilateral disputes such as softwood lumber. Canada was becoming less important to the White House in the long run anyway, and the Iraq and missile decisions were only contributing factors.

67 Richard Sanders, "Canada's 'Open Secret': Deep Complicity in the Iraq War," Coalition to Oppose the Arms Trade, Ottawa, February 2008.

68 United States Department of State, "Issues for [National Economic Council] Discussion re Canada's 'Beyond the Border Accord' Non-Paper" (draft information memorandum), 23 September 2002.

69 United States Embassy Ottawa, e-mail, 25 March 2003.

CHAPTER FOUR

1 See, *inter alia*, Joseph Stiglitz, "The Economic Consequences of Mr. Bush," *Vanity Fair*, December 2007, and Joseph Stiglitz and Linda J. Bilmes, *The Three Trillion Dollar War* (New York: W.W. Norton 2008).

2 United States Department of State, diplomatic telegram 2003 Secstate 74249. Canada had declared $2.73 million in Iraqi assets in June 1991, a very small amount compared with the billions known to be in the United States and Europe.

3 United States Department of State, diplomatic telegram 2003 Secstate 082459.

4 Agence France-Presse, "Think Tank Sees Little Impact of Iraq War," *Financial Times*, 11 November 2002.

5 Brian Milner, "Forget Winning, Just Draw up an Exit Strategy," *Globe and Mail*, 29 October 2004.

6 Quoted in Guy Dinmore, "Powell Gives Bleak Assessment of Iraq," *Financial Times*, 13 January 2005.

7 Bruce Jentleson, "Toe the Line or Buck the Trend," *Globe and Mail*, 23 November 2004.

8 Michael Den Tandt, "Cellucci Proud of Influence on Defence Spending," *Globe and Mail*, 17 March 2005.

9 "Question Period: Interview with Paul Cellucci," CTV Television, 6 March 2005.

10 Bill Curry, "Public Backed Missile Defence Talks in '04 Poll," *Globe and Mail*, 6 July 2005.

11 Alexander Moens, Cassandra Florio, and Sean McCarthy, "Canadian-American Relations in 2007," Fraser Institute Digital Publication, May 2007, 3.

12 United States Embassy Ottawa, e-mail, 27 March 2006.

13 United States Department of State, e-mail, 17 March 2006.

14 Patrick White, "Wallet-Size ID Card Could Be Sufficient for Canadian Travel to U.S.: Wilkins," Canadian Press, 1 February 2006. United States Embassy Ottawa, "Remarks by Ambassador David H. Wilkins – Canadian Association of Importers and Exporters," 10 April 2006.

15 An exchange of e-mails among US officials in early 2008 gives insight into just one of the issues involved in using alternative documents. A US consular official in Canada asked, "How will state issuers [of enhanced drivers' licences, EDLs] know who is a U.S. citizen and who is not, for example? What documents will they accept ... Will there be any method for state EDL-issuing offices and employees to double-check their decisions with a U.S. Federal office?" Another consular official answered, "Essentially, the Passport Office has agreed to train certain DMV [individual US states' Departments of Motor Vehicles] people on citizenship documentation ... If there are any complications, they will decline to issue and refer the person to the nearest passport office ... the last word I had was that [the US Department of] State had determined that the EDLs would NOT be definitive evidence of citizenship (a Federal Authority)." And a DHS colleague commented, "[There is a] distinction between US citizenship adjudicated under federal authority and a verification of US citizenship by a driver's license examiner since only the Departments of State and Homeland Security have legal authority to adjudicate US citizenship. A practical consequence of this important critical dis-

tinction is that the Department [of State] will not accept an EDL issued by a state as proof of citizenship in the context of a passport application. As a driver's license, an EDL will be accepted as proof of identity." United States Mission to Canada, e-mail, 3 January 2008.

16 United States Embassy Ottawa, e-mail, 13 February 2007.

17 United States Embassy Ottawa, e-mail, 13 November 2007.

18 US Representative Charlie Norwood, "Partnering for Success: Securing the Northern Border," submission to the House of Representatives Armed Services Committee, 7 September 2006. What this (along with supporting infrastructure) would cost, and why the government should spend those considerable resources on the Canadian border rather than elsewhere, was not explained.

19 Windsor, Ontario, MP Brian Masse was quoted saying, "If we're going to see weaponization that is used in conflicts like Afghanistan and Iraq put on the Canada-U.S. border, saying that it's required for safety and security, it really changes the nature of the relationship." United States Embassy Ottawa, e-mail, 11 August 2008. See also US Department of Homeland Security, "CBP Opens 5th Northern Border Air and Marine Branch," news release, 8 August 2008.

20 For example, "No Delays as New Border ID Rules Begin," Associated Press, 31 January 2008.

21 United States Embassy Ottawa, e-mail, 5 September 2006.

22 "The Unwelcome Landing of Another U.S. Penalty," editorial, *Globe and Mail*, 2 September 2006.

23 United States Foreign Agricultural Service, US Embassy Ottawa, e-mail, 14 September 2006.

24 Prime Minister of Canada, Letter to the President of the United States of America, 4 December 2006.

25 United States Department of State, e-mail, 26 January 2007.

26 United States Embassy Ottawa, e-mail, 14 December 2007. Passages quoting Minister Emerson are drawn from an e-mail forwarded by reporter Steven Chase. See also Reuters News Service, "U.S. 'Rigidity of Mindset' Hurting Trade: Canada," *Calgary Herald*, 4 December 2007. On the effects of 9/11 on cross-border trade, see Danielle Goldfarb, "Is Just-in-Case Replacing Just-in-Time? How Cross-Border Trading Behaviour has Changed since 9/11," Conference Board of Canada, June 2007. This report sought evidence that security had hurt Canada-US trade, but failed to find any. The author did find some evidence that security had increased costs, but only by 1–2 per cent for trucking, which would have been one of the most affected sectors. The bottom line was that, rather than bilateral trade being reduced, business appeared to be absorbing those costs. This finding was first misunderstood and then (after the Embassy tried to straighten him out) disregarded by a *Globe and Mail* reporter (Steven Chase, "Border Security Chills Trade Relations," *Globe and Mail*, 17 December 2007). Even the conclusion that costs

had increased could have been exaggerated, since it was based mainly on interviews with businesspeople who had incentives to complain.

27 United States Department of State, "Informal Summary of Discussions: Security and Prosperity Partnership Ministerial Plenary, Ottawa, 23 February 2007."

28 United States Embassy Ottawa, internal e-mail, 30 January 2008. The next day in a meeting Ambassador Wilkins thanked me, saying he hadn't changed a word of it.

29 Michael Hart, "Canada Blew It," *Financial Post*, 12 February 2008, and also Terence Corcoran, "U.S. Border Is Killing Free Trade," *Financial Post*, 12 February 2008. My own reaction, which I shared with my colleagues, was cast in simple economic terms: I thought the media were overstating the decline in cross-border trade. The year 2000 had been an extraordinary high in merchandise trade and economic activity, reached after more than a decade of spectacular growth. Much change had been happening in the economy since, including a shift from merchandise toward services and investment, structural changes in the auto sector, and permanent decline in demand for pulp and paper products. The newspapers' presentation of the Hart and Corcoran items seemed to blame all the slowdown in Canada's exports on border measures. I also pointed out the Conference Board study that looked for, but did not find, a negative effect on trade volumes from measures introduced after the September 2001 attacks.

30 United States Embassy Ottawa, e-mail, 12 February 2008.

31 United States Department of State, e-mail, 12 February 2008.

32 United States Department of State, diplomatic telegram 2005 State 125165.

33 Al Kamen, "In the Loop: LES Means More," *Washington Post*, 9 November 2005. The lifestyle of Americans in the Green Zone, on the other hand, was portrayed by journalists as extravagant. For example, see Iason Athanasiadis, "Beer, Bikinis, Baghdad? At Saddam Hussein's Former Republican Palace, Tuesday Is Now Karaoke Night," *Toronto Star*, 5 May 2006.

34 United States Embassy Ottawa, e-mail, 25 January 2007.

35 Paul Richter, "Staffing Crisis at U.S. Foreign Service," *Los Angeles Times*, 6 June 2007.

36 Barbara Slavin, "Study Looks at Diplomats' Well-Being," *USA Today*, 15 June 2007.

37 Notes from the Chairman: A Conversation with Martin Dempsey, *Foreign Affairs*, September/October 2016, 9.

38 Leila Fadel, "U.S. Embassy Employees Fearful over Green Zone Attacks," *McClatchy News*, 15 May 2007.

39 Glenn Kessler, "Embassy Staff in Baghdad Inadequate, Rice Is Told," *Washington Post*, 19 June 2007.

40 Elizabeth Williamson, "How Much Embassy Is Too Much?" *Washington Post*, 2 March 2007.

41 Kessler, "Embassy Staff in Baghdad Inadequate, Rice Is Told." The war-driven scarcity of Foreign Service personnel presumably contributed to the State Department's accelerated efforts to identify ways in which locally engaged staff

could assume more responsibilities at all posts. United States Department of State, diplomatic telegram 2007 State 42193.

42 United States Department of State, diplomatic telegram 2007 State 85014. See also Glenn Kessler, "Rice Orders That Diplomatic Jobs in Iraq be Filled First," *Washington Post*, 21 June 21 2007.

43 Guy Dinmore, "U.S. Twists Civilian Arms to Fill Fortress Baghdad," *Financial Times*, 8 January 2007.

44 Ibid.

45 Williamson, "How Much Embassy Is Too Much?"

46 United States Embassy Ottawa, internal e-mail, 12 June 2007.

47 Rajiv Chandrasekaran, "Defense Skirts State in Reviving Iraqi Industry," *Washington Post*, 14 May 2007.

48 Martin Wolf, "America Failed to Calculate the Enormous Costs of War," *Financial Times*, 11 January 2006. In the same column Wolf remarks, "Whether or not one believes the war was justified, one should still be concerned that a decision to go to war was taken in the absence of any intelligent analysis of the likely costs. Nor can one argue that it was impossible to do such an analysis."

49 Gideon Rachman, "Why the World May Regret the End of the Neo-Con Era," *Financial Times*, 5 September 2006.

50 United States Department of State, "Rapid Response," international media summary, 6 and 12 September 2006.

51 "Five Questions for the Protesters" (editorial), *Ottawa Citizen*, 27 November 2004. This marked a year when protests against trade agreements moved to the background of a more general anti-globalization theme. A policy paper by the Canadian Labour Congress (CLC) said that "it is time to acknowledge that the free trade era as a whole, contrary to some of our most pessimistic predictions, has not been an economic disaster." CLC President Ken Georgetti reportedly explained that the CLC continued to oppose free trade but was proposing ways to work with it because there was no political will to reverse the 1989 FTA or the 1994 NAFTA. Bill Curry, "Hargrove at Odds with CLC over Trade," *National Post*, 23 September 2004.

52 Michael Lind, "How America Became the World's Dispensable Nation," *Financial Times*, 25 January 2005.

53 United States Department of State, "Rapid Response," international media summary, 25 September 2006.

54 United States Department of State, Public Affairs Bureau, "Rapid Response: Reaction to Iraq Study Group Report," 6 December 2006.

55 Statement of Edward N. Luttwak before the Committee on Foreign Relations, United States Senate Hearings on "Securing America's Interest in Iraq: The Remaining Options," 23 January 2007.

56 Testimony of the Honorable Zbigniew Brzezinski before the Senate Foreign Relations Committee, United States Senate, 1 February 2007.

57 Thomas E. Ricks, "McCaffrey Paints Gloomy Picture of Iraq," *Washington Post*, 28 March 2007.

58 David Ignatius, "After the Rock, Diplomacy," *Washington Post*, 7 March 2007.

59 Al Kamen, "Wanted: A Few Good Iraqis. Or Jordanians. Or ... Anybody?" *Washington Post*, 12 February 2007.

60 Helene Cooper, "Few Veteran Diplomats Accept Mission to Iraq," *New York Times*, 7 February 2007.

61 US Mission to Canada, Draft FY2009 Mission Strategic Plan, 30 March 2007.

62 US General Accountability Office, December 2007.

63 Anne Gearan, "White House Opens Doors to Iraq Refugees," Associated Press, 15 February 2007.

64 United States Embassy Ottawa, e-mail, 12 July 2007.

65 United States Embassy Ottawa, e-mail, 27 July 2007.

66 United States Embassy Ottawa, e-mail, 24 July 2007.

67 Keith W. Mines, "After the Surge," Foreign Policy Research Institute E-Notes, 4 December 2007.

68 John Naland, "Implications of Directed Assignments," AFSANET e-mail, 30 October 2007. See also United States Department of State, diplomatic telegram 2007 State 150726 for descriptions of Provincial Reconstruction Team positions then open in Afghanistan.

69 United States Department of State, diplomatic telegram 2007 State 158199.

70 Karen DeYoung, "U.S. to Cut 10 Percent of Diplomatic Posts Next Year," *Washington Post*, 13 December 2007.

71 William Langewiesche, "The Mega-Bunker of Baghdad," *Vanity Fair*, November 2007.

72 US Embassy Baghdad, "Iraq: IDF in the International Zone," Press Guidance, 26 March 2008.

73 United States Department of State, diplomatic telegram 2006 Ottawa 0270.

74 John Ibbitson, "How Kandahar Fits into PM's View of Canada," *Globe and Mail*, 4 March 2006.

75 United States Embassy Ottawa, e-mail, 27 February 2008.

76 United States Embassy Ottawa, e-mail, 26 April 2007.

77 United States Embassy Ottawa, e-mail, 3 May 2007.

78 Conference of Defence Associations (CDA), "Seeking the Truth on Afghanistan," e-mail to federal party leaders and others, 2 May 2007. In the same e-mail the CDA included excerpts from a federal government briefing note that outlined Canada's arrangements with Afghanistan and the fact that Afghanistan, too, was a party to the Geneva Convention.

79 Eugene Robinson, "Fleeting Glory in Albania," *Washington Post*, 12 June 2007.

80 Eric Stover, Victor Peskin, and Alexa Koenig, *Hiding in Plain Sight: The Pursuit of War Criminals from Nuremberg to the War on Terror* (Berkeley: University of California Press 2016).

81 David Beatty, "The 'Canadian Corollary' to the Monroe Doctrine and the Ogdensburg Agreement of 1940," *Northern Mariner* (Journal of the Canadian Nautical Research Society), January 1991, 3–22.

82 Private e-mail, 2006.

83 United States Embassy Ottawa, draft diplomatic telegram, October 2004.

84 United States Embassy Ottawa, e-mail, 9 June 2006.

85 Judy Dempsey, "Defense Secretary, Facing Criticism, Hails NATO's Forces in Afghanistan," *New York Times*, 18 January 2008.

86 J.L. Granatstein, "Wake Up! This Is Our War, Too," *Globe and Mail*, 28 February 2006.

87 Then NDP leader Jack Layton took this view to an extreme when he praised deserters from the US military and advised assisting them (Bruce Campion-Smith, "Canada Should Welcome U.S. Deserters, Layton Says," *Toronto Star*, 5 May 2006). Encouraging and harbouring deserters is a hostile act; it is a way, albeit a mild one, of taking one side of a conflict, that is, it breaks neutrality. The straightforward conclusion is that Layton knew this, viewed the United States to some degree as an enemy, and did not mind saying so because his electorate felt the same way. The charitable but less believable view is that he was simply ignorant of such basic facts about international affairs and military conflict. Layton drew a parallel between assisting Iraq deserters and accepting Vietnam-era draft evaders, but civilians who are avoiding being involuntarily drafted are morally in a very different position from deserters who have already willingly joined a volunteer military and have been active in it for a time.

CHAPTER FIVE

1 Cases where an Embassy employs a citizen of the host country to do analytical and representational work are less common than employing, say, locally hired drivers, cooks or gardeners, but still not unusual. In centuries past, some East Asian empires employed well-connected Westerners to represent them in European capitals, and sometimes accredited these non-subjects as their "Ambassadors Extraordinary and Plenipotentiary." In present-day Ottawa, the Delegation of the European Commission, the embassies of Japan and South Korea, and some high commissions hire local Canadians at a professional level to work alongside their Foreign Service officers.

2 Ottawa is home to people who are nationals of all, or nearly all, countries in the world. During my years there, in addition to its many American and Canadian employees, the US Embassy employed citizens of Argentina, Moldova, Ukraine, Egypt, Pakistan, Germany, Nepal, and various other countries.

3 This is how I came to realize that large segments of Canadian society fundamentally misunderstand our country's situation in the world. Being adjacent to the

United States is, by any sane evaluation, a fabulous piece of good luck. Yet too many Canadians view it as a problem, even a misfortune. This causes them to misunderstand all kinds of policy issues, from the Arctic (where the United States is a vital ally yet is traditionally viewed as a sovereignty threat) to the economy (where the United States underpins our wonderful prosperity but is too often demonized as a looming menace that "wants to own us").

4 This sort of reasoning came more easily to me as a result of my studies in nationalism with Elliott Tepper at Carleton University in the early 1980s. I recall Professor Tepper asking rhetorically, "Why should we express passionate loyalty to Canada? Why should we sing its song and salute its flag? Why not the province of Ontario? Why not the cities of Nepean or Gloucester, why not the Regional Municipality of Ottawa-Carleton? Why not our own neighbourhood?" He pointed out how the symbols, anthems, flags, myths, and allegedly shared "values" and collective loyalties of a nation are, to a large extent, deliberately made up and propagated by the state itself, specifically so that people will go to war for it. Tepper's course conditioned me to think more critically about such questions of loyalty.

5 As a practical matter, my lack of a Secret clearance on the US side was no more than an occasional and minor irritant. It made it awkward to get into the Chancery at nights and on weekends but did not prevent me from attending meetings and exercising substantial influence on Embassy processes and decisions. Indeed, by ensuring that a cleared American officer colleague remained nominally responsible for what I did, it protected me by limiting my own accountability. My lack of clearance also spared me from many administrative responsibilities which were reserved for cleared Americans and which I had no interest in sharing – such as dealing with classified files and computer systems (these played a small role in the US-Canada relationship but were cumbersome to maintain) or being duty officer overnight and on weekends (little good ever came anyone's way as a result of being duty officer).

6 This characteristic of social life in Canada has moderated but not as much as it deserves to. In 2008 I was at a staff meeting of a community organization in Ottawa, one whose mission statement refers to "an open and welcoming Ottawa" and whose announced "values" are to "treat all individuals with dignity and equity," to "believe in everyone's ability to enrich our society," and to cultivate "interdependent, harmonious relationships within our community." In casual chat, a staff member (who knew nothing about me) remarked on the similarity of my name to that of a popular US television comedian who regularly criticized President George W. Bush and whose show the staff member said she enjoyed. As she walked away she added, "I like anything that's anti-American." I found myself counting the strange overlapping ironies contained in this remark: it casually and openly expressed prejudice within a meeting of professedly "welcoming" and

"harmonious" people; it identified Bush's negative qualities with America, even in a context where Bush's critics were American; and the speaker who "likes anything that's anti-American" enjoyed US televised entertainment.

7 United States Department of State, diplomatic telegram 1993 Ottawa 6331.

8 United States Department of State, diplomatic telegram 1993 Ottawa 0118.

9 United States Department of State, "Promoting America: A Proposal for Public Diplomacy," internal non-paper, October 2003.

10 US Ambassador Charles J. Swindells, "Anti-Americanism and Its Discontents," address to the New Zealand Institute of International Affairs, 23 August 2004.

11 Nora Jacobson, "Before You Flee to Canada, Can We Talk?" *Washington Post*, 26 November 2004.

12 Quoted in Paul Gessell, "Foreign Affairs Rife with Anti-Americanism: Gotlieb: One-time Envoy to U.S. Slams Former Colleagues, Says Department Still Harbours Same Sentiments," *Ottawa Citizen*, 29 November 2006.

13 One reason the right to retaliate has never been tested is that the Canadian government has gone to some lengths to tailor its cultural-policy measures so that it need not invoke the cultural exemption to defend them. This makes the measures more legally robust and avoids retaliatory measures.

14 Based on a draft that I saw in May 1996, this three-pronged strategy included responding aggressively to trade agreement violations or instances of discrimination, engaging Canada in a dialog at the deputy ministers' level, and making public international statements to the effect that, while the United States was supportive of efforts to promote national identity through cultural development, "we will not tolerate attempts by our trading partners to shroud commercial protectionism in the cloak of cultural sovereignty."

15 The unfortunate history of this dispute is related in detail elsewhere. John Stewart, "Magazines, Ministers and Monoculture: The Canada-United States Dispute over Magazines in the 1990s," *Canadian Foreign Policy Journal*, vol. 16, no. 1, spring 2010.

16 As this is written more than a decade later, it remains awkward to disentangle "content" goals from industrial goals in Canada's cultural-policy measures. One example is a 2008 controversy over government proposals to deny tax credits to film/video productions with "objectionable" subject matter. The government suggested that different rules would need to apply to "non-Canadian" films and videos being shot in Canada since, in these cases, the policy goal was not to influence content but to attract production activity.

17 After discussing cultural policy with officials at the Department of Canadian Heritage in December 1997, one of the Embassy's senior officers complained to me about Heritage officials' predilection for snide remarks. This exemplarily polite officer was stunned that Heritage officials made it so plain to him that they thought being located next to the United States was some kind of misfor-

tune for Canada. He wondered whether they would prefer to live next door to three hundred million Russians or Chinese.

18 The Canadian media did much the same thing two years later when Giffin was replaced as Ambassador by Paul Cellucci. Writers and editors quickly determined to cast Cellucci as a blunt, tough-talking bully – thus pandering to a crude stereotype of the Bush administration that they had already created. I worked with Giffin and Cellucci for about three years each. I saw both as considerate gentlemen. True, Cellucci did have a more direct style of communication, but because of this he was extraordinarily likeable and a terrific leader. Giffin was not a bit less willing than Cellucci to criticize Canadian positions. The difference was that the media decided immediately to trash Cellucci, on partisan grounds – because he was a Republican and they knew that Canadian readers, seeing Cellucci as a proxy for Bush, would lap up the "bully" story. Years afterward, I encountered people in Ottawa who couldn't recall the name of the ambassador who had preceded David Wilkins, but they did think they "remembered" that he was a rude bully. The media had a free hand in misrepresenting Cellucci because he would not divert energy toward trying to prevent or correct them. When we asked him if it bothered him, he said that the treatment he had received from Boston's press was significantly worse than what he had received from Canadian writers. With similar dignity, the ambassador scaled back the enormous, splashy Fourth of July parties that his predecessor had held. Perhaps that made it even easier and cheaper for reporters to attack him, since they were less likely to get invitations.

19 James Baxter, "Liberals Face Backbench Rebellions over Contentious Magazine Bill," *Ottawa Citizen*, 23 February 1999.

20 United States Information Service Office in Toronto, Direct Video Conference Transcript, 30 November 1998.

21 A further factor reinforcing the belief that cultural conflict would continue was the advent of the Internet, which brought the widespread expectation that media and information technologies would soon "converge." Such technologies had contributed to *Sports Illustrated*'s circumvention of the border ban on split runs in 1993. It was widely thought that these technologies would quickly undercut Canadian cultural-policy measures, bringing Canada and the United States into increasing conflict. In fact, "convergence" took about a decade longer than most players anticipated. Also, Internet-based communications flooded around and past the regulated media in Canada – like a rising tide rather than a tsunami, leaving the regulated sectors in place (though declining in importance) but not devastated. In this way, advancing information technology may actually have somewhat decreased the likelihood of international conflict over cultural policy, though it raised the profile of certain related issues, such as privacy and copyright.

22 For a particularly incorrigible view, see David Crane, "Magazine War Shows the U.S. Wants to Own Us," *Toronto Star*, 29 May 1999.

23 An item published on 7 May 1998 in the *Toronto Star* further illustrates how some Canadian media covered the trade and legal issues at stake in the magazine dispute with biased, emotional language. National-affairs columnist Rosemary Speirs, who probably knew (or ought to have known) better, wrote that the 1996–97 WTO case originated because "Jean Chrétien's new government underestimated the U.S. administration's aggressiveness on behalf of the American entertainment industry." The "new" government had been in office for three years at the time of the case. There was no mention of *Sports Illustrated*'s legitimate complaint about being shut down by a retroactive tax measure. Speirs remarked that "the U.S. won the first round on technical trade grounds," although numerous Canadian trade lawyers stated that the WTO's support of the United States' complaint had been thorough and substantial. Speirs continued, "By making clear that the defence of Canadian magazines is a defence of Canadians' right to read about their own country in their own voices, Copps hopes to win the next round at the WTO," thus inserting a hot-button nationalist buzz phrase into what purported to be a discussion of WTO rules. Such writing did nothing to inform and everything to inflame.

24 "Some Canadian politicians and intellectuals ... engage in constant, unproductive shadow-boxing. They strut around on their home stage, jabbing their fists in our direction, scowling, cursing, threatening to take us on, while virtually nobody south of the border is paying any attention ... Some of Chrétien's senior cabinet ministers have been known to make totally inappropriate or inaccurate comments during visits to Washington. But I'm convinced that they never intended their insults to be picked up or taken seriously. They were intended to impress or appease a small crowd of left-of-center Liberal constituents back home ... Canadian politicians and their advisers would get lured into showing how tough and independent they really are, and would usually end up walking the plank. The final deal, no matter how advantageous to Canada, could never be good enough for the Canadian press. Whatever the ultimate compromise, they lambaste the politicians and negotiators as spineless weasels who have sold out to the Americans or been taken to the cleaners. If an American politician or negotiator has a problem with Canada that becomes highly publicized, however, he or she is generally viewed as ineffective ... That's why, I concluded, high-profile disputes between the United States and Canada are no-win propositions for both sides. They're best resolved calmly and without publicity." James Blanchard, *Behind the Embassy Door* (Ann Arbor, MI: Sleeping Bear Press 1998), 158–9.

25 United States Embassy Ottawa, e-mail, 21 October 1999.

26 With the benefit of hindsight fifteen years later, it is clear that Minister Copps had led and nourished a very unfair multi-country assault on the United States

that was likely no help to culture or to international relations. As a State Department officer wrote internally in 2002: "The charge of U.S. cultural imperialism is often a theme at any discussion in international cultural forums. The term imperialism may not be used, but the dominant effect of U.S. popular culture on other societies is a frequent subtext ... Illicit traffic in cultural property ... causes important chapters in the history of mankind to be irretrievably lost and undermines a sovereign nation's right to protect its patrimony ... The U.S. ... is a major destination for illicitly acquired objects and, citing ethical and moral principles, has become party to the 1970 UNESCO Convention to reduce pillage and illicit trafficking in archaeological and ethnological objects. At the same time it is able to promote access to this material for educational, cultural, and scientific purposes. The most dangerous and irresponsible charge is that the U.S. government is directing some sort of cultural campaign and trying to impose its economic, political, and social views on the rest of the world. Of fundamental concern is that the charge of U.S. cultural imperialism not be used as a basis to restrict the free flow of information and products across borders. The U.S. continues to support unfettered trade in intellectual and cultural products ... Popular culture has become internationalized, drawing from many sources ... In terms of high culture, the trade is international as well ... When American museums and galleries stage art exhibitions, their least concern is the nationality of the artist – quality is the main consideration. Charges of U.S. cultural imperialism also stem from many countries' unease with economic globalization and the need to readjust ways of doing business. The U.S. is unfairly blamed for this phenomenon as well, in order to find a convenient scapegoat for unanticipated dislocations in a nation's economy." United States Department of State, "U.S. Cultural Imperialism," draft memo, 21 February 2002.

27 Keith Acheson and Christopher Maule, "The Culture of Protection and the Protection of Culture: A Canadian Perspective in 1998," Carleton Industrial Organization Research Unit (CIORU), https://ideas.repec.org/p/car/ciorup/98-01.html. See also subsequent work by these authors.

28 United States Department of State, diplomatic telegram 2003 Ottawa 2062.

29 Production revenue of the top ten Canadian film/TV production firms grew by nearly 220 per cent from 1988–99 to 1997–98, while their export revenue grew by over 580 per cent, and this was driven mainly by expanded firm activities, not by mergers. Their full-time employment grew by 274 per cent. At least half of all exports went to the United States. "Focus on Culture," Statistics Canada Catalog no. 87-004-XPB, vol. 12, no. 2, 2000.

30 "This Pregnant Pause: The Future of Cultural Trade Conflict between Canada and the United States," paper presented to the Society of Historians of American Foreign Relations 2000 Conference, Toronto, 23 June 2000.

31 United States Department of State, diplomatic telegram 2003 Ottawa 2873.

32 United States Department of State, e-mail, 10 March 2004.

33 As minister of the environment in 1996, before coming to the Canadian Her-
    itage portfolio, Copps was responsible for launching an attempt to control the
    gasoline additive MMT in Canada. MMT could not be shown to be unsafe, but
    Copps undertook to control it anyway by banning both its importation and its
    trade across provincial boundaries, a law that was disputed by MMT's manufactur-
    er, provincial governments, and others, and eventually failed. Copps's initiatives
    on MMT and split-run magazines had similar results: both found creative ways to
    criminalize innocuous activities that happened to be based in the United States;
    both put Canada on the wrong side of a trade-law issue, thereby corroding
    Canada's credibility in trade policy; both cost a good deal of effort; and both
    accomplished very little.

34 United States Department of State, diplomatic telegram 1999 Ottawa 03599.

35 United States Department of State, e-mail, 25 January 2005.

36 United States Department of State, "U.S. Intervention on the UNESCO Convention
    on the Protection and Promotion of the Diversity of Cultural Expressions, Third
    Inter-American Meeting of Ministers of Culture and Highest Appropriate
    Authorities, Montreal, Canada, 13–25 November 2006."

37 United States Department of State, e-mail, 16 November 2006.

38 A comparison might be drawn to Canada's position around the same time on
    the role of another UN body, the Committee on the Peaceful Uses of Outer Space
    (COPUOS). For a while until 2006, Canada was the most vocal proponent of COPU-
    OS, hoping to divert some of its attention from civilian activities toward protec-
    tions against the "weaponization" of space (proposing voluntary guidelines with-
    out verification). This position irritated the United States and drew limited
    support from other parties because it would be ineffective if implemented.
    Canadian officials backed down at a COPUOS meeting in early 2006, saying the
    existing international regime was sufficient. US Department of State, diplomatic
    telegram 2006 Vienna 191.

39 Dean Beeby, "Starbucks' Music Proposal Eyed for Canadian Content," *Globe and
    Mail*, 3 October 2005, B5.

40 United States Department of State, e-mail, 3 October 2005.

41 United States Department of State, e-mail, 3 October 2005.

42 Jeff Sallot, "Bush Lied in Justifying Iraq War, Canada Right to Stay Out: Poll,"
    Globe and Mail, 15 March 2004.

43 Pew Global Attitudes Project, "U.S. Image up Slightly but Still Negative," Pew
    Research Center, 2005.

44 Jason Fekete, "Manley Critical of Premier, PM: Speech Urges Canada to Work
    with U.S.," *Calgary Herald*, 28 March 2004.

45 United States Embassy Ottawa, e-mail, 2 September 2005.

46 United States Embassy Ottawa, e-mail, 2 September 2005.

47 United States Embassy Ottawa, briefing note for US Trade Representative, 8 September 2005.

48 Jim Brown, "Martin Joins U.S. Ambassador to Mark 9–11 Anniversary, Reaffirm Fight against Terror," *Canadian Press*, 11 September 2005.

49 United States Embassy Ottawa, minutes of weekly economic meeting, 13 October 2005.

50 John Ibbitson, "Poll Shatters Tired, Old Myths," *Globe and Mail*, 9 May 2005.

51 The 105th American Assembly, "Renewing the U.S.-Canada Relationship," 2005.

52 COMPAS poll, week of 15–19 August 2005.

53 Kim Nossal, "The Responsibility to Be Honest," in David Bercuson and Dennis Stairs, eds., *In the Canadian Interest: Assessing Canada's International Policy Statement*, (Calgary, AB: Canadian Defence and Foreign Affairs Institute 2005).

54 Derek Burney, "International Policy Statement – One Hand Clapping?" *The Dispatch*, Canadian Defence and Foreign Affairs Institute, vol. 2, no. 1, spring 2005.

55 United States Embassy Ottawa, weekly economic meeting notes, 3 November 2005.

56 United States Embassy Ottawa, weekly economic meeting notes, 8 December 2005.

57 Ambassador David Wilkins, Address to the Canadian Club of Ottawa, 13 December 2005.

58 *Globe and Mail*, "The Prime Minister Thumps His Chest," editorial, 16 December 2005, A18.

59 United States Embassy Ottawa, weekly economic meeting notes, 15 December 2005.

60 "DCM remarked on the absence of anti-American themes from the Canadian election campaign in recent weeks." United States Embassy Ottawa, weekly economic meeting notes, 5 January 2006.

61 Jeffrey Simpson, "The Dirty Lowdown about Canada's Commitment to Kyoto," *Globe and Mail*, 2 December 2005, A19.

62 Alan Freeman, "McKenna Believes Anti-U.S. Talk Hurt Liberals," *Globe and Mail*, 2 March 2006, A1. As usual, of course, all this turbulence at the political level belied greater continuity below the surface in the massive (but not headline-grabbing) regular business of such a large two-country relationship. Our Embassy's 2005/2006 report on allied contributions to common defence had almost nothing negative to say. "While the [Canadian] government does not participate in stability operations in Iraq, it is a leading contributor to both Operation Enduring Freedom and the NATO-led International Security Assistance Force in Afghanistan" (ISAF). But the report noted that Canada's defence spending as a proportion of GDP remained among the lowest in NATO (at 1.1 per cent) and that "most defense insiders believe Canada will need a defense budget of over US$20 billion by FY2012 to implement [its own February 2005] Defence Policy Statement." It also remarked that "the Canadian Forces has a limited ability to recruit and train new forces. The accession and training of the 5,000 new regular forces will only just fully man existing units and will take five years to

fully implement." United States Department of State, diplomatic telegram 2006 Ottawa 0270.

63   Robert Fulford, "Do Not Disturb," *National Post*, 31 December 2005.

64   United States Embassy Ottawa, e-mail, 17 January 2005.

65   United States Department of State, diplomatic telegram 2005 Ottawa 0153.

66   United States Department of State, diplomatic telegram 2005 Ottawa 0393.

67   United States Department of State, diplomatic telegram 2005 Calgary 0137.

68   United States Department of State, e-mail, 24 January 2005.

69   Michael Taube, "The Harper Era Begins," *Washington Times*, 30 January 2006.

70   United States Embassy Ottawa, e-mail, 17 February 2006.

71   United States Embassy Ottawa, e-mail, 3 May 2006.

72   United States Department of State, diplomatic telegram 2006 Ottawa 513. Another Embassy analysis a few weeks later pointed out that "having the federal government stick to the jobs it was constitutionally assigned is what Harper really cares about. The latter is an uphill battle, because MPs who knock on voters' doors keep hearing about provincial issues like health, education and transport – not about fisheries management or strategic airlift. Harper will have trouble finding a political payoff for cleaning up the jurisdictional overlap. Indeed, provinces are complicit in the overlap. They like it, because it obscures their responsibility for policy outcomes. If there is trouble in health care, for example, they can always blame Ottawa." United States Embassy Ottawa, e-mail, 23 May 2006.

73   United States Embassy Ottawa, e-mail, 1 May 2006.

74   United States Department of State, diplomatic telegram 2006 Ottawa 1322.

75   United States Department of State, e-mail, 3 May 2006.

76   United States Department of State, diplomatic telegram 2007 Ottawa 921.

77   United States Embassy Ottawa, e-mail, 6 June 2005.

78   United States Department of State, e-mail, 19 December 2007.

79   Stephen Fidler, "U.S. Suffers Decline in Prestige, Survey Says," *Financial Times*, 13 September 2007.

80   United States Embassy, e-mail, 13 September 2007.

CHAPTER SIX

1   Canada's economy is growing more slowly than the rest of the world's, and it has a much lower rate of natural-population increase than the United States, though the latter difference is partly mitigated by immigration. Also, according to United Nations data analyzed by the International Institute for Sustainable Development (IISD), among the G-7 countries, Canada had the slowest growth (averaging 0.28 per cent annually) in real comprehensive wealth per capita from 1990 to 2010 – less than half the rate of the United States, which had the next lowest rate in the group. Other studies came to similar conclusions. Canada's

"development model is based heavily on the exploitation of natural capital, and the country cannot sustain another 30 years of natural capital depletion." What growth Canada had was narrowly concentrated in oil and gas and housing. IISD, "Comprehensive Wealth in Canada – Measuring What Matters in the Long Run," December 2016, executive summary.

EPILOGUE

1 Author's diary.
2 Edward Luce, "Beware of the Return of the Clinton Dynasty," *Financial Times*, 6 April 2017.

Index

Acheson, Keith, 185–6

Afghanistan, 102, 112, 155, 158, 159; detainees, 160–1, 163; Harper and, 184, 219; NATO in, 165–6; polling Canadians about, 221; Provincial Reconstruction Teams (PRTs), 257n68; Tarnak Farm incident, 107–9

aircraft industry, 60, 133

air marshals, 106

Alberta: Harper Conservatives, 212, 215–16; Reform Party, 30, 54

alcoholic beverages, 50, 242n9

al-Qaeda, 96, 152, 160

Animal and Plant Health Inspection Service (APHIS), US, 134–5

anti-Americanism: in Canada, 158, 166, 170–5, 194, 200, 233; internationally, 152, 173, 221–2

Arar, Maher, 140, 160, 162–3

Asian economies and trade flows, 12, 26, 68, 74

Asia-Pacific Economic Cooperation (APEC), 26, 60, 63–4, 238n22

automotive industry and Auto Pact, 44–5, 99

aviation, 72, 138; disruption on 9/11, 97–9, 248–9

Axworthy, Lloyd, 54, 109, 246n3

Baghdad, US Embassy in: cost of, 145; living conditions of staff, 143, 146; recruitment for, 142, 144, 146, 154–6

ballistic missile defence (BMD), 114, 121, 129–30, 207

Barlow, Maude, 48, 64, 81

Barrett, David, 51–2

Barshefsky, Charlene, 75

Beatty, David, xiii, 163, 258n81

Beinart, Peter, 96

Berlin Wall, 6, 10

Bhagwati, Jagdish, 61–2, 83

Black, Conrad, 43, 97

Blanchard, James, 32–3, 41–2, 262n24

Bloc Québécois, 29, 31, 213

Bombardier, 21

Borden, Robert, 43–4

border, Canada-US: after 9/11, 67, 71–2, 98, 100–2, 137, 249n27; enforcement of, 104, 114–15, 133; erasing, 90, 223; Obama and, 84; thickening of, 68, 103, 134–6, 139–42. See also Western Hemisphere Travel Initiative

Bosnia, 10, 12

Bouchard, Lucien, 29, 31, 40, 41

bovine spongiform encephalopathy (BSE), 66–7, 198, 214

Breese, Terry, 23

Brussels, 13

Brzęzinski, Zbigniew, 152

Bulte, Sarmite, 189

Burney, Derek, 200–1

Bush, George H.W., xi, 12–13, 88–9

Bush, George W. (administration of), x–xi, 122–3, 127–9, 148, 208, 232; 2004 visit to Canada, 63–4, 71, 73; Canadian politicians' public remarks about, 113; diplomacy and, 78, 109, 112, 116, 117–18, 122, 146, 150, 158; economic and trade policy, 76, 78, 85, 91, 247n8; Kyoto Protocol and, 77, 203; popularity of, 108, 151, 196, 221, 222, 231; terrorism and, 90, 96, 150, 227, 248n16, 248n22

Business Council on National Issues (BCNI), 39

businesses: and Canada-US border, 68, 72, 90, 114; and governments, 47–8, 136, 183, 200, 211, 218–19; and NAFTA improvement efforts, 73–5, 93; and Quebec separatism, 39

cables (diplomatic telegrams), 19, 20, 237n18

Calgary, University of, 54, 212

Canada-US Partnership (CUSP), 91

Canadian Association of American Studies, 170

Canadian Centre for Policy Alternatives (CCPA), 81

Canadian Council of Chief Executives. See Business Council on National Issues, 83, 93

Canadian Defence and Foreign Affairs Institute, 200

Cellucci, Paul, 91–4, 107, 115, 121; 9/11, 97–101; abuse by Canadian media, 261n18; BMD and Canadian military spending, 128–30; Iraq invasion, 120

Central Intelligence Agency (CIA), 21–2

Charest, Jean, 41

Charlottetown Accord, 29–30

Charter of Rights and Freedoms, 116, 162

Chertoff, Michael, 138, 140

Chile, 8, 26, 60, 79

China, 59, 74–5, 196, 218, 233

Churchill, Winston, 5, 14, 163, 235n1

Civil War, US, 31

climate change, 77, 81, 154, 213–14, 217, 220–1, 234, 245n44. See also COP 11, Kyoto Protocol

Clinton, Hillary, 82, 208

Clinton, William J. (administration), xvi, 10, 33, 39–40, 57, 61, 96, 202–3

Cohen, Andrew, xiii, 197

Cold War, 6–8, 10–14, 25–7, 90, 147, 150, 237n16

Collectif Échec à la Guerre (Stop the War Collective), 149

Commerce, US Department of, 15, 20, 71

Commonwealth of Independent States, 10

Conference Board of Canada, 137

Conference of Defence Associations, 161, 257n78

Congress, US, 8; and Bush Administration, 31, 47, 56–7, 75–6, 78–9, 101, 151; and Kyoto Protocol, 202–3

Conservative Party of Canada (or Progressive Conservative Party of Canada): Diefenbaker era, 209; Harper era, 136, 198, 205, 210–13, 216–20; Mulroney era, 175; in Ontario, 214

containment strategy, 95, 248n16

COP 11, 198, 202, 206

Copps, Sheila, 123, 177, 180–90, 262n26

Corcoran, Terence, 139

Council of Canadians, 48, 52, 62, 81

Council of State Governments, 41

counterfeit products, 68

country mandate (manufacturing), 90, 246n5

Country Music Television, 176

Crocker, Ryan, 146, 155–6

Crosbie, John, 51

Cuba, 8, 161

cultural policy, 55–6, 172–93, 260nn13–17, 261n21

currencies and monetary policy, 35, 82

Customs and Border Protection (CBP), US, 133, 135

customs union, xvi, 72, 89–94, 247n9

Czechoslovakia, 1993 division of, 34, 36

dairy products, 33

Defence Policy Statement (2005), 158, 265n62

Defence Production Sharing Agreements, 44, 101

Defense, US Department of, 122, 126, 147, 165

Democratic Party, US, 56–7, 62, 81, 83–4; 2006 and later, 151, 155

Department of Foreign Affairs and International Trade (DFAIT), Canada, 37, 185, 201

detainees, xvii, 140, 160–1

Devils Lake, 77

Dhaliwal, Herb, 113–14, 120–1, 137

dispute-settlement mechanisms: FTA, 49, 59; NAFTA, 61, 67, 70, 79, 85

economic performance of Canada, 65–7, 217, 220; 9/11 impact, 98–100; FTA and NAFTA impact, 59–61, 72, 79; Kyoto Protocol impact, 203

Economist Intelligence Unit, 127

Ehrenreich, Barbara, 89

election advertisements, 205–6

election campaign work, by Canadians in US, 208–9

embassies (other than US), 167

Embassy, US, in Ottawa: building, 9, 15, 24, 238n20; role in State Department, 20, 22, 24–7, 103; staff and organization, 9–23, 74, 88, 104, 161, 168. See also ambassadors by name

Emerson, David, 67, 134, 136

European Union, 90, 179, 247n9

"fair trade," 65

films, 175–6, 178–9, 185–7, 260n16, 263n29

Finance, Canadian Department of, 196, 213, 215

First World War, 8, 44, 97

fiscal imbalance, 211, 213, 215

fiscal policy, 34, 54, 211

Flaherty, Jim, 215–17

Flanagan, Tom, 54

foreign investment, 45–6, 76, 181

Foreign Investment Review Agency, 46

Foreign Service, US, 14–16, 142, 145–7, 154–7, 167–8

France, 122, 179, 137n17, 252n65; Quebec relations with, 36–7

Free Trade Agreement (FTA), US-Canada, xvii, 4, 21, 43, 47–52, 54–5

Free Trade Agreement of the Americas (FTAA), 62–3

Fulford, Robert, 210

Gallaway, Roger, 180

Gandhi, Mohandas K., 8–9

Garten, Jeffrey, 180

Gates, Robert, 153, 165

General Accounting Office (GAO), US, 56, 61

General Agreement on Tariffs and Trade

(GATT), 44. *See also* World Trade Organization
Georgetti, Ken, 256n51
Germany, 10
Gibbins, Roger, 197
Gingrich, Newt, 117, 125
Global War on Terror (GWOT), 90, 96–7, 107–16, 150, 162, 166, 227
Goolsbee, Austan, 83–4
Gore, Al, 57, 108
Gortari, Carlos Salinas de, 50
Goss, Porter, 128
Gotlieb, Allan, 175, 209–10
Graham, Bill, 112–13
Granatstein, Jack, 109, 165
Guantánamo Bay, 161, 163
Guatemala, 7
guns, 114, 201

Harper, Elijah, 29
Harper, Stephen, 54–5, 135–6, 198, 217, 239n13; attacks on, 205–6; economy, 218–19; election of, 211–13; foreign policy, 220–1; ideology and policies, 159–60, 212–15, 266n72
Harris, Mike, 111, 217
Hart, Michael, 61, 101–2, 139, 255
health care, 19, 31, 66, 68–9, 215
Hersh, Seymour, 127
Hillier, Rick, 161
Homeland Security, US Department of, 78, 115–17, 131, 140–2; authority of, 253n15; creation of, 251n54; secretaries of, x, 67, 104, 138, 194
Hurd, Douglas, 11
Hurricane Katrina, 197–8
Hussein, Saddam, 89, 120, 122, 126, 149
Hyde Park Declaration, 44

Ibbitson, John, 199
immigrants to Canada, 165, 227, 233–4

India, 68, 75–6
intellectual-property rights (IPR), 19, 69
International Network on Cultural Policy (INCP), 189–90
Iraq: costs of war in, 125, 145, 148–50, 158; Green Zone, 142, 157; invasion of, x, 113, 117, 119–23; in Kuwait conflict (First Gulf War), 87; occupation and reconstruction, 117, 123–7, 147, 152–3; Provincial Reconstruction Teams, 144; refugees from, 154; Study Group (ISG), 146, 151; "surge," 153, 156
Islam, 9, 152, 236n7

Japan, 12, 25–6, 105, 163, 236n7

Katz, Julius, 49
Kennan, George, 14, 237n16
Kergin, Michael, 93–4
Khadr, Omar, 160–1, 163
Kinzer, Stephen, 236n5
Kissinger, Henry, 148–9
Kohl, Helmut, 11
Krugman, Paul, 243n12
Kuwait, 87
Kyoto Protocol, 77, 112, 202–3, 205, 207

Langeweische, William, 8, 157, 235n4
Latin America, 7, 26–8, 32–3, 57, 79, 242n10
Laurier, Wilfrid, 43–4, 51, 65
Layton, Jack, 258n87
Lévesque, René, 28, 238n28, 239n34
Liberal Party of Canada, 28, 109; electoral campaigns, xi, 30, 43, 113, 205–6, 210–11; leadership, 48, 52, 64, 66, 124, 196, 198; support, policy, and ideology, 51–8, 130, 183, 189, 204, 207–9, 219

Lind, Michael, 150
locally engaged staff (LES), 10, 141–2, 144, 167–9
Loyalist migrations, 89, 174
Lugar, Richard, 12
Luttwak, Edward, 151–2

Macdonald Commission, 47
MacKenzie, Lewis, 110
MacLaren, Roy, 51, 58
magazine-advertising dispute, 123, 176–81; industry strength following, 181, 186; media bias in, 179–80, 182–3; retaliation option, 180
Main Street North America, 92–3
Mandela, Nelson, 12
Manji, Irshad, 9, 236n7
Manning, Preston, 30, 55, 217, 219
Marchi, Sergio, 26
Marshall Plan, 13
Martin, Paul, 66, 70, 124, 183, 196–8, 213; BMD decision, 129–30; COP 11 and Kyoto Protocol, 198, 202–4, 220–1; detainees, 161; election campaign of 2005–06, 20–7, 209; fiscal policy, 215; foreign policy criticized, 200–1; government of, 66, 115, 128, 136, 197, 202–10; Iraq conflict, 123
Masse, Brian, 254n19
Maule, Christopher, 185–6
May, Elizabeth, 81
McCaffrey, Barry, 152
McDonough, Alexa, 63, 72
McGuinty, Dalton, 83, 245n51
McKenna, Frank, 73, 210
McLaughlin, Audrey, 53
Meech Lake Accord, 28–9
Mexico, 4, 50–2, 56–9, 176, 195, 243n12
Merkin, Bill, 182
military intervention/occupation, risk of in Canada, xvii, 105–6, 228

Mines, Keith, 155
Montreal, 22, 41; US Consulate General in, 38, 240n43
Mulroney, Brian, 24, 218, 247n10; on customs union, 91–2; free trade, 4, 47–8; government of, 28–30, 175; Reform Party and, 53–5
Murkowski, Lisa, 131
music industry, 176, 179, 187–8, 192
Muslims, 9, 148–9, 158, 164
Myers, Jayson, 98

Naland, John, 156
National Energy Program, 45–6
National Security Council (NSC), US, 91, 129, 136, 247n8
New Democratic Party of Canada (NDP), 21, 51–2, 59; credibility of, 80–1; on Frank McKenna as ambassador, 73; on military deserters, 258n87; Summit of the Americas, 63–4
New Embassy Compounds (NECs), 157
Ney, Edward, 18
Nicaragua, 8, 235n3
North, Oliver, 230, 235n3
North American Air Defence Command (NORAD), 101, 105, 129–30, 141, 159, 250n34
North American Free Trade Agreement (NAFTA): effects of, 56, 61–2, 65–6, 75, 79–80, 99–100; efforts to improve upon, x, 67–8, 70–3, 78–9, 102; negotiations toward, 4, 50–2, 54; opposition to, 57–60, 80–5; provisions of, xvii, 182, 192; Quebec and, 32–5, 41; side letters to, 58–9
North American Initiative (NAI), 70–7
North American Security and Prosperity (NASP), 93–4
North Atlantic Treaty Organization (NATO), 110, 158, 161, 165, 265n62

Northern Command (NORTHCOM), US,
    104–5, 250n34
Norwood, Charlie, 78, 132–3
Nossal, Kim, 200–1
nuclear energy, 234

Obama, Barack, 209, 232–3; election
    campaign of 2008, 208, 230–1; trade
    policy, 82–4, 246n53
O'Connor, Gordon, 130, 161
Ogdensburg Agreement, 44

Parizeau, Jacques, 32–3, 35, 39
Parrish, Carolyn, 113, 252n62
passports, 77, 130–3, 159, 253n15
Patriot Act, 114, 149
Penson, Charlie, 180
perimeter concept, xvi, 68, 72, 98, 135,
    195, 228; Cellucci and, 92–3; Chertoff
    and, 138; Mulroney and, 91–2; reac-
    tion to, 93–4, 101
Perle, Richard, 122, 252n65
Permanent Joint Board on Defence
    (PJBD), US-Canada, 44, 105, 121
Pettigrew, Pierre, 64, 97–8, 183
pharmaceuticals, 19–20, 68
pipelines, 211–14
polls, opinion: cultural policy, 185;
    electoral, 53–4, 203–4; Quebec, 35;
    terrorism and foreign policy, 97, 108,
    164, 195–6, 199, 221–2; trade policy,
    57, 81
Powell, Colin, 81, 102, 125–6, 128, 185;
    and State Department, 118–19, 145,
    155
presumption of succession (treaties), 36
Progressive Conservative Party, 4, 30, 47,
    214. See also Conservative Party
protesters, 63–5, 149, 256n51
Public Safety and Emergency Prepared-
    ness Canada, 115–16

Quebec: economy, 33–5, 55–6, 239n29;
    foreign relations, 28, 36–8, 216–17,
    240n38, 240n39; referendum in 1995,
    35, 38–9, 239n29; separatism, 21,
    28–33, 39–42, 227, 239n33, 239n44;
    US Consulate in Quebec City, 41,
    212–13, 240n39, 240n43

Rachman, Gideon, 148–9, 235n3, 241n6
Reagan, Ronald (administration of), 7,
    46
Reciprocity Treaty (1854), 223, 228
Reform Party of Canada, 30–1, 54–5,
    218–19, 239n20, 243–4n13
Revolution, American, 31, 89, 174
Ricardo, David, 52
Rice, Condoleezza, 128, 132, 144, 146,
    153–7
Roosevelt, Franklin D., 14, 44
Rumsfeld, Donald, 108, 122, 127, 151
Russia, 10–11, 36, 196, 222, 260–1n17

Sachs, Jeffrey, 11
Safe Third Country Agreement, 162
Sands, Chris, 187
Schott, Jeffrey, 62
Second World War, 3, 25, 163; United
    States and, 6, 95, 105, 151, 237n16
security clearance, 4–5, 169
Security and Prosperity Partnership
    (SPP), 76–82, 138, 160, 244n15
Senate, US, 99, 103, 109, 151, 203,
    249n17
smuggling, 102, 165
softwood lumber, 61, 65, 198, 200, 204,
    214
South Africa, 12
Sports Illustrated, 176–8, 182, 186,
    261n21
State, US Department of: Canada Desk,
    20, 24, 113, 119–20; Economic

Bureau, 103, 245; European Bureau, 20, 27; Intelligence and Research Bureau, 118, 221; Latin American Bureau, 238n27; Near Eastern Affairs Bureau, 142; Western Hemisphere Affairs Bureau, 25–7
Sullivan, Daniel, 85–6
Summit of the Americas (2001), 63, 65

Tarnak Farm incident, 107
Tepper, Elliot, 259n4
Tobin, Brian, 54
Toronto 18 suspects, 164
torture, xvii, 109, 114, 127, 148, 162–3
trade, Canada-US, performance of, 45, 66, 254n26
trade-remedy laws, 57–8, 61, 73, 85
Treasury, US Department of, 4, 20, 216, 247n8
trucking, 99–100, 135, 254n26
Trudeau, Justin, 208, 220
Trudeau, Pierre, 21, 45–7, 175, 210, 238n20
Trump, Donald J., xi, xviii, 232
Turner, John, 48

unemployment, 36, 47, 81, 98

UNESCO Convention on Cultural Diversity, 190–2, 216, 262–3n26
Union of Soviet Socialist Republics, 6–7, 237n16
United Kingdom, 25, 44, 116, 123, 139, 232
United States Trade Representative (USTR), Office of the, 20, 177, 179, 180, 182

Vietnam, 8, 87–8, 152, 156, 158, 235n4

Western Hemisphere Travel Initiative (WHTI), 77–8, 130–3, 135, 184, 225
Weston, Tom, 23
White, Bob, 48
Wilkins, David, 79, 131, 137–9, 158, 198, 202–4, 214
Williams, Jody, 246n3
Wolf, Martin, 148, 256n48
Wonnacott, Ronald and Paul, 45
World Intellectual Property Organization (WIPO), 69
World Trade Organization (WTO), 64–5, 179, 182, 192, 262n23

Yergin, Daniel, 14, 237n16